# Social Policy
## *for*
# Social  Welfare Practice
# in a Devolved Wales

Edited by: Charlotte Williams

BASW website: http://www.basw.co.uk

Published by
VENTURE PRESS
16 Kent Street
Birmingham
B5 6RD
www.basw.co.uk

British Library Cataloguing-in-Publication Data
A catalogue record for this book is available from the British Library

ISBN-13: 978-1-86178-079-9 (paperback)

Printed by:
Hobbs the Printers Ltd
Brunel Road
Totton
SO40 3WX

Printed in Great Britain

# Contents

# List of figures and tables

## Figures

## Tables

# Acknowledgements

With thanks to all the contributors who worked hard to meet a very tight time schedule, to Malcolm Hold for his editorial eye and to Angela Drakakis-Smith for her help in preparing the final typescript. Thanks also to the referees who provided helpful comments on the original book proposal.

# Notes on contributors

**Elaine Davies** is a graduate of UCW Aberystwyth and Jesus College Oxford and worked for several years as a social worker and team manager in Dyfed and in the London Boroughs of Islington and Hillingdon. More recently she has fused her interest in language and social care issues and has published and developed training workshops in the area of language sensitive practice. She now works for the language consultancy, *Cwmni Iaith*.

**Mark Drakeford** is a former probation officer, community development project leader and youth justice worker. He is currently Professor of Social Policy and Applied Social Sciences at Cardiff University. Since 2000 he has been the Cabinet's health and social policy adviser at the Welsh Assembly Government. A former editor of the *British Journal of Social Work*, he has published widely in the fields of poverty, youth policy and social policy in Wales.

**Ian Butler** is Professor of Social Work at Bath University. He is a former social worker and social work manager with experience in both the statutory and voluntary sectors. Since 2005 he has been the Cabinet Adviser on Children's Policy at the Welsh Assembly Government. He was Editor of the *British Journal of Social Work* between 2000 and 2003 and is a member of the Economic & Social Research Council's Research College. He was elected as a member of the Academy of Social Sciences in 2004. He has published widely on social work policy and practice with children and families.

**Anne Crowley** is Senior Policy Adviser with Save the Children. She co-ordinates Save the Children's advocacy and public policy work aimed at influencing decision-makers and duty bearers for the rights of children in Wales. Anne has worked with marginalised young people in both the statutory and voluntary sectors in Wales. She took up her current post with Save the Children in 1999, seeing the creation of the National Assembly for Wales as a key opportunity to develop made-in-Wales policies to benefit the nation's youngest citizens. In 2004/05 she was an adviser to the Parliamentary Welsh Affairs Select Committee for their inquiry into *Empowering Children and Young People in Wales*. In 2006, she co-edited *Righting the Wrongs*, a report reviewing progress on implementing the United Nations Convention on the Rights of the Child in Wales.

**Hefin Gwilym** is Director of Social Work at the University of Wales, Bangor. His main teaching areas are mental health, learning disabilities and the organisation of social care for adults in Wales. Before entering the teaching profession, he had extensive experience of working in social care settings in Wales including as a team manager for a voluntary residential learning disabilities service in Ceredigion, working in the field of mental health for Gwynedd Social Services and as a member of Dwyfor Community Mental Health Team.

**Jayne Neale** completed an ESRC-funded PhD on the welfare needs of young offenders in Wales in 2007. She has wide practical experience of working with children, young people and families within the voluntary and public sector. After completing her undergraduate studies at Bangor University, she took up a post with the York Youth Offending Team (YOT), where she developed and co-ordinated the Bail Supervision and Support Programme and went on to become part of the YOT management team as Court and Accommodation Co-ordinator.

**Richard Pugh** is Professor in Social Work at Keele University and has worked as a residential and field worker in the UK and the USA. He has published widely on minority language issues, childcare, social work theory and rural social work. He has extensive international links with academics and practitioners in Europe, North America and Australia, and is a member of the editorial boards of *Rural Social Work* (Australia) and *Portularia* (Spain). He is currently co-writing an international textbook on rural social work.

**Michael Sullivan** is Professor of Policy Analysis in the School of the Environment and Society at Swansea University. He has written widely on the politics of social policy and, latterly, on devolution and social policy. He has advised the Welsh Assembly Government on matters of health policy, has recently completed research on the contribution of ELWa to education and training in Wales and acted as an adviser to the Organisation for Security and Cooperation in Europe on the development of public policy frameworks in Serbia and Montenegro.

**Charlotte Williams** is Professor of Social Justice at Keele University. She began her career in welfare practice working as a housing officer and later worked as a local authority social worker and finally in social development projects in Guyana, South America before returning to the UK to take up an academic post at Bangor University. She is currently Head of the School of Criminology, Education, Sociology and Social Work at Keele. She has researched and published widely on issues of race and ethnicity in welfare practice, more latterly in the context of devolution.

# Editor's introduction

Devolution has changed the parameters of welfare practice. There is mounting evidence both in terms of legislation, policy and practice that key differences are emerging between Welsh social policies and those that exist elsewhere in the UK. For example, Wales created a Children's Commissioner ahead of Scotland and England, smoking was banned in public places in Wales prior to England, Welsh pensioners have enjoyed free bus travel and Welsh school children free swimming for some years, and all people in Wales now benefit from free prescriptions. Devolution has had an impact in countless ways across the UK and in ways much more fundamental than these apparent policy shifts. Issues of Welsh distinctiveness, identity and nationality have been revitalised following devolution in Wales, with the concomitant effect of a resurgence of English nationalism. There is the assertion that Welsh and Scottish social welfare policy reflects a strong commitment to social democracy by contrast with the neo-liberal agenda of Westminster, creating differences in the style and principles underpinning political choices in the different parts of the UK. It is increasingly claimed that devolution has produced a more inclusive politics, engaging with and empowering a much higher level of involvement by local communities and the general public in matters that affect their well-being. In this way devolution has opened up both a new politics of the UK and the potential for new forms of governance to emerge. Social welfare practice is being, and will continue to be, transformed by these changes.

All the while anxieties grow about the extent to which this policy divergence foreshadows the break-up of Britain. On the one hand there are those who argue that we are witnessing an acceleration of this process. They suggest that policy differences that affect our everyday lives are now substantively different across the UK (take student tuition fees as just one example), leading to growing inter-regional and intra-regional inequalities. On the other hand there are those who suggest that these arguments are overstated and point to the fact that the Scottish Parliament and Welsh Assembly have strictly limited powers, that the public have little appetite for full independence and that despite the differences in policy there is still much more that unites rather than divides the nations of the UK. There is little doubting that these debates will continue to engage those of us concerned with the fortunes of the traditional welfare state.

The Welsh Assembly was established in 1999 under the Government of Wales Act 1998 following a slim win on the YES vote in the referendum of 1997. Now in its third term, the popularity of the Assembly has grown and its powers have been extended as has its tangible presence in the everyday lives of the people of Wales. It has £14 billion to spend flexibly in ways that reflect Welsh priorities and needs and crucially, given its brief, on largely social policy concerns. There is little doubt that differences in policy context across the UK will widen and as social welfare practitioners the responsibility will grow to engage proactively with this policy development and change.

This book arises from the need for students, practitioners and other policy actors in Wales to be attentive to and involved in the creation of indigenous policy-making and shaping. It will appeal to students of social work, nursing, those engaged in health and social care roles, youth and community studies and childcare as well students of social policy, sociology and applied social sciences. The book brings together academics and practitioners from within Wales who bring considerable knowledge and experience from their own first-hand experience of practice in the Welsh context and/or work with the Welsh Assembly Government. They have drawn extensively on research and literature from Wales in compiling their chapters and aim to highlight in an accessible way the emerging policy framework shaping practice.

An overriding theme of the contributions is the Welsh Assembly's ambition to develop a distinctive Welsh approach to policy making: a 'Welsh Way', which reflects particular values, principles and a style of engagement with service users. The chapters are linked by their shared concern with the Assembly's stated aim to produce a fairer society. Chapter after chapter focuses on the potential of the Assembly to translate into concrete practices its ambitions to achieve social justice for all. The chapters outline the policy framework and the political philosophy and values underpinning them. The book is divided into three sections. In the first section three chapters set the scene for the book by discussing key aspects of the devolution project. In Chapter One, I set out to critically explore some of the key assumptions of devolution, arguing that as much as it is a 'hurray' word for many of us there is a need to move beyond attention to policy differentiation to ask questions about discourses and ideologies that are constructed and mobilised in this process of change and that shape how social problems are identified, articulated and selected for policy attention. As students of social policy and practitioners we need to develop a healthy scepticism to political projects in order to question their synergy or otherwise with the core values of the social welfare professions. In Chapter Two, Drakeford takes us further by outlining the development of the Welsh Assembly, its role and remit and indicating the core values and approach the Assembly has taken. Sullivan's concern in Chapter Three is to indicate, using the example of health policy, the nature, extent and implications of policy divergence. In Section Two, key themes fundamental to service delivery in Wales, the Welsh language, poverty, rurality and equalities are explored and their implications for practice are signalled. Finally, Section Three, in a broad sweep, looks at children's, youth and adult policy, highlighting the distinctive nature of the policy framework in Wales. The book concludes by looking at the aspirations of the Assembly to create a coherent framework for social work practice. It is as yet early days in terms of evaluating outcomes but that makes it even more compelling to engage social welfare practitioners' awareness of the policy framework and their potential to shape policy.

It has often been said that devolution is not to be understood as a single event marked by a transfer of powers from Westminster to Cardiff, but as an ongoing and dynamic process. There is little doubt that devolution is a contested terrain, a terrain in which we as writers and academics – but also as citizens of Wales - doubtless have a vested interest. It is easy to emphasise the gains and overlook those nagging questions and puzzles that the devolution project brings in its wake. Concerns that it may act to undermine universal or minimum standards across the UK and create territorial inequalities, concerns that it may operate as a countervailing force to solidarity and social cohesion as ethnic-nationalism gains a greater foothold, and concerns that in the search for a coherent unity branded as a 'Welsh way' or a 'Welsh social policy' new and old exclusions may be compounded. If we are guilty of being over-enthusiastic about the existence of an Assembly for Wales or of talking up the achievements of the Welsh government then so be it. That is for you as the reader to critically discern.

**Charlotte Williams**
**November 2007**

# SECTION ONE

## Understanding Devolution

Chapter 1

# What is Wales?

Charlotte Williams

## Introduction

The question of the distinctiveness of Wales has engaged historians and social scientists alike. In his compelling account of the development of the nation, *When Was Wales?*, the eminent historian Gwyn Alf Williams provides us with the thought-provoking assertion that 'Wales is an artefact which the Welsh produce' (1991:304). This statement invites us to understand Wales as a dynamic entity that is constantly in the process of change and remaking. Since devolution, this process of remaking Wales as somehow distinct from other places has taken on a new urgency. Pragmatic questions of how to appropriately respond to the specific needs of the Welsh population now engage policy makers as does fostering the renewed sense of national identity. In this sense we are experiencing a Wales that is in the process of being remade or, in sociological terms, being *socially constructed*. In speech after speech the First Minister, Rhodri Morgan has appealed for 'doing things the Welsh way' (Morgan, 2002) and the idea of 'Welsh solutions for Welsh problems' has become the mantra of the policy makers. These kinds of ideas are not, however, without contention and beg questions such as: What are Welsh problems? Are they somehow distinct from problems elsewhere? What is special – or indeed different – about Wales? What is Wales? The devolution project begins with the assumption of Wales as a unique entity that displays its own particular characteristics and its own particular needs that require specific responses. It is this set of assumptions that this chapter seeks to explore. It opens by considering the idea of Wales as socially constructed, it explores the arguments related to the notion of policy divergence and concludes by challenging some of the central assumptions of the devolution project.

## Constructing a *'better Wales'*?

In his book *Making Sense of Wales*, Graham Day (2002) offers a contemporary questioning of the idea of Wales, suggesting it as a construction based on competing understandings, myths and visions about what is and what is not Wales, and who is and who is not Welsh. He reviews a variety of stereotypical images of Wales and Welshness that vie with each other in sociological and popular imagining: depictions such as the Celtic imagery of the tourist brochures and the craft artefacts that hark back to an ancient Celtic ancestry; images of a traditional industrial working-class Wales, best symbolised by photographs of the Welsh coal miner; or images of a scenic rural Wales based on ideas about the intimacy and cohesion of small-scale communities (Day, 2002). In doing so Day is problematising the assumption of any comforting consensus on what Wales might be, or indeed any standardised view of what we would like Wales to be. He is suggesting that there are 'multiple realities, intelligible from differing standpoints and anchored in different sets of social experiences and positions' (2002:11). Accordingly, different perspectives and experiences of Wales are mediated through factors of class, place and location, gender, ethnicity or age, as well as other structured social locations. There are, indeed, many ways of viewing Wales, which suggests a complex heterogeneity of positionings rather than any singular reality. Day takes this further, however, by suggesting that these images or constructions have significant import for the ways in which social problems are identified and become the subject of research or not.

Social policy is not divorced from these constructions. How social problems are identified and defined, whether they are responded to and by whom, is not a neutral activity but suffused with values that produce competing and contrasting explanations as to what should or should not be done. In any analysis of social policies it is possible to identify value judgements and specific visions about what steps might be taken to produce a better society. For example, the early strategy document of the Welsh Assembly *Wales: A Better Country* (WAG, 2003) sets out 'our guiding vision of a fairer, more prosperous, healthier and better educated country, rooted in our commitment to social justice' (2003:1).

It is also possible, when considering what policies emerge, to identify a variety of stakeholders and interest groups vying in the public arena to set the agenda on policy priorities, some of which are more powerful than others in shaping outcomes. It is important, therefore, to consider the way in which some ideas about what Wales is, what it should be and what issues require intervention, come to prevail while others do not. As key actors, social welfare professionals are implicated in this process – and increasingly so as opportunities for their direct involvement in policy-making have been opened up in an unprecedented manner by devolution (see Chapter 11).

Since devolution there has been a tendency to contrast an old Wales with a vision of a new and better Wales and to attempt to define some of the essence of traditional Welsh society and Welsh characteristics on which to develop the devolution project. *Wales: A Better Country* (WAG, 2003:3), for example, offers some references to those characteristics considered to be part of the distinctive nature, needs and values of Wales. Wales is regarded as having a unique identity as a small nation and factors such as 'our strong sense of local community', 'our heritage', 'our creative industries and artists' and its own particular language and culture are highlighted (ibid:3). The report flags the ambition to strengthen Wales' cultural identity and create 'a truly bilingual nation' (ibid:3). This type of analysis is not only a feature of government reports. John Osmond, a leading political commentator in Wales, talking about change, identified many of the enduring values associated with Wales as:

> *'The generosity and self-interest associated with a health service free at point of delivery remained common sense, as did a native sense of community solidarity founded on attachment to locality, people and a shared landscape and culture … all these things were mutating back more to what it meant to be Welsh than British.'*
> (Osmond, 1998:3)

The First Minister, Rhodri Morgan, referencing a particular version of Welsh community life, refers to these communities as:

> 'The raw material, the social heritage out of which Welsh
> devolution has been created – and in which we can now
> make our own social policy in Wales, for Wales.'
> (Morgan, 2002)

These ideas about Welsh community life, the national character and national values are all important in fostering a sense of collective spirit and social solidarity. They are also, of course, contestable and relate to the specific mobilisation of sets of ideas that help shape everyday views and promote particular discourses of what a new or better Wales might be. The idea of making and remaking a Wales that appeals to the populace is central to the politicians' task. Delineating a Wales as a point of pragmatic policy interventions is one thing, but this clearly is not the whole story in any discussion of a nation as old as this. Wales is not simply a region, is does not simply come into existence for want of administrative convenience or pragmatic policy making. It is also a product of a history, a culture and a language. It has a collective sense of self as a small nation that is both centuries old and at the same time the product of contemporary re-formation. As citizens and key definers of policy and practice, social welfare professionals in Wales are actively engaged in this process of remaking.

## Devolution and divergence

The story of contrasts and comparisons is growing as devolution matures and each version carries its own selection of supporting evidence. Some commentators argue that the degree of divergence in social policy since devolution has been significant (Chaney and Drakeford, 2004; Greer, 2005; see also Chapter 3 of this volume) while others would suggest that discontinuity with the past is not as striking as it may first seem (Rees, 2005).

It is possible to suggest three key ways of thinking about Welsh distinctiveness post-devolution:

- Policy divergence as a pragmatic response to specific challenges in the Welsh context.

- Policy divergence as based on a particular ideological set of beliefs about welfare delivery and citizenship that are somehow different and reflect 'a Welsh way' of doing things.
- Policy divergence as an expression of self-determination based on ideas about national distinctiveness and national identity.

These perspectives are not distinct but are intimately inter-related and together provide the underpinning rationale for devolution. Devolution was secured on the basis of claims to more accountable, responsive and inclusive policy-making but it also reflected in part a longstanding expression of ethnic-nationalism. On a purely pragmatic level, the socio-economic profile of Wales suggests that there are particular needs and challenges in the Welsh context and these demand specific kinds of responses. It may also be that Wales is different because the values, ideas and beliefs about how we should relate to one another, how we should relate to the state and what we view as a good society, are somehow distinct from other parts of the UK. In addition, the desire to be self-governing and assert Wales as a distinct national entity and somehow experientially different acted a driver for change. These types of factors combine to produce support for policies, institutions and practices that diverge from elsewhere in the UK.

*Welsh distinctiveness*

The demographic profile of Wales presents some very particular challenges for social policy. Historically, the absence of data specifically disaggregated for Wales limited the production of this evidence to guide policy. So comprehensive was social policy analysis based on 'England and Wales' as the organising principle that an immediate challenge for the new Assembly was – and remains – the development of a rigorous evidence base. This situation is improving but in some policy fields the lack of detailed information continues to hamper responsiveness.

Wales is a small nation and it is also very diverse. These divisions are often described in rather stark terms such as north/south, urban/rural, Welsh speaking/non-Welsh speaking, Anglicised/non-Anglicised, white/black and so on. This typification, however, misses the detail of complex differentiation across Wales both within and across its counties and even within wards. The population at the last Census was 2.9 million, two thirds of whom live in the south east. The rural population counts for one third of this total. Almost a quarter of the population are Welsh speaking. Speaking Welsh and indeed identifying as Welsh even without being able to speak the language forms an important interface with issues of welfare (see Chapter 4) as do the more generalised and perhaps nebulous notions of '*ways of life*' or '*Welsh culture*' (Mooney and Williams, 2006).

Wales is also a multicultural society. Traditionally, it has been difficult to assert that issues of race, ethnicity and religion demand a specific response in the Welsh context. Ethnic diversity in Wales is a factor that has been slow to be acknowledged in public policy terms, hampered by the assumption that relatively low numbers means relatively low need (Williams *et al.,* 2002). This policy neglect in itself marks out the need for an invigorated approach in Wales and in particular the collection of appropriate data to accurately predict needs. The majority of people living in Wales describe their ethnicity as white, almost 98 per cent, with the remaining 2.1 per cent being from a broad mix of ethnic backgrounds and comprising some 62,000 people. A breakdown by ethnicity reveals considerable diversity among ethnic groups. One notable factor of the minority ethnic population of Wales is the large number and relatively large percentage of people of mixed race, reflecting long settlement and intermarriage. A quarter of the total minority ethnic population was in the mixed category at the last Census and this is a growing percentage of the minority ethnic population.

There are a number of factors that single out the experiences of the minority ethnic population in Wales from the picture elsewhere in the UK, perhaps the most important features being the degree of dispersal that has meant that few concentrated communities exist outside the crescent of cities in the south. Cardiff has the largest percentage of people from minority ethnic groups with 11.8 per cent of the population describing themselves as non-white, followed by Newport (7.0 per cent) and Swansea (4.5 per cent) (WAG, 2006a). Yet there is no authority in Wales that does not have an minority ethnic presence (Williams *et al.,* 2002). The challenge has been in developing a strategic whole-Wales approach to issues of need and to identifying needs in rural areas. Since the accession of the Eastern European countries to the European Union in May 2005, Wales has been experiencing a major demographic change yet to be properly documented. Now Poles, Lithuanians, Estonians and others are workers and residents in many towns and cities across Wales and in particular the more rural areas (Wales Rural Observatory, 2006). It may well be that communities are no more diverse than ever they were (Day, 2002) but the diversity is now becoming more visible and complex and raising new issues for public services. Religious diversity is also in the mix since its enumeration in the 2001 Census. Beyond the more debated issues of faith schools, faith-based community and welfare organisations play a key role in service delivery and individual preferences in care-giving and care-receiving practices can be shaped by religious affiliation. Nearly three quarters of the Welsh population described their religion as Christian (72 per cent) at the last Census. After Christianity, Islam was the next most common faith. Cardiff has the largest Muslim population (4 per cent of the local population) but in the country overall, Muslims accounted for less than one per cent of the population (22,000 people). Most Muslims were from Asian backgrounds, although nearly 3,000 white people also described themselves as Muslim. Among other faiths the next largest groups were Indian Hindus (over 4,000) and white Buddhists (3,000), followed by White Jews and Indian Sikhs (both about 2,000) (WAG, 2001). The rapidly changing profile of many communities, and in particular rural communities in Wales, presents a number of challenges to welfare practitioners, not least because of the complex patterning of diversity relating to ethnicity, gender, age and nationality and class among other lines of difference.

The Welsh population has been steadily growing, increasing by some 300,000 people since the post-war period and it is forecast to grow slowly but surely over the next 20 years, rising to just over 3.2 million by 2031. These changes in population size relate to changes in the ratio of births to deaths and to flows of inward and outward migration. In common with most European countries, Wales has an ageing population, and it has the highest proportion of people of pensionable age for any part of the UK (21 per cent). In the ten years between the 1991 Census and the most recent Census in 2001 the number of people over working age increased by nearly two per cent while the number of children under 16 decreased by 0.5 per cent. The number of people over the age of 85 has grown five-fold over the last 50 years reaching 59,000 in 2001 (National Statistics Online). For the next two decades the number of older people in Wales is projected to increase both in absolute terms and as a proportion of the overall population. By 2021 one in three households in Wales will include a person aged over 65 and over 50,000 households will be headed by a person aged 85 or older. At the same time the birth rate is falling steadily. By 2018 the number of children is projected to fall by around 6 per cent (WAG, 2007). In some areas of Wales such as Conwy Unitary Authority, over a quarter of the population are now of pensionable age. This changing population structure has far-reaching implications for policy-making not least in relation to the 'dependency ratio' – the proportion of people over pensionable age to those under sixteen.

Many of those of pensionable age live alone. Wales has a high number of one-person households (29 per cent) and just over half of those living alone are pensioners (15 per cent). The tendency to live alone increases sharply with age. Almost half of the over 75s live alone. Over 20 per cent of pensioners live in poverty and poverty is especially high among single pensioners (JRF, 2007).

The implications of this profile for health and social services are perhaps obvious (see Chapter 10 on adult services) particularly in relation to the care and support of elders and their well-being. Expectations of social services are constantly raised as people's rights awareness grows, as more careful assessment of services highlights gaps in delivery, or the need for more sophisticated responses, and as awareness of new social problems and needs becomes apparent. The number of people in Wales receiving a social service grew by 50 per cent (from 100,000 to 150,000) between 2001 and 2005. Alongside publicly provided services, an army of some 340,000 people provide unpaid care for family members, one in five of the population and including some 7,000 children (WAG, 2007).

The Welsh Assembly Government report *Fulfilled Lives, Supportive Communities* (WAG, 2007:12) acknowledges that these demographic trends will mean a number of vulnerable adults requiring increased support from social services, but it also suggests that the scale of increased demand could be reduced if services could be changed to reduce dependency.

Another issue related to the dependency ratio that has attracted somewhat contentious debate in Wales and has been subject to competing constructions is the problem of migration. By far the biggest migration issue facing Wales is the out-migration of young people and yet in the popular mind in-migration and the challenge this poses to small communities across Wales is perceived as the problem (Davis, 2004). Rural depopulation and now the influx of European Union migrant workers to rural areas of Wales (see Chapter 6) poses challenges for policy-makers in responding to issues of social integration and welfare provision.

One of the most critical issues in the demand for social services relates to the poor health of the nation. In Wales 23 per cent of all adults report having a limiting lifelong illness compared to 18 per cent in England and 20 per cent in both Scotland and Northern Ireland (WAG, 2007). Trends indicate that by 2018 there will be an increase by 12 per cent in the number of adults with at least one chronic condition. Black and minority ethnic groups are particularly prone to ill-health with the highest proportion experiencing life-limiting long-term illness (WAG, 2007). Welsh distinctiveness is also marked out by the high number of disabled people in the population by comparison with elsewhere in the UK, with 23 per cent of the working-age population having a work-limiting disability, one in five (National Statistics Online).

Perhaps the state of the nation's health is a factor that has attracted the most headline news of all the demographic features of Wales. The legacy of heavy industries and the facts of poverty combine to produce some of the poorest regions in the whole of Europe with two thirds of the Welsh population covered by Objective One status for the period 2001-06 and with all areas of Wales covered by European Structural funding. Seventeen (almost 10 per cent) of the poorest areas of the UK are in Wales. The low level of earnings in Wales contributes directly to the low Gross Domestic Product (GDP) and hence the need for European Structural fund help (Brooksbank, 2006). Wales remains a low-pay economy. Thirteen per cent of male full-time workers and 18 per cent of women full-time workers are in the low-paid sector, about a quarter higher than the figures for England (JRF, 2007). The Joseph Rowntree Foundation report *Monitoring Poverty and Social Exclusion in Wales* (JRF, 2007) found that poverty rates and unemployment in Wales were falling slowly towards the UK average but there were still many who are economically inactive and who wanted work, especially disabled people and lone parents. Long-term unemployment is identified as a continuing problem and some 350,000 working-age adults are living in poverty (JRF, 2007). While child poverty rates in Wales have improved, they are still among the highest in Europe (see Chapter 5).

What this overview of the demographic profile of Wales reveals is a relatively poor country characterised by visual contrasts and detailed differentiation by class, ethnicity, age and other social locations as well as by differences in locality and identities. Deep patterns of inequality are also evident, which are proving resistant to change (see Chapter 6). The gap in the life chances of particular groups means that social justice concerns would inevitably come high on the agenda of the Assembly keen to make real citizenship rights. These issues present core challenges for social services in Wales, a sector where concerns about variable standards of delivery, increased expectations and gaps in the skills mix and size of the social care workforce have prompted a comprehensive modernisation strategy (see Chapter 11).

*A Welsh way?*

It is now not too difficult to accumulate a body of evidence to demonstrate a measure of policy divergence in Wales from elsewhere in the UK. The First Minister has argued for 'innovation not imitation' in the direction of policy-making (Morgan, 2002) and Welsh policy divergence has been growing steadily if perhaps in an *ad hoc* fashion. Figure 1. indicates some of the details of Welsh-specific policy-making.

---

**Figure 1.1: Welsh-specific policy making**

- UK's first Children's Commissioner and an Older People's Commissioner.
- Creation of 22 Local Health Boards to work alongside Wales' 22 local authorities.
- Abolition of school league tables.
- Free medical prescriptions for all.
- Free bus travel for pensioners.
- Free school milk for children under seven years of age.
- A Welsh Baccalaureate.
- Free nursing home care.
- Free swimming for the young and the old.
- Free breakfasts in primary schools.
- Assembly learning grants for Welsh students to attend universities of their choice across the UK.

In addition to these policy areas the Welsh Assembly Government has also taken a number of actions that signal differences of approach, such as reforms of public services to achieve better coordination and cooperative working (see Chapter 2), a rejection of the Best Value performance culture imposed on local government and the establishment of new-style regulatory bodies such as the Care Standards Inspectorate for Wales.

These apparent differences in policy, however, belie more complex questions about the nature of change. Adams and Robinson (2002:199) refine the blanket assumption of distinctiveness by offering a framework for considering divergence. Their argument is that divergence 'is not all of the same character' and suggest a useful way of considering differences along five trajectories: values, structures, decision-making, changes to policy and outcomes. This framework invites a consideration of different values and ideologies that may exist between the different nations of the UK. It raises questions about the nature of change to administrative structures, to the institutional framework and to the processes of decision making. It asks: What new policies are emerging and is devolution producing different outcomes in various policy areas? This leads us to more detailed questions about the nature of the divergence and its implications in terms of a distinctively Welsh approach.

The issue of values and ideology is one taken up by Drakeford (Chapter 2) and is a theme that permeates many chapters of this book. It is often suggested that Wales, like Scotland, has adopted a more social-democratic style of politics that marks it out significantly from the strategies and approach of New Labour. It is argued that this reflects a strong Welsh social-democratic tradition that is collectivist and communitarian, upholding strong support for the public sector as opposed to English (Blairite) neo-liberal modernism. As such, the claims are made that Welsh politics represents a defence of the traditional welfare state and it is the English that are diverging from it. The First Minister has said:

> '*The actions of the Welsh Assembly Government clearly owe more to the traditions of Titmuss, Tawney, Beveridge and Bevan rather than those of Hayek and Friedman. The creation of a new set of citizenship rights has been a key theme in the first four years of the Assembly – and a set of rights which are as far as possible: free at point of use, universal and unconditional.*'
> (Morgan, 2002)

This statement was made in what has become known as the *Clear Red Water Speech*, delivered just prior to the Assembly elections for the second term of office. This speech has become probably the most cited reference point for the value-base underpinning the direction of Welsh social policy. The speech sets out what Morgan refers to as 'clear red water' between policy in Wales and policy emanating from Westminster. In this speech the First Minister describes himself as 'a socialist of the Welsh stripe' and constructs his argument around what he identifies as three particular 'ideological fault lines' in approaches to social welfare: universalism versus means testing, equality versus choice and equality of opportunity versus 'the fundamentally socialist aim of equality of outcome' (see Chapter 2):

'Our commitment to equality leads directly to a model of the relationship between the government and the individual which regards the individual as citizen rather than consumer. Approaches which prioritise choice over equality of outcome rest, in the end, upon a market approach to public services, in which individual economic actors pursue their own best interests with little regard for wider considerations.'
(Morgan, 2002)

There is now ample evidence to underpin this commitment. The universal policies of free school milk, free nursery places for every three-year-old, free bus travel for pensioners, free breakfasts for all primary school children, free swimming and free prescriptions are good examples. Major policy strategies such as *Making the Connections* (WAG, 2004) and *Fullfilled Lives, Supportive Communities* (WAG, 2007) open with vision statements reiterating this commitment to a model of public service delivery that differs markedly from the market-orientated approach of New Labour. The language of policy papers in Wales stresses citizenship, equality of outcome, universality and collaboration rather than competition and consumerism.

There are, however, a number of caveats worth considering in relation to this forthright positioning. While there are many examples to support the universalist direction, there are also many examples of the limitations of universalism. Assembly Learning Grants are means tested, the Communities First (anti-poverty strategy) is geographically determined (disadvantaged areas) and some would argue that initiatives such as free swimming and free breakfasts for primary school children are hardly revolutionary. Wyn Jones and Scully (2004) have pointed to the fact that the *Clear Red Water Speech* stopped short of discussing redistribution as one of the fundamental pillars of the traditional welfare state. In addition, universal policies cost money and there are obvious limitations posed by the Welsh funding formulae, as the anomaly of 'Scandinavian-style' politics on an 'Anglo-American tax funding base' will be difficult to square (see *Agenda*, 2007). Mackay's analysis suggests clearly that 'relative devolved spending is already too low in Wales' (2006:251). Notwithstanding, the general orientation in this direction is marked and the collectivist *aspirations* are a core feature of social policy-speak in Wales.

This raises a second issue. The coherence of this ideological differentiation must also be open to debate. The new politics of Wales is characterised by a much more open and pluralist decision-making process with a shift from government, top-down policy-making to governance based on networks of policy-making (see Chapter 2). In this respect it is difficult to see how one *big* idea can hold sway without an emphasis on the top-down, bureaucratic and centralised social-democratic stateism that became the focus of such criticism in old-style welfare politics. Perhaps more telling is what might appear to be a mismatch between this political orientation and public sentiment. The basis of the ideological rift argument rests on the assumption of a particular version of the Welsh radical tradition that may not be borne out in reality. The idea that the people of Wales have a more progressive or more left-wing set of values than those in England is clearly unfounded (Jeffery, 2005). In their empirical test of this sentiment, Wyn Jones and Scully (2004) found little evidence to suggest widespread public radicalism underpinning the policy agenda committed to *Clear Red Water* and concluded that the Welsh might not be as radical as they like to believe. It appears that the Welsh or indeed the Scots are not more left wing than the English; indeed the evidence suggests that the Welsh are the least left-wing (Jeffery, 2005).

Others have suggested that what is more apparent in devolved politics is a change of style rather than a clear shift away from the overarching neo-liberal agenda of New Labour politics (Mooney, *et al.,* 2006). Martin Laffin (2004), for example, contests the idea of a radical departure from mainstream Labour Party values. He agrees that Welsh Labour has fought shy of the market-driven solutions favoured by central government but suggests that the policies of the Welsh government more truly reflect 'reasonable and pragmatic policy adaptations' (ibid:16) rather than a distinct *Welsh way*. However, Laffin does find Welsh policy overall much more willing to demonstrate ideological divergence than the Scottish who he argues are moving closer to Westminster policy.

The ability to hold a steady course on the ideological bent of policy in Wales has been assured by two successive Labour administrations and the party's place in the current co-alition government. This may not always be the case and it remains important in the future for welfare professionals to retain a critical and reflective stance in relation to ideologically driven politics (see Chapter 11).

*Structures, decisions and outcomes*

Other changes are everywhere in evidence. In terms of structures, while there has been a radical departure from the pre-devolution situation, it is important to note that Wales has had a degree of administrative devolution for some time. Early in the development of the Welsh-language policy in education, for example, Wales-specific structures were set up to oversee Welsh education practice. A Secretary of State for Wales was established in the 1950s and in 1964 the Welsh Office was set up to manage Welsh affairs. Unlike Scotland, however, Wales did not have its own legal system and areas like social work were not independent of the English system in the way that they were in Scotland. Devolution has now brought considerable changes to institutions in Wales even beyond the formal departmental structure of the Assembly itself.

Wales has a relatively small institutional infrastructure. For example, there are just 22 local authorities, 22 local health boards, 220 secondary schools, four police forces and six regional areas as identified by the Wales Spatial Plan: *People, Places, Futures* (WAG, 2004). These six distinctive regions provide the framework in which the Welsh Assembly delivers on its vision for the economic, social and environmental development of Wales. Proximity and familiarity characterise inter-agency working within such a small country. There are close and informal relationships between many public agencies and the extent of collaboration is being formally encouraged by the Welsh Assembly Government initiative *Making the Connections* (WAG, 2004). The co-terminosity of the structures of local authorities and local health boards is seen as particularly advantageous in responding to need and is expected to produce significant impacts in frontline services (see Chapter 3).

The Assembly has also been instrumental in creating and funding a number of new bodies with a Wales-wide remit: particularly consultative bodies such as the Interfaith Council, the All Wales Ethnic Minority Association and the Wales Women's Coalition. In 2006 it disbanded the so-called quangos or Associated Public Bodies and brought agencies such as the Family Court Advisory Service and the Welsh Development Agency, within the Welsh Assembly Government structure. In 2009 the Assembly will open its offices in North Wales. Many of these developments are aimed at making decision-making more transparent and bringing decisions closer to the people. In turn, a significant degree of institutional realignment with the Welsh border has occurred in the voluntary and private sectors. Organisations previously managed from England have restructured their administrative arrangements and functioning to reflect a focus on Wales as a distinct entity. Organisations such as Citizen's Advice Wales, Stonewall Cymru, Barnados and others, now manage their affairs on this basis. Many of these developments have been prompted by new relationships between the Assembly and the voluntary sector (Chaney, *et al.,* 2001; Day, 2006) and between the various stakeholders in the mixed economy of welfare.

In terms of decision-making, much has been made of the Assembly's ambitions towards greater inclusivity and towards a new more open style of politics (Chaney *et al.,* 2001). A number of innovations indicate the shift towards governance (discussed in Chapter 2) including the creation of consultative bodies, civic forums, public consultations, the use of statutory partnerships with the voluntary sector and the deliberative nature of the committee system of the Assembly, which have a greater degree of power than their counterparts in Westminster (Adams and Robinson, 2002). A wider range of stakeholder groups from the voluntary sector and from business are now invited into the policy-making process in a way not hitherto possible (Day, 2006). A large number of task and finish groups have been used during the life of the Assembly such as the Child Poverty Task Group (2005) and the Older People's Strategy Task Group (2003), which were made up of a range of professionals and lay experts. The ability of the Assembly to engage successfully with citizens is seen as something of a triumph. Regional committees across Wales have been well attended and direct access to politicians is unprecedented. As a symbol of open and inclusive decision-making the Assembly building itself in Cardiff Bay is a shining beacon of transparency.

Has the Assembly paid dividends? Outcomes are inevitably a more tricky issue to assess. Outcomes such as lower waiting lists, lower rates of morbidity and greater social inclusion are notoriously difficult to attribute to specific public policy measures. No assessment can be made here about particular policy fields, although later chapters provide some evaluation of developments. The point should be made, however, that it takes a number of years for policy changes to realise into measurable outputs and outcomes for people in Wales. What is clear is that in terms of policy prioritisation Wales has a highly permissive divergence achieved by block grant funding rather than ring-fenced funding. It has £14 billion to spend and can use this money as it sees fit and reflecting its own priorities, approaches and styles of working.

The focus on divergences in policy alone is to take too simplistic an approach to thinking about policy in post-devolution Wales. What is more likely is that we are experiencing a complex patterning of both divergence and convergence of policies across the nations of the UK. As much as we can identify divergences there are equally a number of forces of convergence shaping policy preferences. Public opinion is an important factor in limiting policy divergence as expectations of a measure of common standards across the UK shape priorities (Jeffery, 2005). An example of this might be concerns over health service waiting lists for treatments such as breast cancer or hip replacements that often make headline news. The interdependency between the labour market in the UK and its largely common tax regime is another factor prompting convergence. The portability of qualifications and their relevance across the UK and beyond is yet another example. This means that qualifications such as the Welsh Baccalaureate have not proved to be popular. And the amount of policy transfer and policy learning between areas of the UK means roughly common approaches to common issues, for example in child poverty strategies (Lohde, 2005). Convergence in policy strategies can be a good thing as policy experimentation in one part of the UK can provide important lessons that can be transferred elsewhere. It may also allow for strategic responses to issues that cut across national boundaries, for example, in responding to the needs of asylum seekers or migrant workers, or it may standardise good practices, for example in relation to equalities.

## A contested devolution

There is little doubt that devolution has brought considerable change to policy and practices across the UK. It heralds a greater democratisation in welfare delivery with a plethora of new points of engagement for ordinary citizens in shaping policies that impact on their well-being. Novel approaches to ensuring citizenship rights are being tested out in attempts to produce a much more deliberative democracy. It has provided an arena for policy experimentation and policy learning and perhaps above all an increased sense of ownership on the part of the Welsh public in the running of their own affairs.

Gradually the public in Wales have warmed to the Assembly (Wyn Jones and Scully, 2004). There are, however, a number of critical lines of inquiry to be pursued in thinking through the devolution project. This is not to suggest that devolution is a 'good thing' or a 'bad thing' but to offer it as a dynamic process, one that is evolving and one that is worthy of critical reflection.

As has been suggested, the idea of policy divergence is central to the devolution project. The notion that particular circumstances require particular policy responses is a given and by implication the suggestion that policy-making is somehow new and novel. This assumption is, as the starting point, itself contestable. I have indicated how a degree of administrative devolution was present prior to constitutional change. Several policy commentators have identified deep continuities with past policy-making or influences that stretch forward to ensure specific policy paths are maintained such that policy innovation might not be as great as it seems. Gareth Rees (2005:34) refers to 'assumptive worlds' and 'conventional ways of thinking' that shape debates on educational policy and relationships between the Welsh Office and institutions in Wales that have lain down particular 'policy pathways' that will be hard to shake off. Greer (2005) has suggested the important influence of established policy communities on the nature of contemporary restructuring of the health service and Wincott (2005) notes the history of abuse scandals in Wales that have led to much more rights-based approaches to early childhood education and care policies for children. These all suggest a measurable degree of continuity in the practices of policy-making that shape and constrain policy development. When thinking about policy developments, therefore, it is useful to consider the extent to which they are derivative of what has gone before rather than radically distinctive or innovative. Perhaps more importantly, in the endeavour to construct a sense of a new and better Wales, there is a tendency to obscure continuities with the past that reflect deep inequalities, divisions and polarities. In the search for what the First Minister has called the 'powerful glue of social solidarity' (Morgan, 2002), it is easy to overlook what has long been recognised: that social policies can structure, sustain and even promote social inequalities.

Devolution has become a *hurrah* word for many of us in Wales and there is indeed much to be proud of. However, there are a number of issues devolution raises in relation to social justice that must be of critical concern to welfare practitioners. Jeffery (2002), for example, raises the point that devolution could be seen to lead to the lowering of standards across the UK as opposed to pushing them up. Rather than the four-nation UK reflecting 'virtuous circles' of policy making, policy learning and policy transfer, one view suggests that a fragmented UK might slide into a 'race to the bottom' where restraints and cutbacks in one part of the UK become the justification for constraints and cutbacks in another (Adams and Robinson, 2002:212). There is concern that policy divergence may lead to different standards of public services across the UK and serve to undermine citizenship rights and a sense of solidarity fostered by UK-wide institutions such as the National Health Service (NHS). In this sense some would argue that devolution undermines the idea of the British welfare state and the principles on which it is based. Further, it has been pointed out that devolution raises a number of concerns about widening economic disparities, territorial inequalities and two-tier systems across the UK. Is it reasonable to expect free prescriptions in Wrexham but not in Warrington, just 35 miles apart – or to have long-term support for older people in one area of the UK and not another? For these reasons the question must arise: is devolution as progressive as might be suggested in social justice terms?

This important question is not easily answered in the absence of any constitutionally agreed set of common standards or formal minimum standards set by the UK centre, or indeed any set of institutions charged with 'holding the ring'. There is arguably an important role for

Westminster politics in maintaining the balance between diversity and equality, between the demands of subsidiarity, autonomy and particularity on the one hand and solidarity, standardisation and universalism on the other. These, of course, are longstanding tensions in welfare delivery but ones that are now being felt more acutely under devolution.

As yet, there has been no real evidence of resistance and conflict between the centre and the devolved nations to the extent that Adams and Robinson (2002:219) argue 'the effects of divergence so far have been remarkably benign' and have not threatened the solidarity of the UK. While these tensions may become more evident if the dominance of Labour administrations across the nations is weakened, as in the recent change of government in Scotland and as the powers for indigenous policy-making increase as in Wales, it is also clear that devolution was never intended to produce different sets of citizenship rights across the UK and a number of mechanisms, including most importantly the electorate themselves, operate as a countervailing force.

Perhaps the focus on policy divergence itself should be held up for critical inspection. While the norm has been to compare things happening in Wales with things happening in England, this centre-periphery axis is but one dimension for comparison. England is just one of four constituent parts of the UK and not the 'norm' against which all are contrasted. Wales can now look to international influences in the development of its policies. There are also points of comparison to be made within as well as across the nations. Wales' longstanding concerns about a north/south divide have come to the fore post-devolution and in response to this Chaney and Drakeford (2004:17) have argued that 'devolution is not about a transfer of power from London to Cardiff, but onwards from Cardiff to the whole of Wales'.

All this begs the important question as to whether nation itself is the appropriate unit for welfare delivery (for a broader discussion of this see Clarke, 2004) and brings us full circle in our consideration of the question: What is Wales? Increased globalisation and associated migrations across nations pose a number of challenges for any social policy and social welfare practice based on provision ringfenced by national borders. National boundaries by definition involve inclusions and exclusions and as a key instrument of nation building, social policies reflect particular sets of assumptions about who is an insider and who is an outsider. For this reason it is important to look beyond a focus on traditional policy domains and beyond a focus on institutional structures towards an assessment of the social relations of welfare that emerge within these new regimes. Mooney and Poole (2004), writing in the context of Scotland, argue that the focus on 'institutional approaches' is limiting in terms of assessing the potential for a distinctively Scottish social policy and suggest that 'divisions and relations of welfare matter more' (2004:479). Adopting such an approach allows those of us involved in welfare delivery to ask, who is being included and who is not?, but more critically to turn the lens towards constructions of the Welsh nation and ask, inclusion into what? What is Wales?

## References

Adams, J and Robinson, P (2002) (eds.) 'Divergence and the centre' in Adams, J and Robinson, P *Devolution in Practice* London, Institute of Public Policy Research.

*Agenda* (2007) 'Editor's introduction', *Agenda* Winter, Cardiff, Institute of Welsh Affairs, p.13.

Brooksbank, D (2006) 'The Welsh economy: a statistical profile' *Contemporary Wales* 18 pp. 275-97.

Chaney, P and Drakeford, M (2004) 'The primacy of ideology: social policy and the first term of the National Assembly for Wales' in Ellison, N, Bauld, L and Powell, M (eds.) *Social Policy Review* 16 Bristol, The Policy Press, pp. 121-42.

Chaney, P, Hall, T and Pithouse, A (eds.) (2001) *New Governance, New Democracy*? Cardiff, University of Wales Press.

Clarke, J (2004) *Changing Welfare, Changing States* London, Sage Publications.

Davis, C (2004) 'Migration, identity and development' *Agenda* Summer, Cardiff, Institute of Welsh Affairs, pp. 4-7.

Day, G (2002) *Making Sense of Wales: A Sociological Perspective*, Cardiff, University of Wales Press.

Day, G (2006) 'Chasing the dragon? Devolution and the ambiguities of civil society in Wales' *Critical Social Policy* 26(3), pp. 642-55.

Greer, S (2005) 'The politics of health-policy divergence' in Adams, J and Schmeuker, K (eds.) *Devolution in Practice 2006* London, Institute of Public Policy Research, pp. 98-120.

Jeffrey, C (2002) 'Uniformity and diversity in policy provision: insights from the US, Germany and Canada' in Adams, J and Robinson P (eds.) *Devolution in Practice: Public Policy Preferences within the UK* London, Institute of Public Policy Research, pp. 176-97.

Jeffrey, C (2005) 'Devolution and divergence: public attitudes and institutional logics' in Adams, J and Schmeuker, K (eds.) *Devolution in Practice 2006* London, Institute of Public Policy Research, pp. 10-28.

JRF (Joseph Rowntree Foundation) (2007) *Monitoring Poverty and Social Exclusion in Wales* York, Joseph Rowntree Foundation.

Laffin, M (2004) 'A brand that binds' *Agenda* Autumn, Cardiff, Institute of Welsh Affairs, p. 15.

Lohde, L (2005) 'Child poverty and devolution' in Adams, J and Schmeuker, K (eds.) *Devolution in Practice 2006* London, Institute of Public Policy Research, pp. 172-95.

Mackay, R (2006) 'Identifying need: devolved spending in Wales, Scotland and Northern Ireland' *Contemporary Wales* 18, pp. 236-55.

Mooney, G and Poole, L (2004) 'A land of milk and honey? Social policy in Scotland after devolution' *Critical Social Policy* 24(4), pp. 458-83.

Mooney, G and Williams, C (2006) 'Forging new ways of life? Social policy and nation building in devolved Scotland and Wales' *Critical Social Policy* 26(3), pp. 608-29.

Mooney, G, Scott, G and Williams, C (2006) 'Introduction: rethinking social policy through devolution' *Critical Social Policy* 26(3), pp. 483-97.

Morgan, R (2002) Speech to the University of Wales, Swansea, National Centre for Public Policy Third Anniversary Lecture, 11 December.

National Statistics Online, www.statistics.gov.uk/STATBASE/ssdataset.asp?vlnk=5955

Osmond, J (1998) (ed.) *Introduction in the National Assembly Agenda: A handbook for the first four years* Cardiff, Institute of Welsh Affairs.

Rees, G (2005). 'Democratic devolution and education policy in Wales: The emergence of a national system?' *Contemporary Wales* 17, pp. 28-43.

Wales Rural Observatory (2006) *Scoping Study of Eastern and Central European Migrant Workers in Rural Wales,* www.walesruralobservatory.org.uk

WAG (Welsh Assembly Government) (2001) Census of Population: *Religion,* http://new.wales.gov.uk/topics/statistics/wales-figs/population/2001religion

WAG (2003) *Wales: A Better Country* Cardiff, Welsh Assembly Government.

WAG (2004) *Wales Spatial Plan: People, Places, Futures* Cardiff, Welsh Assembly Government.

WAG (2006a) *Local Labour Force Survey,* www.statswales.wales.gov.uk/TableViewer/tableView.aspx?ReportId=3091

Welsh Assembly Government (2004) *Making the Connections* Cardiff, Welsh Assembly Government.

WAG (2007) *Fulfilled Lives, Supportive Communities* Cardiff, Welsh Assembly Government.

Williams, C, Evans, N and O'Leary, P (2002) *A Tolerant Nation? Exploring Ethnic Diversity in Wales,* Cardiff, University of Wales Press.

Williams, G A (1991) *When Was Wales?: A History of the Welsh* (3rd edition) London, Penguin Books.

Wincott, D (2005) 'Devolution, social democracy and policy diversity in Britain: the case of early-childhood education and care' in Adams, J and Schmeuker, K (eds.) *Devolution in Practice 2006* London, Institute of Public Policy Research, pp. 76-97.

Wyn Jones, R and Scully, R (2004) *Devolution in Wales: What does the Public Think?* Devolution Briefings No. 7, ESRC Devolution and Constitutional Change Programme, www.devolution.ac.uk/pdfdata/Scully_RLJ_Briefing7.pdf

## Chapter 2

# Governance and social policy

### Mark Drakeford

## Introduction

For anyone involved in social welfare services in Wales, the nature and pattern of governance in the post-devolution era has to be a matter of continuing interest. Other than to those directly involved in such issues, much of what makes up the landscape of public administration has little intrinsic fascination. The reason why social workers and other social welfare practitioners need to know these things is different. It is because, boring and arcane as some of the detail may be, effective practice depends on being able to navigate a path through these developments in a way that delivers the best possible outcomes for users. In the post-devolution era, change has been rapid and multi-faceted. The relationships between different tiers of government have altered; the basic foundations of the Assembly itself have been radically reformed; the underlying approach to public service provision, particularly as regards Wales and England, has become increasingly divergent; and different practical policies have emerged, as a result.

Other chapters in this volume will provide the necessary detail of these changes in relation to specific services – health, social services and so on. Here, my aim is four-fold:

- to set out an account of the changing powers, responsibilities and internal arrangements of the National Assembly itself;
- to explore the relationship between the Assembly Government and local authorities in Wales, particularly as far as social welfare services are concerned;
- to suggest some of the ideological distinctiveness of social policy making in a post-devolution Wales, again concentrating on those aspects that make a difference to social work and social welfare;

- to provide an account of what is, at the time of writing, the most recent statement of future Assembly Government intent, as far as such services are concerned.

## The developing Assembly

The unsteady origins and troubled birth of Welsh devolution have been well traced by a variety of different authors (Andrews, 1999; Osmond, 2003). After eighteen years of Conservative administration, in which Welsh voters consistently rejected Conservative candidates in increasingly large numbers, the Labour Party Manifesto at the 1997 General Election promised the establishment of a Scottish Parliament, and a Welsh Assembly, provided that such a proposal was confirmed in a post-election referendum. The 'democratic deficit' had been exposed in a series of examples where either policies had been imposed on Welsh voters despite their clear rejection of them – water privatisation and the poll tax, to cite just two examples – or where policies that were widely embraced in England – such as grant-maintained schools and fund-holding GPs – were largely ignored, despite some hefty financial inducements to do so.

It was largely this experience that appeared to have brought about a major shift in Welsh public opinion. The 1979 referendum, in the dying months of the Callaghan government, had seen devolution proposals rejected in Wales by a landslide. Even the most enthusiastic supporters of the idea concluded that it had been settled for a generation or more. Yet, less than 20 years later, the proposition was put again to the voters. In some ways, this history ought to have served as a warning that devolution was always going to be a more contentious proposition in Wales than in Scotland. The Labour Party itself continued to hold both devo-enthusiasts and devo-sceptics, as they came to be known. The 1997 proposals, on which the referendum was held, were a careful balancing act in which the principle of an Assembly was hedged about by a series of limitations on its powers. The close-run nature of the September 1997 referendum vote was claimed, by both sides, as a vindication of their views. Enthusiasts believed that the second-best nature of the Welsh proposals had blunted voters' willingness to support devolution. Sceptics regarded the vote as a vindication of their caution, believing that voters were largely unconvinced of devolution, with the scale of doubt growing in proportion to the scale of change.

*Essential elements of the 1999 Assembly*

Despite the narrow margin of victory, the referendum provided the go-ahead for preparation of the Bill that was to become the Government of Wales Act of 1998. The main features of the Assembly it created were for 60 members (smaller, therefore, than most Welsh councils), elected by a form of proportional representation (and thus a self-denying ordinance, stripping Labour of the built-in majority that it would have enjoyed through a first-past-the-post form of election). The Assembly was to represent a form of 'new politics', in which old, tribal dividing lines were to give way to fresh forms of less partisan dialogue and debate, in which the best talents of all parties would combine to put Wales first. The Act set out the 'functions', or areas of policy responsibility that were to be devolved to Wales. Essentially, these comprised the great domestic agenda of health, education, housing, social services, local government, sports and arts, the Welsh language and agriculture. There were substantial areas of responsibility, also, in the field of economic development. These did not include, however – as was the case in Scotland – an ability to vary taxation levels. Indeed, the whole of the macro-economy – taxation, social security, interest rates, government borrowing and so on – remained the responsibility of the Westminster administration. All matters relating to defence and foreign policy were similarly un-devolved. By chance, rather than by design, the result has been that total public expenditure in Wales has been divided more or less evenly between Westminster and the Assembly.

For social workers, and others involved in welfare professions, the main conclusion to be drawn from this division of responsibilities under devolution, is that the National Assembly is, overwhelmingly, a *social policy* body. Anyone engaged in asserting the rights to essential services of the most disadvantaged citizens – surely one of the core purposes of social work – needs to understand that the rule book for access to such services, in health, education, housing and so on – is now written in Wales. Progress towards rebalancing the social contract in favour of the least well-off thus depends on the policies adopted, the financial decisions taken and the legislation passed at the National Assembly. Dry, dusty and detailed as matters of governance often are, they remain an essential focus for any social welfare worker with a serious interest in social change and a practical, rather than simply rhetorical, commitment to addressing discrimination and disadvantage.

Other chapters in this volume will look in more detail at the Welsh Assembly Government's record in relation to policy development. At this stage, it is important to emphasise that, from the outset the Assembly has been provided with substantial legislative powers, through which the statute book in Wales has departed from that which applies in England. Because, in the terms used by lawyers, and parliamentary drafters, these have been 'secondary' powers, it has often been assumed that 'secondary' must mean 'insubstantial'. In fact, a 50-year trend in UK law-making means that, more and more, Acts of Parliament passed at Westminster have set out principles and frameworks, leaving the detail of policy development and implementation to 'secondary' legislation. Thus when, in Wales, means-testing was abolished for Disabled Facilities Grants for children, or when prescription charges are abolished, or when additional payments are made to the Child Trust Funds of looked-after children, then these measures – which apply only in Wales – are the result of secondary legislation in action.

*Early days*

The narrowness of the 1997 referendum in Wales was, of itself, likely to mean that devolution in Wales got off to a halting start. This sense of uncertainty was, however, much reinforced by a series of unforeseeable events that soon followed. By the time actual elections to the new body took place, in May 1999, Ron Davies, the Secretary of State at the time of the referendum, and responsible for much of the detail of the 1998 Government of Wales Act, had made his celebrated incursion into Clapham Common, and resigned, on the wholly novel basis that he had been a victim of crime. The struggle within the Labour Party to succeed him became a matter of very public acrimony and resulted in the imposition of Downing Street's preferred candidate, Alun Michael, over that of the membership of Welsh Labour, Rhodri Morgan. Election of a minority Labour administration followed and, within a year, the instability inherent in such circumstances had contributed to the loss, and replacement, of three of the four Assembly Party leaders.

From these very unpromising beginnings, a slow but steady recovery got underway during 2000. This recovery had two main dimensions. On the one hand, the new First Minister, Rhodri Morgan, used the enormous political capital at his disposal to bring the Liberal Democrats into government, as junior members in a 'partnership' – or coalition – administration. With a secure overall majority, ministers were able to face a series of immediate challenges – widespread flooding, fuel protests, foot and mouth disease – in a way that combined clear leadership and competent administration. A firmer divide between 'government' on the one hand and 'opposition' on the other also emerged so that, *de facto* if not *de jure* the Assembly came to turn its back on the 'corporate body', in favour of a more classically parliamentary model. As the Welsh Assembly Government, as it now became known, found its feet, so the second dimension of institutional recovery became apparent. Public opinion, which had been so ambivalent at the Assembly's birth, began to move more positively towards it, as discussed more fully below.

*Next moves*

One of the specific points included in the 2000 partnership agreement was a commitment to review the experience of the first Assembly, focusing on the legislative powers at its disposal and its form of election. A group was drawn together, combining nominees from all the Assembly's political parties, and experts selected through open competition. The Richard Commission, as it came to be known, was chaired by Lord Ivor Richard of Ammanford – former Labour government minister, UK ambassador to the United Nations, Leader of the House of Lords in the first Blair administration – and reported early in 2004. It recommended a strengthened Assembly, with full legislative powers and 80 members, elected in multi-member constituencies using the Single Transferable Vote. The Commission emphasised that it had reached these far-reaching and unanimous conclusions because of the *success* of devolution to date, rather than because of any limitations in the Assembly's original design. Not all the Richard recommendations were to be accepted by government, but the Report undoubtedly provided the catalyst for a second Government of Wales Act, passed into law in July 2006. Briefly summarised, the Act contained the following provisions:

- it confirmed a 60-member Assembly, and left unchanged its semi-proportional electoral system;
- it reshaped the Assembly in law, so that responsibilities were newly allocated between an 'executive' – or government – and an opposition ;
- it provided a new mechanism by which enhanced legislative powers could be drawn down from Westminster to Wales; and
- it enshrined in law the process by which the Assembly could, in future, acquire full primary powers, without the need for any further Act of Parliament.

The Government of Wales Act thus provides a further potential staging post on the road to full Welsh devolution, rather than, necessarily, its final destination. The third Assembly, elected in May 2007, inherited the new constitutional arrangements that the Act provides and the prospect of additional powers that it offers. The new administration was able to bring forward a legislative programme in a way that was not previously possible – and as discussed in more detail below. The result will be that, to a greater and more apparent extent, the statute book, as well as policy and practice in Wales, will become distinctive and divergent from that in other parts of the UK.

## The Assembly and local government

As already noted in this chapter, the coming of devolution in Wales was hedged about with ambivalence. One of the major sources of that hesitation was to be found among the leaders of local government in Wales. A number of reasons were combined in this feeling. In the first place, with the Conservatives lacking democratic legitimacy in Wales during the Thatcher and Major years, leaders of local authorities took on a new importance, as individuals who did, at least, carry the authority of the ballot box. It was easy enough to suspect that 60 new, full-time elected politicians at Cardiff Bay would rival, rather than complement, the importance that Labour local authority leaders (and, by the end of the Conservative period in office, almost all 22 local councils in Wales were Labour-led) had come to enjoy. More generally, the limited nature of the Welsh devolution settlement – 'Mid Glamorgan County Council on stilts', to quote one of the disparaging accusations regularly made against it – gave rise to a suspicion among local authorities that the Assembly would attempt to establish itself, not by drawing down power from Westminster, but by sucking up power from local councils.

Against that background, it was perhaps fortunate that so many of those members elected to the Assembly in 1999 (and particularly members of the governing Labour Group) had their background in local government. A majority of the first Labour Cabinet was drawn from individuals who had either worked for local authorities or had been elected to them. They brought with them an understanding of the internal workings of councils and a strong defence of localism.

Why should this be of importance to social workers? In governance terms, the answer is simply that the relationship between local and central government remains the key to understanding the administrative shape of the service by which most social workers are employed, as well as many other services on which social work users rely. The worst fears of local government in Wales have not been borne out by the experience of devolution. The Assembly Government has developed an approach to local service delivery that emphasises cooperation over competition, and partnership over contestability. All this has been in sharp contradistinction to England. There the former Seebohm social services departments have been dispersed to Primary Care and Children's Trusts as part of the 'managed decline' that Blairite ministers have preferred for local authorities. In Wales, by contrast, social services remain a core function of local councils, with adult, children and mental health workers continuing – in most instances – to operate within unified departments.

From time to time, and over individual issues, such as delayed transfers of care and the state of children's services in some Welsh local authorities, Assembly Government ministers have expressed impatience at the lack of progress that local councils seem capable of achieving, and at the weakness of levers that appear to lie in the Assembly's hands for bringing about improvement. The inability of the Assembly, for example, to 'fetter the discretion' of local councils in areas such as charging for domiciliary care services frustrated ministers' attempts to create a fairer charging regime across Wales, ironing out some of the wider disparities between different charging regimes in different local authorities.

Two specific developments, of a governance variety, have emerged, against that background. First, the Assembly Government and the Welsh Local Government Association have agreed a Protocol, in which Assembly ministers are enabled to intervene in local service delivery, where 'serious concern' has been independently verified. Second, the first legislative programme of the May 2007 administration has used the new powers of the 2006 Government of Wales Act to strengthen its hand in being able to insist on local government implementing particular policies when these are underpinned by the legislative authority of the Assembly, and where funding has been provided to allow them to be put into practice.

Two further, and more general policy thrusts have shaped the relationship between the Assembly and local government in Wales, and seem set to do so for the foreseeable future.

The first approach is captured in a key Assembly Government publication, *Making the Connections* (WAG, 2004), which sets out the shape and rationale for Welsh public service development and improvement. The document rehearses different models of public service reform, including the marketisation and consumerist agenda pursued at Whitehall. From the perspective of social welfare services it reaches three key conclusions. First, it comes down, unambiguously, in favour of cooperation rather than competition as the best means of securing better performance from public services. In a Welsh context, in particular, the document points to the advantages of scale that a small country possesses, as the basis for working across sectoral and organisational boundaries. Second, it endorses the need to increase the influence of users on the design and delivery of public services, but identifies amplifying the collective *voice* of users rather than individual choice in the marketplace, as the best means of doing so. Third, it models the relationship between providers and users of public services as one based on *reciprocity*, rather than mutual suspicion. In this model, the different qualities that both parties bring to social welfare transactions are equally valued, and grounded in a climate of mutual respect. Finally, it confirms the ongoing need for a mixed economy in the provision of welfare services, emphasising the need for balanced and managed markets in which voluntary sector services complement, rather than replace, those provided in the public sector.

The second approach is derived from a report produced by the Beecham Committee (WAG, 2006a), established by the Assembly Government in order to advise on practical ways of securing better performance from public service organisations in Wales. From the point of view of this book, the following conclusions of the Beecham exercise are the most significant. In governance terms, the report concluded that structural reform of local government and other public service boundaries did not provide the best route to improved delivery. Rather, the future lay in far greater working across boundaries, both between organisations of the same sort – between local authorities, between Local Health Boards (LHBs) and so on – and across sectors – councils working with their LHBs, LHBs working with Community Safety Partnerships and so on. In the Beecham prescription, such cross-boundary work is to be pursued through new Public Service Boards (PSBs), in which organisations will pool sovereignty and commit resources in pursuit of common goals.

The impact of these developments on social work will be direct. High on the agenda of the new PSBs will be delayed transfers of care, bringing together local councils, LHBs, National Health Service Trusts (NHSTs) and the voluntary sector in a renewed attempt to provide the fabled 'seamless service' that governments have pursued without real success for more than half a century. The Welsh recipe for social work (as set out more fully below), envisages the retention of Seebohm-like local authority departments. Beecham developments, however, if successful, may suggest a new model in which formalised joint working may come to predominate.

## Ideology

No fully informed understanding of governance can be obtained without some reference to ideology. Few higher education courses now claim to offer 'social administration', as though the wheels of bureaucracy ran on, regardless of the political context in which they turned.

Devolution was, by itself, an intensely political act. It transferred to Wales not simply a set of policy responsibilities, but the political authority to exercise them. Uniquely, in a UK context, Wales has remained a predominantly left-wing country for more than 150 years. The nineteenth century witnessed the triumph of Liberalism over the Conservative Party. The 20th century saw Liberalism displaced by the Labour Party. In successive General Elections in 1997 and 2001, Wales remained a Tory-free zone, without a single Conservative candidate returned to Westminster.

The upshot is that, within the National Assembly, the essential contest has been between three parties, each of which would self-describe as belonging to the political left, with Conservative members forming less than a quarter of the institution as a whole. While within the first eight years the Assembly Government has been variously formed by a majority Labour administration, two minority Labour administration, and a coalition between Labour and the Liberal Democrats (Lib Dems), the ideological path pursued has been one that reaches out to at least three quarters of the Assembly's make-up. The 2007 Assembly elections once again left Labour as by far the largest party, albeit – at 26 seats – well short of an overall majority. Nearly ten weeks of negotiations followed in which a concerted attempt was made to bring about a coalition involving the Conservatives, along with other non-Labour parties. In the event, that attempt failed, very largely because of the enduring hostility, in significant parts of Plaid Cymru and the Liberal Democrats, to opening the door for the Tories to walk back into power in Wales. By the end of July, a new Labour-Plaid Cymru coalition was in place, led by Rhodri Morgan, and with at the least the prospect of stable, left-of-centre, administration over the four years of the third Assembly term.

Given the hundreds and thousands of decisions which make up the day-in-day-out activity of any administration, there is something fool-hardy in suggesting that there may be some unifying ideological themes which, standing back from the canvas, can be discerned in this mass of activity. Inevitably, there will be examples which could be cited as contradicting any picture which claims to do so. What follows, however, is an attempt to identify a set of underlying principles which, it will be argued here, are characteristic of Assembly Government policy-making and which, together, amount to a particularly distinctive context in which to practice social work.

In the space available here, six core principles will be set out (for a fuller discussion of these ideas see Drakeford (2007):

The first of these may be summarised as *good government is good for you*. Now, to many readers, this may seem like a statement of the entirely obvious, yet there exists a very clearly articulated political position which concludes exactly the opposite to be the case (see, for example Butler 2007; Seldon 2007). Mrs Thatcher famously advised Members of the House of Commons to read the works of von Hayek, her favourite philosopher, and a determined advocate of 'small' government for whom Government did best when government did least. In the hands of the neo-conservatives public services, and public servants, were part of the problem faced by the UK – or 'knaves' as Le Grand (2003) famously termed them – rather than part of the solution. Government, in this analysis, was at best a necessary evil, at worst a force for evil, in itself.

That line of argument has never run successfully in Wales. Here there is an enduring belief that when competently organised and delivered, government continues to provide the platform for promoting and protecting the best interests of the greatest possible mass of people. That first key principle of Welsh policy-making is, of course, one that has long formed the foundation of the case for social work itself, as a function of government.

The second major theme of Welsh policy-making has been the adoption of *progressive universalism* as a guiding principle. Thus, wherever possible, the Assembly Government has a preference for universal measures – abolishing charges to museums and galleries for everyone, making prescriptions free for every patient, providing free breakfasts in every participating primary school, providing free swimming for children in school holidays and so on. While at a UK level, behavioural conditionality has become the hallmark of a qualified and restricted approach to social entitlement, the Assembly's approach has been to make services available to all, based only on residence. Universal services are preferred, where possible, in Wales because, as has been so long known, services designed to be a pauper's safety net, reserved for poor people, very quickly become poor services. As First Minister Rhodri Morgan has said on a number of occasions, universal services help provide the glue that binds together a complex modern society and gives everybody a stake – the articulate, as well as those who find it difficult to make their voices heard, the well informed as well as the less well off – in making those services as good as possible.

In addition to universality, however, policies in Wales also draw on a form of targeting, to provide additional help, over and above the universal measure, to those whose needs are greatest. A single example will be provided here in relation to children and young people. In the 2006 budget, the Chancellor of the Exchequer provided substantial new funding for schools which, in England, he directed to be distributed directly to head teachers on a simple formula based on school size. In Wales, the Assembly Cabinet decided to concentrate the same funding exclusively on those schools serving the most disadvantaged areas and on the education of looked-after children.

Universal services, with a progressive twist, combine the advantages of the classic welfare state with some of the benefits that can be claimed for targeting. The approach matters to social work because it identifies vulnerable citizens as having a *greater* not lesser call on public services. The sense in which the fate of any one of us affects the fate of us all remains close to the heart of the Welsh approach to social welfare. Progressive universalism is a key to retaining the widespread support on which the survival of that understanding depends.

The third principle to be identified here is that, as far as the Assembly Government is concerned, in the design, delivery and improvement of public services, *co-operation is better than competition.* This position is well rehearsed in the document, *Making the Connections* (WAG, 2004), in which the First Minister sets out what he calls the 'respectable case' for both models, before concluding that co-operation provides a better fit with the needs and circumstances of Wales. Behind this conclusion, of course, lies a very substantial contemporary debate in which the ethic of consumerism has been rejected in favour of an ethic of citizenship.

The fourth major principle is linked to the third, and concerns the *ethic of participation* that is pursued in the Welsh context. Devolution is, of itself, a major experiment in increasing the leverage that people who live in Wales have over the government that serves them. But, if social work is rooted in a commitment to the equal worth of every individual, then the need to draw on the talents of all our citizens applies as much to government itself as to any other aspect of life.

The most important corollary of all this, for social work, is that Assembly Government action in this area is characterised by a unifying preference for improving collective voice rather than relying solely on individual choice. Where public service participation is modelled on the mechanisms of the market, then those who already possess economic and social advantages will, inevitably, do best while others get left further behind. The preference for collective voice, as, for example, in the decision to retain and strengthen Community Health Councils in Wales, is grounded in an understanding that this provides the best way of ensuring that participation produces shared and wider benefits, rather than simply individual advancement. It means that user participation in the design and delivery of social work services is also to be based on capturing and responding to the collective experience of users, rather than confined to improving mechanisms for dealing with individual complaints or grievance.

The fifth principle identified here is that, in shaping the relationship between the citizen and the state, policy-making in Wales is predicated on the creation of *high-trust not low-trust* relationships, in which users of services, and those who provide them, are regarded as essentially engaged in a joint enterprise (see Chapter 11).

Quasi-commercial relationships of marketised services are based, inevitably, on low-trust foundations. The Latin tag *caveat emptor* – 'buyer beware' – reminds us that a self-interested sense of scepticism has underpinned markets for 2,000 years and more. By contrast, collective and co-operative approaches rely on high-trust relationships between those who combine their efforts in the hope of improved outcomes for all. In doing so, they draw on the fundamental recognition that success in public services depends on reciprocity. It seems difficult to imagine a closer alignment with this approach than that which underpins effective social work (see Butler and Drakeford [2005] for a wider discussion of this point). Trust is, surely, the pivot around which co-production turns, generating qualities of reciprocity and respect and cementing the sense of social solidarity on which the basic premise that one human being may be of assistance to another depends.

The sixth and final principle to be explored here is, perhaps, the most ambitious but the one that provides the most distinguishing feature of Assembly Government policy making. On a series of occasions the First Minister has endorsed the notion that, as far as Wales is concerned, greater equality of *outcome* is an ambition that has overtaken the more conventional pursuit of equality of opportunity. Recent figures published by the Chief Medical Officer of Wales show that, in Wales today, a child born in the least well-off part of Wales will live, on average, for five years less than a child born not one hour's travel away (Chief Medical Officer of Wales, 2006). In a lecture at Swansea, and in response to that finding, Rhodri Morgan reaffirmed the Assembly Government's position in this way:

> *'Inequality is the most insidious form of injustice because it prevents individuals from achieving their full potential. And every time inequality prevents any of our fellow citizens from exercising their talents, or accessing the services to which they are entitled, the total stock of freedom available to all of us is diminished.'*
> (Morgan, 2006)

The pursuit of greater equality provides the backdrop against which it is possible to retain some optimism about the pursuit of fruitful social work (see Chapter 7). More equal societies enjoy better health (Wilkinson, 2005), where health is understood as the product of being cared for by others. More equal societies enjoy lower levels of crime and, even more importantly, are marked by lower levels of fear of crime. There is a sense of individual validation and social solidarity that greater equality brings. Moreover, the sum of freedom in a more equal society will always be greater than in unequal societies, where freedom is unfairly divided.

Taken together, the argument of this chapter is that Wales remains a place where the wider purposes of government and governance remain focused on improving the prospects of the least fortunate, and doing so in a way that reaches out positively to individuals, families and communities where help is most needed. It offers a chance to practise social work in a way that goes with the grain, rather than against the tide, of social policy-making.

## Social work itself

This chapter now turns to the fourth and final purpose identified at the outset – a brief description of the main principles which inform the Assembly Government's approach to social work itself.

In the summer of 2006, the Health Minister, Brian Gibbons, published for consultation a social services policy statement, *Fulfilled Lives, Supportive Communities* (WAG, 2006b), designed to set out a ten-year agenda for development and improvement. The document received widespread support. It embodied the following key conclusions:

- that social services should remain a core responsibility of local authorities, in order to place social workers at the heart of a range of wider services, such as housing and education, on which their users need to draw;
- that local authorities should remain key providers of social services, as well as taking responsibility for overall planning, and commissioning some services from others;
- that the focus of social work and allied professionals should be re-orientated towards preventative strategies, wherever possible, both in relation to children's services and social care. The Welsh Assembly Government will set specific targets for reducing the proportion of children received into the 'looked-after' system, and invest in new services for older people, designed actively to counteract the loss of independence;
- that new arrangements will be put in place to strengthen the influence of users, and carers, on what services are provided, and how they are delivered;
- that the staff needed for the future of social services should be regarded as a single workforce, well-trained, well-motivated and informed by up-to-date evidence and research. Workers in social services in Wales will be capable of exercising *critical judgement* and expected to do so in the unique circumstances of each individual user;
- that the new powers of the Government of Wales Act 2006 should be used actively, where these lead to better outcomes for users.

Taken together, these conclusions set out a future for social work as an occupation in its own right, actively involved in influencing national and local policy through speaking up alongside users; utilising and developing the wider community and neighbourhood networks that strengthen the wider social fabric; and enabling individuals and their families to obtain the help they need.

## Conclusion

This chapter has mapped out a wide canvas, moving through the mechanics of government in a devolved Wales, through the key relationships between different levels of administration, outlining some linking characteristics of post-devolution social policy-making and setting out the specifics of that policy approach in relation to social welfare services.

Other chapters in this book will deal in more detail with other policy dimensions, and contextual factors. The conclusion drawn here is that, in relation to social work, Wales remains a place in which worthwhile practice can be pursued; where the broad policy purposes of greater equality, and reciprocity provide a solid foundation from which the positive promotion of individual progress can be undertaken and where the preference for a unified, publicly provided, critically informed profession allows for some optimism that social workers, as well as social welfare, have a future worth searching out and helping to shape.

## References

Andrews, L (1999) *Wales Says Yes* Bridgend, Seren Books.

Butler, I and Drakeford, M (2005) 'Trusting in social work' *British Journal of Social Work*, 35(5), pp. 639-53.

Butler, E (2007) *Adam Smith: a Primer* London, Institute of Economic Affairs.

Chief Medical Office of Wales (2006) *Chief Medical Officer's Report Series 2: Health in local areas, a compendium of maps* Cardiff, Welsh Assembly Government.

Drakeford, M (2007) 'Devolution and social justice in a Welsh context', *Benefits*, 19(2), pp. 173-180.

Le Grand, J (2003) *Motivation, agency and public policy: Of knights and knaves, pawns and queens* Oxford, Oxford University Press.

Morgan, R (2006) *Twenty First Century Socialism: A Welsh Recipe* London, Compass.

Osmond, J (ed.) (2003) *Birth of Welsh Democracy* Cardiff, Institute of Welsh Affairs.

Seldon, A (2007) *Capitalism: A Condensed Version* London, Institute of Economic Affairs.

WAG (Welsh Assembly Government) (2004) *Making the Connections* Cardiff, Welsh Assembly Government.

WAG (2006a) *Beyond Boundaries – Report of the Beecham Commission* Cardiff, Welsh Assembly Government.

WAG (2006b) *Fulfilled Lives, Supportive Communities* Cardiff, Welsh Assembly Government.

Wilkinson, R (2005) *Impact of Inequality: How to make sick societies healthier* London, Routledge.

# Chapter 3

# Post-devolution health policy

Michael Sullivan

## Introduction

This chapter provides a detailed example of policy differentiation in the UK following the 1999 political devolution settlements. It charts the development of health policy from pre-devolution to post-devolution Wales and, *en passant*, makes glancing comparisons with the other UK nations. It suggests that policy differentiation or divergence has sharpened considerably since 1999, considers why this should be so and looks at how policy divergence in social policy has been crafted by an Assembly that, until June 2007, functioned without primary law-making powers. It suggests that part of the answer to this latter question is that politicians and officials have worked together to create a 'Welsh way', which places health policy at, or near, the centre of the agenda for health organisations, local government and communities.

After making some general points, we move on to focus on the effect of devolution on health policy innovation in Wales. Political devolution has led to significant differences in policy between the devolved administrations and between those administrations and the Westminster government. This is no surprise: on one reading, at least that was one of the intentions. In Wales, which rejected devolution in the 1979 referendum, one of the main claims for it in 1997 was that it would allow 'Welsh solutions to Welsh problems'. This appears to have resonated with an impulse among the Welsh electorate, which had, since 1979, consistently voted for non-Conservative parties only to see the writ of Conservative governments run as far as – and beyond – Cathays Park! What we have observed since 1999 is far more than the policy anomalies claimed by some political pundits. We need, therefore, to analyse the extent and nature of policy divergence and its relationship to the devolution project.

## Asymmetrical devolution

As a glance at the Acts establishing devolved government will indicate, political devolution in the UK is asymmetrical with distinct differences between the settlements for Wales, Scotland and Northern Ireland.

The Scottish Parliament and the Northern Ireland Assembly have powers in relation to all matters not specifically reserved to Westminster.

Scotland has a single list of reserved matters, while in Northern Ireland there is a distinction between reserved matters, which may be devolved in the future, and excepted matters, which are to be reserved permanently for Westminster.

Both bodies have primary legislative powers over non-reserved matters, as well as executive responsibility for matters where the primary responsibility remains with the centre.

The Welsh Assembly, on the other hand, had only secondary legislative and executive responsibility for a list of powers devolved from Westminster and was required to obtain parliamentary approval for any changes in primary legislation. The second Government of Wales Act – so good they named it twice! – in 2006 addressed this imbalance and created a situation in which the Assembly may now make primary legislation in all but name.

## Policy divergence before devolution

Devolution in the UK builds on an existing and deep-rooted system of administrative devolution in which each of the UK countries had a distinct way of making or adapting policy and delivering services.

While the Scottish Office and its associated agencies acted within the limits of overall UK policy, there were areas in which it was allowed to develop policy and practice (for example in relation to education policy). The Welsh Office, on the other hand, was more extensively integrated into Whitehall networks, tended neither to sponsor legislation nor to initiate policy. However, even in this very restrictive relationship, policy divergence was both possible and, occasionally, actual. The development, during the 1980s, of an all-Wales mental handicap strategy both marked a divergence from the UK policy map and led the way in community care arrangements for people with learning disabilities. Government in Northern Ireland was an inheritance from the Stormont power-sharing regime, which had extensive devolved powers although it tended to imitate British welfare state provision. However, immediately preceding devolution, clear differences (in emphasis at least) emerged. This is nowhere more evident than in relation to health policy where, perhaps, we see in Wales and Scotland precursors of a new inclusive politics.

In the context of, and run up to, political devolution to Wales, Scotland and Northern Ireland, three White Papers appeared in 1998 on the refurbishment and modernisation of the NHS (Department of Health, 1997; Scottish Office, 1997; Welsh Office, 1998). Each of them was informed by a set of values reflecting the key concerns of the UK Labour government. While the foreword to the English White Paper talks of the importance of 'modernisation', the Welsh and Scottish versions focus on the need to 'restore' the NHS. In Wales, this was expressed as 'reaffirming its founding principles and devising new responses to the challenges which face it' (introduction to section 1) while in Scotland the aim was 'to restore the National Health Service as a public service working co-operatively for patients' (Foreword).

These aims are underpinned by a number of key principles, chief among them being a new emphasis in all three White Papers on accountability. This perhaps illustrates UK New Labour's emphasis on the 'third way'.

## The 'third way'

As far as the NHS is concerned, this 'third way' is described in the foreword to each of the White Papers as replacing the internal market with integrated care, combining efficiency and effectiveness with fairness and partnership. There is, however, some difference between the English approach on the one hand, and the Scottish and Welsh on the other. Whereas the English White Paper identified the need for partnership between health and local authorities as one of six key principles (chapter 2), the need for partnerships at a number of different levels is spelled out in both the Welsh (paragraph 1.15) and Scottish (paragraph 8) versions, which describe the need for collaboration between:

- government and the electorate;
- patients and professionals;
- the NHS and other statutory and voluntary bodies;
- NHS organisations.

This difference in emphasis is best seen as reflecting the perceived need to re-negotiate relationships between politicians, health and social services agencies and the public in Wales and Scotland in response to the imminence of the Welsh Assembly and the Scottish Parliament.

While the Welsh and Scottish White Papers share the English version's unquestioning faith in the transformative power of IT, information and advice lines, their approach implies a more proactive model of user and public involvement. The Welsh White Paper, for example, is permeated by references to the importance of the patient focus and contains numerous *requirements* for involvement at all levels:

- 'Steps *must* be taken to find out what patients and communities want' (paragraph 3.31, emphasis added).
- 'The NHS *should* give the highest priority to looking at services from the patient's perspective' as well as responding to their perceptions (paragraph 3.18, emphasis added).
- 'Service planning and delivery *should* be designed through the eyes of the patient' (paragraph 3.4, emphasis added).
- 'Particular emphasis should be placed on involving patients in clinical decision-making' (paragraph 3.18) and 'NHS organisations are *required* to examine new approaches to care which focus on the patient's journey through the process' (paragraph 3.27, emphasis added).
- 'Patient evaluation of services is to be measured against the same criteria as those of professionals and managers' (paragraph 3.20) and 'clinicians need to maximise the potential of audit by recognising the importance of patients' views/ experiences' (paragraph 3.29).

In Wales, as Drakeford (2006:549) has noted, the Welsh White Paper represented three main policy cleavages with England. First, it heralded the end of general practitioner (GP) fund-holding in Wales and established Local Health Groups (LHGs), later transformed into Local Health Boards (LHBs) and made up of GPs, other healthcare professionals, social services and the voluntary sector, to develop services to meet local needs and priorities The geographical boundaries of both LHGs and the later LHBs were coterminous with those of Welsh unitary authorities. Greer (2001) describes this departure as a 'grudging acceptance' of the purchaser–provider split in which commissioning remained a possible, but minor, feature of the system. The second cleavage was that a new imperative was placed on the reduction of health inequalities through a renewed obligation to 'protect and improve health as well as respond to illness and disability' (Welsh Office, 1998). Greer sees this as an intellectually coherent agenda which recognised that many of the major health challenges in Wales, such as coronary heart disease, were the product of lifestyle and economics (Greer, 2001). In Drakeford's words, it 'positioned the NHS as but one powerful tool in a far wider set of measures needed to address the determinants of health' (Drakeford, 2006:550). Finally, both described a model of patient and public involvement that flew in the face of the consumerist mode that had already begun to emerge in the parallel English system.

## Policy divergence post devolution

If some differentiation characterised the politics of health policy in the pre-devolution period, this tendency has been sharpened since the formation of the Welsh Assembly and the Scottish Parliament. During the first term of devolved government, each of the administrations introduced a raft of policies in relation to health. Wales, England and Scotland produced plans for the NHS, setting the trajectory for health policy over the next ten years.

*Improving Health in Wales: a plan for the NHS with its partners* (National Assembly for Wales, 2001) sought, *inter alia*, to put policy meat on the rhetorical bones of public involvement . It also aimed to translate the NHS into an agency for the development and implementation of a new health policy trajectory in Wales, which emphasised the primacy of public health. In her *Foreword* to the Plan, the Welsh Minister for Health and Social Services wrote:

> '*I am delighted to introduce proposals, which place the citizen at the centre of the NHS and, building on an enviable record in Wales, establish firm lines of accountability to the people and communities of our nation. The NHS will, as part of its renewal, truly become the people's NHS. This involves not only maintaining the patient-centred focus of our services but also making the NHS answerable to all citizens – patients and potential patients alike. It also means involving communities in the collective development of policies for health and well being and makes the process of health policy making inclusive.*'
> (National Assembly for Wales, 2001:6)

This dramatic commitment was given substance in chapter 3 of the document – entitled, echoing Bevan, *The People's NHS* – where the scope of and mechanisms for involvement are addressed. A close examination of them indicates an interesting emphasis on the nature of the contract between administration, NHS and citizens in Wales. Put simply, the contract implied in the Welsh renewal of the NHS is one that stresses the connections between government, service planners and providers and communities of citizens. This is enhanced by the Welsh administration's abolition of health authorities and the relocation of power closer to the citizen in LHBs which have coterminous boundaries with local authorities.

As an academic involved in the drafting and development of policy in relation to the Welsh plan, I remain struck by the strength of a number of key emphases:

- an emphasis on participation;
- an emphasis on partnership;
- an emphasis on citizenship;
- an emphasis on health inequalities;
- an emphasis on the social determinants of health.

All the above were underpinned by an emphasis on population health: turning the NHS from an illness service to one actively involved in promoting health.

The Plan is also intriguing as it is unique, in the global context, in its development out of an essentially public health document that placed the NHS at, or near, the centre of a partnership network of policy actors engaged in the development of policy and practice rooted in the social and economic determinants of health. This contrasts with both the Scottish Plan and the English Plan. The Scottish Plan – while rhetorically committed like its Welsh counterpart to consultation and involvement and to a public health agenda – retained existing structural arrangements intact and saw the NHS, rather than the NHS with its partners, as driving the health policy trajectory. Interestingly, the ownership of the Service is couched in the language of participation while, largely, the NHS is still regarded as the legitimate concern of three groups of stakeholders: politicians, professionals and managers. A close reading of the Scottish document also suggests an implicit contract. However, unlike the Welsh approach, it is an orthodox contract between government and the individual citizen. The English Plan, sometimes seen as the master document is relatively straightforward. It encapsulates a commitment to improving the health service – rather than health or health policy. It implies a contract between government, service and customer (rather than citizen or communities) and its horizons stretch little further than more effective service provision.

The Plan was also significant in that it indicated that the Welsh way in relation to health policy and improving health was to be rooted in a localist political impulse. To express this sharply, comparatively and succinctly, we might argue the following:

- Scotland tended towards a system based on *professionalism* in which it tried to align organisation with the existing structure of medicine. This meant reducing layers of management and replacing them with clinical networks, thereby increasing the role of professionals in rationing and resource allocation.
- England's model is a *market* model in which independent trusts, similar to private firms, are contracted with each other for care.
- The Welsh NHS system, by contrast, entrenched an ethos of *localism*. This meant integrating health and local government in order to coordinate care and focus on the determinants of

health rather than simply on treating the sick. It sought to use this localism as the lever to make the NHS into a national health service rather than a national sickness service (see Greer, 2004:128-58).

In Wales the publication of the plan was followed by the emergence of policy, that complemented its objectives. Those objectives might be summarised as follows:

- an emphasis on a primary care-led preventive and publicly engaged NHS as opposed to the hospital-dominated, treatment-focused and managerially driven emphasis in the NHS Plan for England;
- an emphasis on the NHS and its partners working collaboratively to diminish health inequalities;
- an emphasis on population health and the social and economic determinants of health;
- an emphasis on the accountability of the NHS to citizens as communities rather than to citizens as individual consumers;
- an emphasis on partnership between health bodies, local government and the voluntary sector.

To facilitate these objectives, the Welsh Assembly Government, engaged during its first term in policy developments that included the following:

- A new evidence-based formula for the allocation of resources to health bodies was commissioned and introduced, based on evidence of social, health and economic need (the so-called Townsend formula).
- A twin-track approach – tackling the causes of poor health and focusing services on results – was also introduced. This followed the advice of Townsend's (2001) report, *Targeting Poor Health*, that such an approach was the optimal route to the reduction of the sharp differences in health that characterised the Welsh NHS.

- A policy commitment both to strengthening local authority Community Strategies and partnerships with local government were seen as tools to ensure health improvement while modernising services. In 2002 the Welsh Assembly Government's *Wellbeing in Wales* reinforced the commitment to integrated policies and programmes to tackle the causes of poor health, disability and poor quality of life. This aim was reflected in *Wales: A Better Country* (WAG, 2003).
- A health inequalities fund was introduced to pump-prime initiatives intended to diminish health inequalities.
- Organisational reform of the NHS in Wales was undertaken to ensure that commissioning of services takes place within geographical and political entities that are coterminous with local government boundaries. The clear intention here was that such geographical coterminosity between health organisations and local government would contribute to the creation of a seamless web of care. It would facilitate joint working, joint (or pooled) funding and the closer interaction of professionals across organisational boundaries and, maybe, encourage greater interaction at the level of professional education between health professionals and social welfare professionals.

Commissioning a report by Derek Wanless (2003) and considering the implications of it on the progress being made towards its aims. A major development post-Wanless was the preparation of Health, Social Care and Wellbeing Strategies by local authorities and LHBs. These, based on a rigorous assessment of needs, serve as the basis for developing services.

During its second term, we have seen the publication and part implementation of the Welsh Assembly Government's ten-year strategy document, *Designed for Life* (WAG, 2005), which includes implementation milestones for the achievement of a redesigned health policy by 2015. The re-modelling of the NHS along the lines alluded to in the introduction to this chapter are intended to achieve three principal objectives:

- *Lifelong health:* including a focus on health and well-being, rather than illness, through the promotion of healthy communities and the encouragement of individual action to promote health.
- *Fast, safe and effective services:* This was seen as necessitating action to get supply and demand into balance; ensuring that demand is better managed, both at primary and secondary care level; and freeing up capacity to ensure that patients and clients are treated in the right place at the right time by the right people.
- *World-class care*: including the creation of services that support people at home, or as close to home as is safely possible; a focus on assisting the highest level of independence and personal potential services that are accessible; and fast, safe, effective and simple to understand services.

## Why policy divergence?

Implicit in the divergence that has occurred, and is occurring, is a differentiated Labour Party and Labour-dominated administrations in England, Scotland and Wales with different 'takes' on the political philosophy of Labour. At the English (or UK) level, the politics of New Labour seem to have predominated in the making of health, and more widely social, policy.

There is, it seems, little argument that the election of Tony Blair as leader of the Labour party in 1994 and the election of Labour to government in 1997 marked a transition from the old post-war Labour politics to a new approach to Labour's traditional concerns. Tactically, the decision, by its leaders to re-brand the party as New Labour signalled this shift. Hard on the heels of the General Election, Blair published a Fabian Society pamphlet entitled *The Third Way: New Politics for a New Century* (Blair, 1998) and this was to be followed in 1998 and 2000 by two books, *The Third Way: the Renewal of Social Democracy* (Giddens, 1998) and *The Third Way and its Critics* (Giddens, 2000) written by Blair's intellectual guru, another Tony, Tony Giddens (formerly Professor of Sociology at Cambridge University and currently director of the London School of Economics and Political Science). One of the central arguments of these publications is that what is new about New Labour is that it has renewed social democracy: it has refined it and revised it to meet the social and economic challenges of new times. Accordingly, they argue that the core values of the new or modernised social democracy remain those of its previous post-war incarnation. The politics of that old social democracy, its top-down approach to policy development, its emphasis on class struggle and its bureaucratic tendencies had, along with other things, made Labour unelectable for nearly two decades. The politics needed changing, opined the two 'Tonies', but the values of social democracy – its commitment to social justice, greater equality of opportunity, as opposed to Welsh Labour's commitment to equality of outcome, and a civilised society – remained.

## Reforming the welfare state

The first Blair government introduced a crusade for welfare reform. The Prime Minister argued, in the debate on the government's programme, that the British public were no longer willing to fund an unreformed welfare state and were similarly unimpressed by proposals that suggested raising taxes further and investing more public money in welfare state services. Instead, the New Labour government set its face towards a new contract between government and people rooted in a concept of social citizenship at some distance from post-war formulations. This much is clear in the social policies of New Labour governments. UK New Labour sees the aims of the welfare state it has created as:

- contributing to economic growth rather than as redistributing resources from rich to poor and providing individual routes out of dependence on state benefits rather than seeing collective provision as a safety net capable of catching those in economic free fall (in other words, New Labour has replaced old social democracy's commitment to the centrality of welfare with a new commitment to the centrality of paid work – it is in this context that we should understand the development and extension of New Deals for young people, single parents and disabled people);

- emphasising the *responsibilities* of citizenship as equally, if not more, important than the *rights* that old social democracy had conferred (again the New Deals, and the increasing compulsion to work being introduced for all those deemed capable, have the effect of eclipsing a rights- or entitlement-based welfare regime with one that changes the balance between rights and responsibilities);
- targeting social provision on an identifiably meritorious or deserving section of the population rather than upholding welfare rights as *universal rights*;
- redefining the role of government in addressing the problem of poverty – the effects of poverty (social exclusion – the inability of poor people to share in the opportunities of society) rather than poverty itself is seen as the legitimate concern of government social policy;
- finally, embracing a conception of the legitimate role of the state as a *guarantor of social provision* rather than as always the *provider* . Here the example of diagnostic treatment centres (in England) comes to mind. They are privately-funded, privately owned, privately staffed and privately run, but they draw their entire income stream from the public purse.

In contrast, Labour, or Labour-led, administrations in Cardiff have retained old Labour's commitment to the welfare state as an engine of equality, social justice and social inclusion based on the political values of universality, social solidarity and free services. To this, they seem to have added a more modern – but also older – set of emphases on collaboration, participation, communities and partnership.

The reality is that the Labour administration in Cardiff has fused an old Labour tradition with a renewed quasi-syndicalist impulse (Sullivan, 2000:19-20) – a sort of forward-to-the past rather than back-to-the-future! It highlights the collective nature of the contemporary politics of health policy in Wales and contrasts with an English Blairite emphasis on consumerism and individualism (although in the New Labour lexicon these concepts are re-branded as a new form of citizenship). Welsh health policy since 1999 has been driven, and continues to be driven by a sort of 21st century collectivism; this explains First Minister Morgan's emphasis on the individual as citizen rather than as consumer. As such, it opens the door to the development of joined-up or cross-cutting policies to impact on health inequalities: social determinants of health therefore become a legitimate concern of health policy and, more significantly, of NHS policy; the NHS becomes accountable to citizens as members of communities rather than as individuals. Here, Greer's analysis of the health reforms as placing the collective at the centre of health policy – rather than the individual consumer (England) or the medical profession (Scotland) – has particular salience (Greer, 2004:224-44). Put another way, Morgan's emphasis on a health service (and welfare state) underpinned by the principles of equality, universality and collaboration potently indicates the extent of 'clear red water' (Morgan, 2002) between Labour in Cardiff and Labour in London.

This is the backdrop for treading a 'Welsh way'. In a lecture in Swansea in 2002 Morgan described this approach to health and social policy in the following way:

> 'The thread which links these and all our other, social policy efforts together is a belief that a complex modern society such as ours can only operate effectively when held together by a powerful glue of social solidarity. Indeed, our commitment to equality leads directly to a model of the relationship between the government and the individual that regards that individual as a citizen rather than as a consumer. Approaches which prioritise choice over equality of outcome rest, in the end, upon a market approach to public services, in which individual economic actors pursue their own best interests with little regard for wider considerations.'
>
> (Morgan, 2002:22)

These, then, are the social politics of old Labour modernised and integrated with new impulses for collaboration, participation and inclusion. They draw succour from a sort of social democracy that characterised post-war Britain. Following the Second World War and the election of a Labour government in 1945, the UK Labour party set about creating a reasoned and moral case for social democracy.

The values underpinning post-devolution health – and indeed other social – policy in Wales have a reasonably long pedigree. For Labour – or Labour-led – administrations in the Welsh Assembly they are, however, contemporary as well as historical guides. The Welsh way is seen by the Welsh Assembly Government as a further redefinition of Welsh democratic socialism, which distances the administration in Cardiff from some of the principles and many of the policy actions of the UK New Labour project.

## References

Blair, A (1998) *The Third Way: New Politics for a New Century* London, Fabian Society.

Department of Health (1997) *The New NHS: Modern, Dependable* London, Department of Health.

Drakeford, M (2006) 'Health policy in Wales: making a difference in conditions of difficulty' *Critical Social Policy* 26(3), pp. 543-61.

Giddens, A (1998) *The Third Way: The Renewal of Social Democracy* Cambridge, Polity Press.

Giddens, A (2000) *The Third Way and its Critics* Cambridge, Polity Press.

Greer, S (2001) *Divergence and Devolution* London, Nuffield Trust.

Greer, S (2004) *Territorial Politics and Health Policy* Manchester, Manchester University Press.

Morgan, R (2002) National Centre for Public Policy Annual Lecture, Swansea, University of Wales.

National Assembly for Wales (2001) *Improving Health in Wales: A Plan for the NHS and its Partners* Cardiff, National Assembly for Wales.

Scottish Office (1997) *Designed to Care: Renewing the National Health Service in Scotland*, Cm 3811, December, London, The Stationery Office.

Sullivan, M (2000) *Labour, Citizenship and Social Policy: A Retreat from Social Democracy?* (Inaugural lecture) Swansea, University of Wales.

Townsend, P (2001) *Targeting Poor Health* Cardiff, National Assembly for Wales.

WAG (Welsh Assembly Government) (2003) *Wales: A Better Country* Cardiff, Welsh Assembly Government.

WAG (2005) *Designed for Life: Creating World-class Health and Social Care for Wales in the 21st Century* Cardiff, Welsh Assembly Government.

Wanless, D (2003) *Review of Health and Social Care in Wales* Cardiff, National Assembly for Wales.

Welsh Office (1998) *NHS Wales: Putting Patients First* Cardiff, Welsh Office.

# SECTION TWO

## Key Themes in Service Delivery

# Chapter 4

# Language-sensitive practice

Elaine Davies

## Introduction

Any attempt to address language-sensitive practice from the standpoint of the Welsh language in Wales relates to three core issues. First, it requires individual practitioners to address the affective or the subjective, an exploration of their personal attitudes, values and perceptions of the language. This links with personal experiences, family histories and group identities and requires an honest exploration of each. Second, it has to do very clearly with the social domain of the Welsh language and an understanding of the complex factors that affect language use in Wales. This helps ensure that social welfare policy and practice may be grounded in a firm understanding of factors that relate to the history, status and current use of the language. And third, and most importantly, it has to do with an appreciation of power, disempowerment and empowerment as they affect Welsh speakers.

Language-sensitive practice also requires the adoption of basic principles, inclusivity being foremost. Rather than building barriers and creating fortresses, as has sometimes happened in the past, it is vital to identify common ground and to look at ways of forging alliances and engaging people who would otherwise be on the outside of the issue. This means recognising the role not only of Welsh-speaking practitioners, but also of non-Welsh speaking colleagues, in the task of furthering language choice for bilingual users. The vision of 'one Wales' is also central as opposed to the more traditional tendency of seeing Wales as a country divided by its geography and economy, its language and culture. By locating language-sensitive practice firmly in the context of empowerment, it becomes more possible for old misunderstandings to be aired and resolved and for language-sensitive practice to be given a rightful place on the diversity agenda in Wales.

Discussions of power, empowerment and their links with language-sensitive practice raise vital questions about the relationship between the periphery and the core. Fishman (1990) sets this in a sociolinguistic context with reference to 'centralising the periphery' and working on the 'cultivation of marginality'. Reflecting on this relationship between the periphery and the core, he states that:

> 'The periphery magnifies and clarifies. Above all, it refuses to take matters for granted. It refuses to confuse peripherality with unimportance, or weakness in numbers or in power, with weakness vis á vis equity, justice, law and morality.' (Fishman, 1990:113)

It is this tension between the periphery and the core, between marginalising and mainstreaming, which underpins much of the following discussion. To this end, the chapter aims to address why social welfare practitioners in Wales need to engage with the Welsh language and language choice in their work with bilingual service users. It will also discuss what they need to know about the Welsh language and its speakers, that is, the knowledge base needed to inform policy and practice, as well as touching on how social care providers can strengthen the delivery of bilingual services.

## The legislative and policy drive

It is the Welsh Language Act, 1993 that sets the legislative framework with its aim to 'promote and facilitate the language in Wales, in particular in the conduct of public business and the administration of justice on the basis of equality with English'. As well as introducing the principle of equality, the Act also requires public sector providers to prepare statutory Language Schemes stating the steps they intend taking to implement this principle in their service provision. It also established the Welsh Language Board with the duty of overseeing the implementation of these Schemes and promoting the language in a wider sense.

In the context of social care, it is important to refer to the guidance provided by the Welsh Language Board to agencies preparing Welsh Language Schemes:

*'... in circumstances where stress, vulnerability, illness or disability are key factors, not being able to communicate in their first language may place those concerned at personal disadvantage. Given the sensitive nature of many of these discussions, it is important to offer language choice wherever possible.'* (Welsh Language Board, 1996:26)

The Act has no doubt heightened awareness of the language. For many public sector providers it now registers on the radar for the first time, with the production over the last decade of Welsh Language Schemes setting out changes in relation to the way these providers operate. Many voluntary sector providers have also produced similar sets of policies and strategies. But, despite these attempts to afford the language greater equality, there is scant evidence of any real change in the ease and extent of language choice made available to bilingual users across Wales as a whole. There is a considerable body of anecdotal evidence suggesting that bilingual users are still faced with the dual block of low personal expectations and correspondingly low levels of actual bilingual provision. The little empirical evidence available confirms this clearly as in the Welsh Consumer Council report prepared by Misell (2000) and Thomas' (1998) research on Welsh-speaking women and bilingual maternity services.

With a growing lobby of opinion in Wales now in favour of new and more robust Welsh language legislation to encompass the private sector and, among other things, to strengthen the rights of Welsh speakers, a cursory evaluation of the 1993 Act may conclude that among its successes has been the creation of a more positive climate for the language generally. But this is offset by its failure to bring about any real improvement in the bilingual services available to users in Wales as a whole, and especially to social care users, often vulnerable and marginalised and least able to invoke their linguistic rights.

While recognising the limitations of the 1993 Act, it has to be acknowledged that devolved government has given a new drive to the process of addressing the status and use of the Welsh language. In 2003 the Welsh Assembly Government published its strategic document, *Iaith Pawb*, in which it outlined its vision of creating a bilingual Wales:

> *'Our vision is a bold one and was set out in our policy statement on the Welsh language, Dyfodol Dwyieithog: A Bilingual Future published in July 2002. Our aspiration is expressed in the title of that document – a truly bilingual Wales, by which we mean a country in which people can choose to live their lives through the medium of either or both Welsh or English and where the presence of the two languages is a source of pride and strength to us all.'*
> (WAG, 2003:1)

This bold and challenging affirmation of bilingualism – of a society in which both languages co-exist with one another and of the need to accommodate this inter-relationship in public policy – is significant and helps set the tone for the development of the inclusive, equality-based social policies that were touched on in the introduction to this chapter.

*Iaith Pawb* also emphasises the rights of the individual to use the Welsh language. This reference to the rights agenda as an aspect of public policy regarding the Welsh language is seen for one of the first times in *Iaith Pawb* with the assertion that, 'The Welsh Assembly Government aims to safeguard and promote the right of individuals to use the Welsh language' (WAG, 2003:47).

The strategy goes on to identify the importance of language-sensitive provision in health and social care, referring to the specific needs of certain user groups, for example, older people, young children, people with learning difficulties and people with mental health problems, and states its determination '… to impress the importance of being able to deliver services in the service users' language of choice in key service areas such as health and social care' (WAG, 2003:47).

So, the Welsh Language Act and, more significantly perhaps, the *Iaith Pawb* strategy, create an impetus for addressing language-sensitive practice. For local authority providers, the Generic Equalities Standard is also significant, offering as it does a framework for mainstreaming and monitoring performance in relation to the four statutory equalities in Wales – race, gender, disability *and* language. (A revised Standard for Wales is expected towards the end of 2007 to reflect changes to equality legislation and the local government policy context since its launch in 2002.)

In relation to local government and social welfare policy, the unifying strand in much Welsh Assembly Government policy during recent years has related to citizen-focused services that are responsive to the needs of individuals and communities. References to the Welsh language dimension are often explicit and set firmly in the context of the need to develop services shaped by the specific needs of individuals and communities. This is seen, for example, in the publications presented in Figure 4.1.

**Figure 4.1:**
**Welsh Assembly Government's policy on the Welsh language**

*Making the Connections: Delivering Better Services for Wales* (WAG, 2004)
Among the principles guiding the development of public services in Wales is the need to place the citizen at the centre and to promote equality and social justice. The publication states that services focusing on citizens' needs are not universally available in Wales and that changes are needed in the way in which services are designed, planned and delivered. Actions needed include *'radical approaches'* to the way in which services are delivered to particular groups, including Welsh speakers.

*Beyond Boundaries: Citizen Centred Local Services for Wales* (WAG, 2006)
This reaffirms the importance of citizen-centred policies and models of service delivery that create '… new opportunities to respond more flexibly and creatively to the diversity of Wales's communities: the particular mix of rurality, industrial valleys and urban areas, as well as its unique language and culture' (paragrah 7.8).

*Fulfilled Lives, Supportive Communities, A Strategy for Social Services in Wales over the Next Decade* (WAG, 2007)
The thrust of this policy document relates to the '… need to shape services around users and to rebalance services towards the community' (paragraph 2.2).
'The Welsh language is an essential part of the Welsh culture and life. It must be reflected in developing effective social care strategies as well as in planning, delivering and improving services for individuals whose language of preference is Welsh' (paragraph 3.29).

Public policy therefore firmly supports the provision of services sensitive to the needs of individuals and communities. More specifically, the Codes of Practice and the National Occupational Standards for social care professionals offer a further thrust towards integrating language-sensitive practice with their recurring themes of cultural sensitivity, respect for diversity, appropriate communication, individual rights and interests, and service user choice. These all offer a sound rationale for getting to grips with language, bringing it in from the periphery to the core.

On the wider stage, the UK is a signatory to the European Charter on Regional and Minority Languages with its underpinning principle of respect for diversity, language rights and equality of opportunity.

## Language-sensitive practice: the knowledge base

*Language, identity and communication*

In the mid-1990s the Central Council for Education and Training in Social Work (CCETSW) published training materials whose title *They all Speak English Anyway* (Davies, 1994), summed up a not uncommon assessment of language use among bilingual Welsh-English speakers in Wales. Underpinning this assertion that 'they all speak English anyway' is an assumption that language is merely a means of communication.

At the time of publishing the CCETSW materials, and contrary to this popular view, there was a wealth of anecdotal evidence from bilingual speakers themselves and a growing body of international research on bilingualism (Grosjean, 1989, 1994), suggesting that language use among bilingual speakers is complex and multi-dimensional. Shortly before the publication of *They All Speak English Anyway*, the Anglo-Welsh writer, John Barnie, had described his experience of learning a second language, saying:

> '... I had the common experience that speaking another language alters the "I" that is being expressed. I had not realized before that who you are is partly formed by what you speak.' (Barnie, 1992:119)

Almost simultaneously with the CCETSW publication in 1994, Aitchison and Carter were also affirming the link between language, ethnicity and identity:

> '... language is much more than a means of communication. Not only does it carry a view of the environment, using that word in its proper inclusive sense, but through its vocabulary and its structure, through the associations generated by its literature, through the symbol which it is and the symbols which it transmits, it creates a distinctive identity which is at once a derivative of tradition and an expression of the present.'
> (Aitchison and Carter, 1994:6)

Language was therefore seen as something that powerfully roots speakers in their past, helps them make sense of their present and creates a sense of affinity and shared territory, all themes that were echoed in Fishman's work:

> 'Language was also the surest way for individuals to safeguard (or recover) the authenticity they had inherited from their ancestors as well as to hand it on to generations yet unborn, and finally, that worldwide diversity in language and in culture was a good and beautiful thing in and of itself...' (Fishman, 1972:46)

Since the mid-1990s, researchers have drawn on evidence to firmly challenge the notion that language is merely a vehicle of communication. Emotion and expression, they argue, are often shaped by the social and cultural context in which they are experienced. Altarriba and Morier, for example, draw on research of language use among bilingual service users in mental health settings; much of this is based on work with Hispanic users and other minority communities in North America. They come to the conclusion that in psychological assessment and diagnosis, '... a bilingual may appear to present him or herself in different ways depending on the language used' (Altarriba and Morier, 2004:252).

They quote Guttfreund who had already concluded in 1990 that:

> 'for the Hispanic population the therapeutic process may
> be far more meaningful in Spanish, because members of
> this population are likely to feel more comfortable
> expressing their feelings in Spanish.'
> (Guttfreund, 1990:606)

Altarriba and Morier conclude that:

> '... past experiences are often coded in the language in
> which they occurred and that the appropriate language can
> be used successfully as a retrieval cue when engaging in
> dialogue with a bilingual client.'
> (Altarriba and Morier, 2004:274)

A recent publication, edited by Pavlenko (2006), draws together research and analysis from several communities addressing more fully these links between language and meaning, expression and emotion, language and self. The questions raised address whether bilingual and multilingual people experience themselves as different people to some extent when speaking different languages. Do they behave differently in their different languages? And are they perceived differently by those with whom they speak?

Based on several strands of empirical research among bi-lingual and multilingual speakers, Pavlenko concludes that:

> 'Reflections and explorations by linguists and
> psychoanalysts show that languages may create different,
> and sometimes incommensurable, worlds for their
> speakers who feel that their selves change with the shift in
> language.' (Pavlenko, 2006:26-27)

Some bilingual and multilingual people may perceive the world differently, she says, and change perspectives, ways of thinking, and verbal and non-verbal behaviours when switching languages:

'Yes, when I am using Italian especially. I am more emotional and use my hands more. My husband has also commented that I adopt the Icelandic attitudes when I am using Icelandic especially when speaking to officials. If you pick up the language in the country where it is spoken then you pick up the traits and habits of those people.'
(Wendy, aged 30, speaks English – French – German – Italian – Icelandic)

'I feel much more sophisticated when I speak English probably because I learnt it from sophisticated people in private college in York some time ago. When I speak Dutch I feel like a more precise person. I learned to use it in a very precise and accurate way and for example never to mix up one word with another.'
(Clement, aged 18, speaks French – Dutch – Italian – English)

'In Welsh I'm more confident and in control. The words flow more easily. In English, I struggle more to express myself. I always think that I sound authoritative in Welsh; in English I sound less intelligent and less in control.
'Some things are far easier to discuss in Welsh. I can talk about business matters in English, no problem. In many ways, it's easier to talk about things like this in English. But when it comes to talking about my personal life – ill health, worries about my family, anxieties about the future … all of these things have to happen in Welsh to have any meaning.'
(Jenny, aged 45, speaks Welsh – English)

[Pavlenko, 2006:12]

It could be argued that this body of work has helped cast a more favourable light on the previously discredited sociolinguistic work of Sapir and Whorf (1929), often referred to as the Sapir–Whorf hypothesis, based on the view that the language we speak directly influences the way we think. For several years people argued that if the Whorfian hypothesis were true and if languages created different worlds for people, then bilingual and multilingual people would be doomed to confusion and difficulty in translating meanings and making sense of different language-related experiences. And yet the work of Pavlenko and others suggests that the dismissal of linguistic relativity in the work of Sapir and Whorf may be misplaced, because:

> '... *our respondents tell us that their thinking, behaviour, and perception of the self and the world do change with the change in language.*' (Pavlenko, 2006:13)

Clearly in relation to social welfare practice in Wales, this shift away from seeing language merely as a medium of communication is significant. Language use for bilingual speakers is complex; shifts in language use create subtle shifts in the tone, texture and nature of what is being said. To be authentic and meaningful, some experiences and emotions are bound to be related in one language rather than the other.

This is summed up by a bilingual Welsh–English speaker relating her experience of operating a telephone helpline for a large voluntary organisation in Wales:

> '*Welsh speakers often phone for advice. They often start the conversation by asking for factual or practical information and then move on to talk about a far more personal problem which is more difficult to discuss. Although it is difficult to put one's finger on the reason why, I get the impression that they move on to the second subject, often the real reason for phoning, because they are able to speak Welsh. The nature of the service would be different if I was unable to speak Welsh.*' (Davies, 1999:9)

It is this relationship between language, experience and expression that was described by the bilingual service users quoted in the 1994 in full then bracket abbreviation (CCETSW) publication. Asked why they would value a Welsh-speaking social care worker, they stated:

*'Dwi'n meddwl ei fod e'n bwysig iawn achos fel gweithiwr cymdeithasol 'dach chi eisio cael allan o rywun y teimladau dwfn y mae rhai'n cael trafferth i ymdrin â nhw. Ella bod nhw'n corddi yn ei feddwl a'i fod yn cael trafferth, fel dwi'n cael rwan, i siarad. Ond swn i'n gorfod siarad Saesneg rwan, swn i byth yn gallu gwneud hynny.'*

(I think that it's important because as a social worker you want the client to be able to express those deep feelings which s/he has difficulty coping with. They could be causing a lot of turmoil and the person has trouble expressing himself, just as I'm having now. But if I had to speak English now I'd never be able to say what's troubling me.) [38-year-old man with physical disabilities]

*'Dyw llawer o bobl ddim yn deall eich bod chi'n hapusach yn siarad Cymraeg. Er fy mod i'n siarad y ddwy iaith ... dwi'n llawer mwy cartrefol yn siarad gyda rhywun sy'n Gymro.'*

(Many people don't understand that you are happier speaking Welsh. Although I speak both languages... I'm much more comfortable talking with a Welsh speaker). [75-year-old woman] (Davies, 1994:72)

*Language and power*

Issues to do with power are at the core of each and every language. John Edwards sets this in context:

*'While there exist something like 5,000 languages in about 200 countries ... only a quarter of all states recognise more than one language. Also, even in those countries in which two or more varieties have legal status, one language is usually predominant, or has regional limitations, or carries with it disproportionate amounts of social, economic and political power.'* (Edwards, 1994:1-2)

In the relationship between one language and another, the power dimension is a force to be reckoned with. This is especially salient, as Edwards suggests, when one of those languages has a recognised status and the other has less status and prestige.

In her analysis, Siencyn (1995) differentiates between perceptions of high-status, high-prestige languages on the one hand, and low-status, low-prestige languages on the other. Figure 4.2 presents the common perceptions to which Siencyn refers.

---

**Figure 4.2: Perceptions of high- and low-status languages**

| High status languages | Low status languages |
|---|---|
| Easy to learn | Difficult to learn |
| Pure, with no borrowed words | Full of borrowed words |
| Widely used | Of limited use |
| Easy on the ear | Full of strange sounds |
| Sophisticated and modern | Old fashioned |

*Source:* Siencyn (1995:25)

---

According to Siencyn, people often reach ill-founded conclusions based on perceptions such as these, for example, that:

• some languages are more important than others;
• some languages are more modern and relevant than others; and
• some languages are of limited use and of little value.

When perceptions such as these are aired consistently over time they tend to influence speakers of the language; negative judgements are internalised. And when individuals feel that they are the butt of criticism, insecurities are generated and confidence is drained. They are then more likely to change or adapt behaviour in order to reduce anxiety and embarrassment. This helps explain in part why Welsh speakers are often so ready to switch language and why they often play down and denigrate their ability to speak Welsh. A fluent speaker will often say, for example:

'Cymraeg talcen slip sydd 'da fi'
(My Welsh is just street-corner Welsh)

'Tydi 'Nghymraeg i'n dda i ddim'
(My Welsh is good for nothing)

All these characteristics are significant for bilingual users of social welfare services in Wales. Added to that, their personal circumstances may mean that they feel particularly fragile and disempowered. In this respect it is worth referring to Dafis' (1996:12) between weak and strong linguistic contexts (see figure 4.3).

---

**Figure 4.3:**
**Distinction between weak and strong linguistic contexts**

| **Weak linguistic contexts** | **Strong linguistic contexts** |
|---|---|
| • When the situation/context is unfamiliar and where there is no training or preparation. | • When there is training and preparation. |
| • When there is a sense of threat | • When there is no threat. |
| • When there is anxiety, fear and negative emotions. | • When there are no obvious emotions and when the speaker is relatively neutral. |
| • When power and authority back up the other speaker. | • When the speaker has power and authority. |

*Source:* Dafis (1996:12)

---

Romaine (2004) summarises this discussion of language and power in a bilingual society with her analysis of what is known as 'diglossia' – a distinct differentiation in the function of both languages. And Wales offers an excellent example of a society in which both languages have occupied very distinct and separate domains:

'Many bilingual communities are characterized by diglossia, a term used to refer to a kind of functional specialization between languages (referred to as High and Low) so that the language used within the home and in other personal domains of interaction between community members is different from the one used in higher functions such as government, media, education.'
(Romaine, 2004:393)

*The shadow of history*

Bilingual service users in Wales will be influenced unconsciously by several of the factors discussed above. Deep-seated structural and attitudinal obstacles help explain why, for many, their language is something to be kept under wraps. The disproportionate power allocated to the Welsh and English language in Wales was nowhere more acutely expressed than in the language clauses of the Acts of Union of 1536 and 1542. At this time, Wales was incorporated within England and it was legislated that English would be the only official language of Wales; people using the Welsh language were not to hold any '... manner of office or fees within the Realm of England, Wales or other of the King's dominions.'

The language clauses had a profound effect on the Welsh language. It was marginalised and came to occupy the private, unofficial sphere of everyday life. The historian John Davies (1990) describes the impact on Welsh speakers in these terms:

'Ni allai Cymro uniaith lai na theimlo'n anfreintiedig o dan drefn o'r fath, a thros y canrifoedd byddai'r ymwybyddiaeth hon o fraint siaradwyr y Saesneg yn meithrin agweddau at y Gymraeg a fygythiai einioes yr iaith.' (Davies, 1990:225-6)

(A monoglot Welsh speaker could only feel underprivileged under such a system and over the centuries this awareness of the privilege of English speakers would nurture attitudes towards the Welsh language which would endanger the existence of the language).

As the domains of the language shrank it lost its status and Davies argues that, over the centuries, this had a marked effect on attitudes towards the language. For example, on:

- *Where and when to use the language:* Welsh speakers learned not to use the language when dealing with public bodies and with authority. Interestingly, a National Opinion Poll (NOP) survey commissioned by the Welsh Language Board showed as recently as 1996 that among Welsh speakers confidence in using their language was highest at home and while socialising with friends and family, and far lower when making more formal contact with public and private sector organisations – the council, the bank, the privatised utilities, for example.
- *The self-confidence of Welsh speakers:* Welsh speakers historically lack confidence in their ability to speak Welsh. Through the language clauses of 1536 and 1542, the language took a severe battering and, as a result, so did the linguistic confidence of Welsh speakers.
- *The readiness of Welsh speakers to change language:* over the course of centuries, Welsh speakers became acutely aware of the lack of status attributed to their language; this in turn created a sense of inferiority and shame. The language tended to be a source of unease and embarrassment, something to be kept hidden.

A very cursory exploration of some of the more significant milestones in the history of the language has to take into account the events of 1847. In that year a report was published on the condition of Education in Wales; it came to be known as *Brad y Llyfrau Gleision*/The Treachery of the Blue Books. The following quote, lifted from the report itself, is characteristic of its tone and findings:

> '*The Welsh language is a vast drawback to Wales and a manifold barrier to the moral progress and commercial prosperity of the people. It is not easy to over-estimate its evil effects.*' (Reports of the Commissioners of Inquiry into the State of Education in Wales, 1847)

Writing of the significance of the report almost 150 years later, the historian Gwyn A. Williams comments that:

> 'The Education Report of 1847, accurate enough in its exposure of the pitiful inadequacy of school provision, moved on to a partisan, often vicious and often lying attack on Welsh Nonconformity and the Welsh language itself as a vehicle of immorality, backwardness and obscurantism. The London press, led by a racist Morning Chronicle, called for the extinction of Welsh.' (Williams, 1985:208)

Soon afterwards came the 1870 Education Act which made no provision at all for the teaching of Welsh in elementary schools in Wales. During the last quarter of the nineteenth century and the first quarter of the 20th century came evidence from several parts of Wales of children being punished for speaking Welsh. They had to wear a block of wood around their neck with the letters WN (Welsh Not) carved on it. When a child wearing the Welsh Not heard another speaking Welsh s/he would eagerly pass it on, keen to be rid of its stigma. This would continue throughout the school day and the child wearing the Welsh Not at the end of the day would be chastised by the teacher before being sent home:

> 'The Welsh Not slung around a child's neck to accompany his or her punishment for speaking his or her own language has become notorious. It was not very effective but it enormously reinforced the image of Welsh as an inferior and gutter tongue.' (Williams, 1985:246)

The Welsh Not was not in any way unique. A similar device – a small wooden clog – was used in Brittany to deter Breton-speaking children from using their language in school.

By the end of the nineteenth century, English was the language for getting on in the world. With the growth of industrialisation Wales saw an emerging middle class, the owners and managers of the new iron and coal works, who were predominantly English-speaking. This became a further threat to the Welsh language as working people aped the mores and language of the middle class. They attached little economic value to the Welsh language and saw little point in transferring the language to their children. What then followed was a rapid decline in the number and percentage of Welsh speakers throughout the 20th century.

At the beginning of the 20th century almost 50 per cent of the population of Wales was Welsh-speaking, close on one million people. By the end of the century, the number of Welsh speakers had dropped by almost a half and the loss in proportionate terms was even greater:

> 1901 – 929,800 (49.9 per cent)
> 1951 – 714,700 (28.9 per cent)
> 1971 – 542,400 (20.8 per cent)
> 1991 – 508,098 (18.6 per cent)

It is this stark demographic trend that is reflected in the personal and family history of hundreds of thousands of Welsh people for whom the language was lost during the last century. Many, however, are now regaining the language and this is witnessed in the changing demographics of the 2001 Census.

*Implications for service provision today*

The 2001 Census showed an upturn in the number and percentage of Welsh speakers, from 508,098 (18.6 per cent) in 1991 to 575,640 (20.5 per cent) in 2001. It also confirmed a trend that was already beginning to emerge in 1991, with boundaries shifting eastwards beyond the traditional heartland of the Welsh language in north and west Wales.

The 2001 Census confirmed that 60 per cent of Welsh speakers now live in urban areas, with very significant numbers living in the urban and industrial centres of south Wales. Aitchison and Carter (2004) refer to two key areas, one stretching from Kidwelly, through Pontyberem, Ammanford and Gwaencaegurwen to Ystradgynlais, and the other in Cwm Tawe, the Swansea Valley, spreading from Ystalyfera, through Pontardawe and Clydach to Swansea and westwards to Gorseinon and Llanelli. Jointly these two areas include 100,000 Welsh speakers. Aitchison and Carter also refer to the density of Welsh speakers in Cardiff, with over 30,000 speakers. Just as significant, they say, are a cluster of wards in Newport and parts of the south Wales valleys with substantial numbers of Welsh speakers:

> '... while it is customary to identify the Welsh speaking community with rural areas of north and west Wales (Y Fro Gymraeg), the actual heartland of that community in terms of absolute numbers lies in south Wales, embracing longstanding Welsh-speaking communities of the former western coal-field and the burgeoning areas to the east, with Cardiff as a powerful focal point.'
> (Aitchison and Carter, 2004:56)

However,

> '... [in these areas] whilst there are some strong clusters where Welsh speakers are locally dominant, these are relatively small in number. The great majority of Welsh speakers are widely scattered and live in areas where percentages are still relatively low.'
> (op. cit: 53)

When considering the implications of these demographic trends for service planning it is important to avoid the temptation of concentrating Welsh medium service delivery solely on those areas with a substantial percentage of Welsh speakers, the traditional Welsh-speaking areas, such as Ynys Môn (Anglesey, 59.9 per cent), Ceredigion (51.8 per cent) and Gwynedd (68.7 per cent), for example. Alongside these, it is essential to consider the needs of Welsh speakers in south and north east Wales where percentage rates may be low but where actual numbers are significant. For example, Swansea – 28,581 (13.2 per cent), Rhondda Cynon Taf – 27,505 (12.3 per cent) and Flintshire – 20,277 (14.1 per cent).

In his review of the Welsh language in the health service, Misell teases out the service provision implications in the following terms:

'It should be remembered that it is as an individual that patients approach the National Health Service for treatment, rather than as representatives of communities, and the needs and wishes of each individual patient are equally important. From this viewpoint, the linguistic 'Welshness' or otherwise of the region a patient is living in is wholly irrelevant when considering whether provision should be made for him or her through the medium of Welsh.' (Misell, 2000:15)

Misell compares the situation of the Welsh speaker with speakers of other minority languages in Britain and draws on the work of Balarajan and Raleigh (1995) who refer to the risk of concentrating resources wholly on those areas with a density of minority language speakers:

'The issue is important not just for health authorities with large black and minority ethnic communities, but also for authorities where the numbers are smaller and hence there is a risk that their needs will be overlooked.'
(Balarajan and Raleigh, 1995, quoted in Misell, 2000:15)

In interviews with healthcare professionals, Misell hears about the experience of service users – 'the hidden Welsh' as he calls them – in parts of Wales thought of as non-Welsh- speaking areas and where the needs of the Welsh speaker are often overlooked. In an exhortation to those responsible for planning local services, Misell comes to the conclusion that:

'... there is not, and never has been, such a thing as a 'non-Welsh speaking area' in Wales, and such old-fashioned ideas about the geographical territory of the Welsh language can only stand in the way of any attempts to increase and develop the provision of services through Welsh. Welsh speakers are to be found in all parts of Wales and it is in some of the most Anglicised areas that the greatest growth of the Welsh language is to be found. There is therefore no point attempting to justify restricting Welsh language provision to certain parts of Wales.' (Misell, 2000:15)

The other significant demographic trend that needs to be considered in relation to social care provision is the growth in the number and proportion of young Welsh speakers. In the early 1990s when analysing the 1991 Census data on Welsh speakers, the *Western Mail* carried the headline, *The Welsh Language is Getting Younger.* This trend continued, and the 2001 Census witnessed a further increase in the number of young Welsh speakers with 31.2 per cent of 3 to 15-year-olds reported as having an ability to speak Welsh (Aitchison and Carter, 2004:87), compared to 22.3 per cent in 1991 (Aitchison and Carter, 1994:104).

In parts of south and south east Wales the percentage of young Welsh speakers, as a proportion of the local Welsh-speaking community as a whole, is striking. For example, in Torfaen 69.5 per cent of Welsh speakers fall into the 3-15 age group; 70.2 per cent in Newport; 54.5 per cent in Caerphilly and 68.2 per cent in Blaenau Gwent.

Each speaker's individual language profile will vary: some will speak Welsh at home; others will be fluent in Welsh through school but may not use the language at home, and others may be learning the language without yet being fluent. But from what is known about complex patterns of language use among bilingual speakers, and the inter-relationship between language, expression and emotion, it is argued that questions regarding language choice should always be addressed in any work with bilingual children and young people. Language-sensitive practice is key to securing the child's voice, enabling sound assessment and ensuring the best outcome.

## Language-sensitive practice – the way forward

Bringing about a shift in the profile of the Welsh language and the availability of services in the user's language of choice – a shift from the margins to the centre – requires social welfare agencies to engage with language as a mainstream issue. In guidance published in 1996, the Welsh Language Board stated that:

> 'The key to providing a high quality service through the medium of Welsh is to make the language a natural, integral part of the planning and delivery of that service.'
> (Welsh Language Board, 1996: guideline 2)

Since then, the Welsh Assembly Government has firmed up the theme of mainstreaming and embedding language-sensitive provision in many of its policy statements (WAG, 2003, 2004, 2006, 2007). The language, rather than being a problematic afterthought, becomes a core consideration in all aspects of policy implementation, planning and monitoring.

Using workforce planning frameworks offers one way of doing this. This may result in an audit of workforce language skills; the compilation of data on the language profile of the local community as a whole, and of users and carers in particular; and an identification of the match or mismatch between staff capacity and user need. It then becomes possible to identify skill deficits and to consider the adoption of recruitment policies that may include affirmative action in relation to the recruitment of a bilingual workforce. Such frameworks may also highlight education and training issues, some of which may be addressed in the short-term through in-service training, for example language skills training to top up the language competence of the existing workforce. Other issues, such as the promotion of the social welfare professions among bilingual speakers and the development and support of appropriate educational frameworks, may need to be addressed on a longer-term basis and in collaboration with sector skills councils and higher education institutions.

Another core consideration in terms of mainstreaming and embedding Welsh language-sensitive practice relates to the role of users and carers. By placing language-sensitive practice firmly in the context of empowerment, it follows that the drive for change has to be rooted very much in the perspective of users and carers. Based on the available sociolinguistic evidence of the inter-relationship between language, experience and expression, as well as evidence regarding the historical disempowerment of Welsh speakers, the development of language-sensitive practice becomes much more than just a concession or a marginal consideration. It becomes a core practice issue – a matter of hearing the voice of those who are otherwise silenced.

An inclusive approach towards both language communities in Wales, and an accompanying focus on equality and empowerment, also secures a role for all social welfare practitioners, regardless of language.

At one end of the continuum will be those who are able to work with users through the medium of the Welsh language. At the other end will be those practitioners who may not be able to speak the language but whose values are sound and who have a vital role to play in identifying need and advocating on behalf of Welsh-speaking users and carers. Across the continuum there will be opportunities for practitioners to acquire different levels of linguistic skill appropriate to their professional capacity, and for all to embrace practice that is informed by principles of equality and empowerment.

Williams (2000) sets this in the context of devolved government in Wales with an affirmation of the importance of inclusivity and equality:

> *'If the National Assembly is to succeed as a political institution people from all over, and from both main linguistic groups, must be able to engage with it and feel a sense of shared ownership. In order for this to occur, the potential sensitivities of the linguistic politics of Wales will need to be recognized and addressed. If, however, the Welsh language is seen in terms of a resource rather than as a problem or, indeed, simply a matter of rights and entitlements, then this will be an important contribution to the development of a common Welsh civic identity – the emergence of which is surely a precondition for the success of the National Assembly and ultimately for the complete rehabilitation of Welsh as co-equal language of everyday life in Wales.'* (Williams, 2000:377)

## References

Aitchison, J and Carter, H (1994) *A Geography of the Welsh Language* Cardiff, University of Wales Press.

Aitchison, J and Carter, H (2004) *Spreading the Word: The Welsh Language 2001* Talybont, Y Lolfa.

Altarriba, J and Morier, R G (2004) 'Bilingualism: language, emotion and mental health' in Bhatia T K & Rithcie, W C (eds.) *The Handbook of Bilingualism* Oxford, Blackwell.

Balarajan, R and Raleigh, V S (1995) *Ethnicity and Health in England* London: NHS Executive, quoted in Misell, A (2000) *Welsh in the Health Service* Cardiff, Welsh Consumer Council.

Barnie, J (1992) 'Foreigners' in Davies, O and Bowie, F (eds.) *Discovering Welshness* Llandysul, Gomer.

Dafis, Ll (1996) 'The need to be understood: an introduction to language sensitivity' in Barnes, J (ed.) *Human Development, Language and Practice* Cardiff, CCETSW.

Davies, E (1994) *'They All Speak English Anyway' – The Welsh Language and Anti-Oppressive Practice* Cardiff, CCETSW.

Davies, E (1999) *The Language of a Caring Service* Cardiff, Welsh Language Board.

Davies, J (1990) *Hanes Cymru – A History of Wales in Welsh* London, Allen Lane, Penguin.

Edwards, J (1994) *Multilingualism* London, Penguin.

Fishman, J A (1972) 'Language and Nationalism' Rowley, MA, Newbury House quoted in Garcia, O and Schiffman, H, 'Fishman sociolinguistics (1949 to the present)' in Garcia, O, Peltz, R, Schiffman, H & Fishman, G S (eds.) (2006) *Language Loyalty, Continuity and Change* Clevedon, Multilingual Matters.

Fishman, J A (1990) 'My life through my work: my work through my life' in Koerner, K (ed.) *First Person Singular* (vol. 2, pp. 105-124) Amsterdam, Benjamins, John quoted in Garcia, O and Schiffman, H, 'Fishman sociolinguistics (1949 to the present)' in Garcia, O, Peltz, R, Schiffman, H & Fishman, G S (eds.) (2006) *Language Loyalty, Continuity and Change* Clevedon, Multilingual Matters.

Grosjean, F (1989) 'Neurolinguists, beware! The bilingual is not two monolinguals in 'One Person' *Brain and Language*, 36, pp. 3-15.

Grosjean, F (1994) 'Individual bilingualism' in Archer, R E and Simpson, J M (eds.) *The Encyclopaedia of Language and Linguistics* Oxford, Pergamon.

Guttfreund, D C (1990) 'Effects of language usage on the emotional experience of Spanish-English and English-Spanish bilinguals' *Journal of Consulting and Clinical Psychology*, 58, pp. 604-7, quoted in Altarriba and Morier (op. cit.).

Misell, A (2000) *Welsh in the Health Service* Cardiff, Welsh Consumer Council.

Pavlenko, A (2006) 'Bilingual Selves' in Pavlenko, A (ed.) *Bilingual Minds: Emotional Experience, Expression and Representation* Clevedon, Multilingual Matters.

Reports of the Commissioners of Inquiry into the State of Education in Wales, *Brad y Llyfrau Gleision*/The Treachery of the Blue Books (1847), Part II, p. 66, London.

Romaine, S (2004) 'The bilingual and multilingual community' in Bhatia, T K and Ritchie, W C (eds.) *The Handbook of Bilingualism* Oxford, Blackwell.

Sapir, E and Whorf B L (1929) 'The status of linguistics as a science' in Mandelbaum, D (ed.) (1945) *Selected Writings of Edward Sapir in Language, Culture and Personality*, pp. 160-6, Berkeley, University of California Press.

Siencyn, S W (1995) *A Sound Understanding: An Introduction to Language Awareness* Cardiff, CCETSW.

Thomas, G (1998) *The Experience of Welsh Speaking Women in a Bilingual Maternity Service*, unpublished MSc dissertation, The School of Nursing Studies, University of Wales College of Medicine, Cardiff.

Welsh Language Board (1996) *Welsh Language Schemes: Their Preparation and Approval in Accordance with the Welsh Language Act, 1993* Cardiff, Welsh Language Board.

WAG (Welsh Assembly Government) (2003) *Iaith Pawb: A National Action Plan for a Bilingual Wales* Cardiff, Welsh Assembly Government.

WAG (2004) *Making the Connections: Delivering Better Services for Wales* Cardiff, Welsh Assembly Government.

WAG (2006) *Beyond Boundaries: Citizen Centred Local Services for Wales* Cardiff, Welsh Assembly Government.

WAG (2007) *Fulfilled Lives, Supportive Communities, A Strategy for Social Services in Wales over the Next Decade* Cardiff, Welsh Assembly Government/NHS.

Williams, C H (2000) 'Conclusion: economic development and political responsibility' in Williams, C H (ed.) *Language Revitalization: Policy and Planning in Wales* Cardiff, University of Wales Press.

Williams, G A (1985) *When Was Wales?* London, Penguin.

Chapter 5

# Child poverty in Wales

Anne Crowley

*'The true measure of a nation's standing is how well it attends to its children – their health and safety, their material security, their education and socialisation, and their sense of being loved, valued and included in the families and societies into which they are born.'* (UNICEF, 2007)

## Introduction

A 'national disgrace' is how the UK's first Children's Commissioner in his first annual report described child poverty in Wales (Children's Commissioner for Wales, 2002). And so it is. Child poverty scars the lives of too many children and young people living in Wales. It limits their future life chances for employment; training; enduring, positive family and social relationships; good physical and mental health and longevity (Bradshaw and Mayhew, 2005) and it affects their childhood experiences profoundly. In research recently conducted on behalf of Save the Children with 1,500 families living on a low income across the UK, eight out of ten parents said their children missed out on activities such as after-school clubs, school trips and inviting friends for tea (Save the Children, 2006). Difficulties in making ends meet meant that children in at least a quarter of these households went without warm coats in winter, proper meals and heat in the home. Poverty is the single biggest threat to the well-being of children in Wales. Poor children often have little or no space to play and live in areas with few shops or amenities; children from the bottom social class are four times more likely to die in an accident and have nearly twice the rate of long-standing illness than those living in households with high incomes. Children who grow up in poverty are far less likely to do well in school and are much more likely to leave the education system with no qualifications at all (Bradshaw and Mayhew, 2005).

It is perhaps now universally agreed that child poverty in Wales and across the home nations of the UK is a social injustice. The UK is a wealthy country yet over one in five children are living in households below the commonly agreed poverty threshold of 60 per cent median income. Among the 25 European Union countries only Italy, Portugal and the Slovak Republic have higher levels of child poverty (UNICEF, 2007).

The latest figures suggest that there are some promising signs of progress in tackling child poverty in Wales. The proportion of children living in income poverty has fallen more dramatically over the last decade than in either Scotland or any of the English regions (Kenway et al., 2005). The child poverty rate in Wales (which was one of the worst in Britain in the mid-1990s) is now at 28 per cent – the same level as Britain as a whole. Wales now has a lower rate of child poverty than a number of English regions including London, the North East and the West Midlands (DWP, March 2007).

Efforts to eradicate child poverty have, of course, to be understood in the wider context of overcoming poverty and social exclusion. At this point in time there seems to be a broad political consensus that poverty and disadvantage in the UK are avoidable and need to be tackled with persistence and co-ordination and that the starting part should be about helping everyone play full economic and social roles. The variation in approach comes when we try to define just how much help, of what sort and for whom; the relative value of economic and social roles; and what should be done to support those who are unable to flourish in the market economy (Darton et al., 2003).

The 'Welsh' approach set out in a think-tank piece published by Joseph Rowntree (Timmins et al., 2004) has been to look at how the collective condition of disadvantaged communities can be improved in a holistic and participative way; looking for long-term solutions that develop social economies to create a range of social capital. This community approach is, it is argued, more appropriate for the deep-seated structural problems affecting the Welsh economy (particularly in the South Wales Valleys but also in rural Wales) featuring relatively high levels of economic inactivity fuelled by a low skill base and the relatively high incidence of limiting long term illnesses (23.3 per cent of the population in Wales compared to 17.9 per cent in England).

Notwithstanding the need to understand the wider context of poverty and disadvantage in Wales, tackling *child* poverty in Wales has become a real political issue. For a nation, setting its sights on renewed prosperity, children and young people assume particular importance for its future economic value. A focus on children and the development of skills in the next generation are essential to the vision of a vibrant and prosperous Wales as set out in the Welsh Assembly Government's strategic plan *Better Wales* (Thomas and Crowley, 2007). Child poverty is seen as especially wasteful carrying huge costs both for the children and families involved and also for society.

This chapter will examine some of the facts and figures and something of the reality of child poverty in Wales today; chart the rise of tackling child poverty as the urgent social policy issue of this decade; outline the current Welsh Assembly Government initiatives to tackle child poverty and set out what more needs to be done if we are to succeed in eradicating child poverty in Wales.

## Raising the stakes

The high rates of child poverty are a legacy of the 1980s when the gap between rich and poor grew faster in the UK than in almost any other industrialised country (see Figure 5.1). Income inequality remains high with income and employment opportunities not evenly shared.

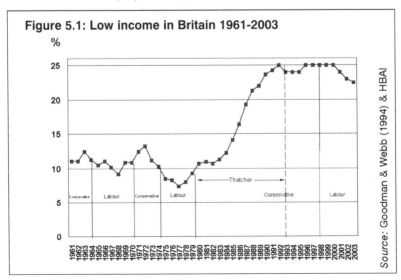

Figure 5.1: Low income in Britain 1961-2003

In 1995, the United Nations Committee on the Rights of the Child expressed concern at the increasing number of children and young people living in poverty in the UK (United Nations Committee on the Rights of the Child, 1995). Four years later, the Prime Minister, Tony Blair, set out a commitment to end child poverty forever:

> *'And I will set out our historic aim that ours is the first generation to end child poverty forever, and it will take a generation. It is a 20-year mission but I believe it can be done.'* (Blair, March 1999)

It was never very clear how this ambitious and welcome target was to be played out in Wales, not least because as devolution progressed, more and more of the family and child-specific indicators used to measure progress in the UK government's annual report on tackling poverty and social exclusion (*Opportunity for All*) related either to England-only policy initiatives or contained England-only statistics (DWP, 2006; WAG, 2006b). However, in 2003 the Assembly Government stepped up to grasp the gauntlet thrown down by the Children's Commissioner's 'national disgrace' comment and the challenge of Tony Blair's historic aim and signalled its intention to develop a strategy to tackle child poverty in Wales.

The first move was to establish a Task Group to advise the Welsh Assembly Government on a strategy. This Task Group on Child Poverty chaired by Dr Charlotte Williams and populated by non-governmental organisations and campaign groups from the End Child Poverty Network Cymru as well as other academics, experts and civil servants, sparked renewed attention on the issue of child poverty in Wales. Deliberations were informed by a series of consultations with children and young people.

The Task Group reported in June 2004 with a number of recommendations on key devolved policy areas that impact on child poverty, including education, health, housing and the environment and skills and employment. Evidence provided to the Task Group indicated that poor children in Wales can feel isolated, left out at school and generally stigmatised by their socio-economic status. Poor children reported being bullied because of their 'difference' from other children accentuated by their receipt of free school meals and by no proper school uniform. We return to consider children's experi. poverty later in the chapter.

In February 2005, the Welsh Assembly Government published its own strategy for tackling child poverty entitled *A Fair Future for Our Children* (WAG, 2005). The strategy stated the Assembly Government's commitment to the target of eradicating child poverty by 2020 and its contributions to meeting that target. Building on a set of core values in line with the United Nations Convention on the Rights of the Child, the strategy includes key action in policy areas where the Assembly Government has devolved responsibility.

The Assembly Government reported that it had made representation to the UK government on levels of Child Benefit. Encouragingly, the strategy recognises the importance of a public education campaign to dispel myths about child poverty and sets out action to try to reduce the stigma and shame felt by poor children. The strategy included an additional £50 million targeted on early years, in the most deprived areas of Wales with at least one integrated centre in each local authority area.

The proposals on the £50 million spend were subsequently developed into the *Flying Start* programme, an Assembly Government initiative running from 2007-11 that targets funding on effective early years provision for nought-to-three-year-olds living in the most disadvantaged communities across the country. The local, strategic children and young people's partnerships receive funding to provide free, part-time quality childcare for two-year-olds and evidence-based early years services such as enhanced health visitor support and parenting programmes (WAG, 2006c). Cymorth is a larger, more longer-standing Welsh Assembly Government funding programme designed to support the same local strategic partnerships to deliver targeted support for vulnerable children aged 0-25 within a network of universal services. In 2007-08, the fund of over £70 million supports about 1,000 projects that aim to specifically improve the life chances of children, young people and families living in the most disadvantaged areas of Wales (WAG, 2007).

The Deputy Minister for Social Justice and Regeneration in the Welsh Assembly Government produced an action plan to deliver the strategy

(WAG, 2006a). This had been a long time in coming – the draft action plan appeared for consultation in April 2006, some three years after the government had set up its Task Group to advise it on producing a strategy. As recommended by the Task Group, the final action plan (published in October 2006) is accompanied by a set of targets and milestones to measure progress on tackling child poverty in the devolved policy fields of housing, health, education and childcare as well as in employment and household income (WAG, 2006b). Progress in meeting these targets and reaching the milestones will be reported to the National Assembly through the Assembly Government's annual Social Justice Report.

The action plan itself includes additional, cross-cutting policy proposals in line with the need to tackle child poverty in the mainstream as well as with targeted initiatives. The intention is to ensure that resources across government are directed towards the needs of the poorest children. All policy is to be proofed as it develops to examine impacts on child poverty even in policy areas not traditionally associated with children – such as transport and economic development. Programme bending is lauded whereby mainstream government programmes are 'bent' to favour child poverty. This follows the approach within the Welsh Assembly Government's existing, flagship anti-poverty programme *Communities First*. This is a long-term 'bottom-up' regeneration programme, involving expenditure of £83 million over the first three years (2002-05) targeting 142 of Wales' most disadvantaged communities. *Communities First* reflects the principles of the community-focused, 'Welsh' approach described on page 88. It aims to improve the living conditions and prospects of people in the most disadvantaged communities in Wales. Further to the publication in 2006 of an interim evaluation of *Communities First* carried out by a Consortium led by Cambridge Policy Consultants (WAG, 2006d), Plaid Cymru, the main opposition Party in Wales at that time, criticised the Assembly Government's management of the *Communities First* programme and the fact that the programme has not delivering on the regeneration outcomes that were (and still are) its main aim (*Western Mail*, 7 December 2006).

The Assembly Government's child poverty action plan also includes proposals to work more closely with local government on tackling child poverty. The Assembly Government has announced funding of a number of corporate local authority pilot schemes working with the Welsh Local Government Association, Save the Children and other members of the End Child Poverty Network Cymru. Consideration is also being given to pursuing the new law-making powers available to the National Assembly under the Government of Wales Act 2006, to develop legislation that places a duty on public bodies to make and demonstrate their contribution to tackling child poverty.

Prior to formulating a specific strategy to tackle child poverty, the Welsh Assembly Government introduced provision to finance free swimming for children in the school holidays. Younger children, however, must be accompanied by a paying adult, which impacts on low-income families' ability to participate. In November 2004 the Assembly Government gave a commitment to provide all primary school children with free school breakfasts. While this is welcome, the Assembly's initiative will need to put sufficient focus on the nutritional content of the breakfasts and ensure that sufficient funds are available to meet demand.

It is not only Labour (New or Old) who has upped the anti on tackling child poverty in Wales in recent years. In the run-up to the last elections to the National Assembly for Wales in April 2007, all the main political parties identified child poverty as a key issue that had to be tackled by the third government of Wales. Plaid Cymru challenged the extent to which child poverty can be tackled without more radical reform to raise low incomes and the inadequacy of the benefit system, laying the responsibilities for key action to tackle child poverty most squarely at the feet of the UK government. We will return to a more hard-nosed appraisal of the evidence as to what has to be done to reach the 2020 target later in the chapter but while there is undoubtedly truth in the argument that reforms to tax and benefits (a non-devolved area) are likely to make the largest single contribution to eradicating child poverty, there is also much that can be done by the devolved administration. Childhood poverty and social exclusion are multi-dimensional and are not just about low income. As the Task Group noted in its review of the available evidence:

> *'Action to mitigate the effects of poverty calls for a cross cutting approach which considers service poverty and participation poverty as well as income poverty.'*
> (WAG, 2004a)

## The reality of child poverty in Wales

*What do the statistics tell us?*

The most recent comprehensive study on poverty and social exclusion in Wales shows that Welsh poverty rates (including child poverty) have fallen faster than those in England or Scotland in the past decade and are now no worse than the average for Britain as a whole (Kenway *et al.*, 2005). Unemployment almost halved in the same period, to around 3.5 per cent of the working-age population. The fall in the level of child poverty is from 37 per cent in 1995-96 to 28 per cent in 2004-05 (DWP, 2007).

But 28 per cent of children in Wales, more than one in four children, continue to live in poor families and there are significant levels of poverty throughout the country. *Monitoring Poverty and Social Exclusion in Wales 2005* (Kenway *et al.*, 2005) shows that roughly a third of the 170,000 children in homes below the poverty threshold live in the Valleys, a third in Cardiff and the rest of the south, and a third in north, west and mid-wales. A fifth of poor children in Wales live in couple households and more than half live with lone parents.

The report highlights that while worklessness is still the single most important reason for poverty in Wales and economic inactivity levels and incidence of limiting long-term illness in some part of Wales (notably the Valleys and parts of west Wales) are some of the worst in the UK, there are growing concerns about the numbers of households in in-work poverty. Parents in low-paid work have undoubtedly been helped and in many cases households lifted above the poverty line by the introduction of Child and Working Tax Credits but still across Britain, half the children in poverty are living in households where paid work is being done. This is the same proportion as when Labour started in the late 1990s and comes about despite the help that is available from tax credits (Kenway, 2006).

Perhaps most worryingly, the report also highlights the intransigence of the most severe child poverty. Research undertaken by the Centre for Research in Social Policy at Loughborough University reveals that over 10 per cent of children in the UK live in severe poverty (defined as those living in households with below 50 per cent median income and going without adult and child necessities) and that the chances of living in severe child poverty are highest if you live in London, Wales or Northern Ireland. The results also show that there is a relatively high likelihood of severe poverty among children living with workless parents; whose parents have low educational attainment; living in rented accommodation; whose parents have no savings/assets; in large families of four or more children; from minority ethnic groups, especially of Asian origin; and in families with a disabled adult(s) (Adelman *et al.*, 2003; Magadi and Middleton, 2005, 2007).

Using this measure, in Wales, there are estimated to be around 70,000 children living in severe poverty with very low incomes – on average a couple and a child will be living on £134 per week after housing costs. Out of this all food, clothes, heating, other bills, transport and school uniforms among other items must be purchased.

Furthermore, the research shows that while some 600,000 children have been lifted out of child poverty across the UK since 1998/99 (DWP, 2007), these are children living in households nearest to the poverty line. Governments will need to identify particular solutions for tackling severe and persistent child poverty if they are to meet their targets:

> '...within the context of target-driven policies such as a reduction of child poverty by one-quarter by 2004, most improvements had been among those who were easiest to help, this is those children who were closest to the poverty line and therefore, arguably easiest to raise above it. Humanitarian concerns would suggest that policy had failed, since the group of children who were experiencing the most severe poverty had been left behind. Indeed if child poverty is to be eradicated, it is essential to maintain focus on dealing with children who are facing the most difficult circumstances and to ensure that policy interventions benefit this group'
> (Magadi and Middleton, 2005:1)

*Outcomes for children*

Research has provided insights into some of the outcomes of poverty for children, including poor health, low self-esteem, poor educational achievement and homelessness (Bradshaw and Mayhew, 2005). Figure 5.2 shows the outcomes for children strongly associated with child poverty.

| Figure 5.2: Outcomes associated with child poverty | |
| --- | --- |
| **Outcome** | **Associated with child poverty** |
| Mortality | Yes, strong association with social class |
| Morbidity | Yes, strong association for most diseases |
| Accidents | Yes, for fatal accidents (but not accident morbidity) |
| Mental illness | Yes |
| Suicide | Yes |
| Child abuse | Yes, except sexual abuse |
| Teenage pregnancy | Yes |
| Environment/ housing conditions | Yes |
| Homelessness | Yes |
| Low education attainment | Yes |
| School exclusions | Don't know |
| Crime | No |
| Smoking | Mainly after childhood |
| Alcohol | No |
| Drugs | No |
| Child Labour | No |

*Source:* Bradshaw and Mayhew (2005)

UNICEF's latest report card on the well-being of children in rich countries states that:

'The evidence from many countries persistently shows that children who grow up in poverty are more vulnerable: specifically, they are more likely to be in poor health, to have learning and behavioural difficulties, to underachieve at school, to become pregnant at too early an age, to have lower skills and aspirations, to be low paid, unemployed and welfare dependant.' (UNICEF, 2007:5)

The UNICEF report reveals that children growing up in the UK suffer greater deprivation, worse relationships with their parents and are exposed to more risks from alcohol, drugs and unsafe sex than those in any other wealthy country in the world. The UK is bottom of the league of 21 economically advanced countries on indicators relating to material well-being; health and safety; educational well-being; family and peer relationships, behaviours and risks; and the young people's own perceptions of their well-being.

In Wales, despite progress in reducing the numbers of children living in relative poverty, the proportion of 16-year-olds who fail to achieve five GCSE passes has remained unchanged since 2000, at 15 per cent. The 7.5 per cent who get no GCSE passes at all is worse than in any English region (Kenway et al., 2005). Among secondary schools with low proportions of pupils entitled to free school meals, just 6 per cent fail to achieve five or more GCSEs. This compares with 27 per cent in schools where a high proportion of students come from low-income families.

Figure 5.3 illustrates trends in respect of a number of key outcome indicators for children in Wales compared to the rest of the UK (Bradshaw and Mayhew, 2005; Save the Children, 2005). It is a mixed picture. Although the overall child poverty rate in Wales has improved to be on a par with the rest of the UK, in comparison to the rest of the UK, Wales has the lowest proportion of children who eat fruit and vegetables, the highest proportion to have taken up smoking especially girls, and the highest rate of boy obesity. It also has the lowest proportion of children expressing life satisfaction, the highest proportion who do less well at school, the highest proportion of unfit dwellings, yet the lowest infant death rate.

**Figure 5.3: Key child well-being trends at a glance – Wales**

| Improving | No change | Deteriorating |
|---|---|---|
| *(Also improving across UK)* | *(Also stable across UK)* | *(Also deteriorating across UK)* |
| • Infant mortality | • Child mortality[1] | • MMR vaccination |
| • Smoking – boys | • Whooping cough immunisation | • Diabetes |
| • Adoptions (from care) up | • Diphtheria, tetanus and polio immunisation | • Young people's alcohol consumption |
| • Daycare nursery places | • Teenage conception rate | • Obesity |
| • Out-of-school places | • Youth crime[2] | • Childminder places |
| • Educational qualifications | | • Playgroup places |
| • Narrowing class differential in attainment | *(Deteriorating across UK)* | • Drug and violent crime[2] |
| • Housing conditions | Still-births[1] | • Girls offending[2] |
| • 15-24 suicide rate[2] | | • School exclusions |
| | | • Child homelessness |
| | | |
| | | *(Stable or improving across UK)* |
| | | • Numbers playing sport[3] |
| | | • Smoking – girls |

| Better than UK rate | Similar to UK rate | Worse than UK rate |
| --- | --- | --- |
| • Infant mortality<br>• Low birth rates<br>• Diabetes – boys<br>• Consumption of sweets and soft drinks<br>• Some physical activity rates<br>• Bullying[4] | • Alcohol consumption<br>• TV watching – boys | • Child poverty before housing costs[5]<br>• Teenage conceptions<br>• Diabetes – girls<br>• Reporting good health<br>• Consumption of fruit and vegetables<br>• TV watching – girls<br>• Looked-after children with mental disorder/conduct disorders<br>• Achieving 5 GCSEs[6]<br>• Achieving 2 A-levels[6]<br>• Leaving school with no qualifications<br>• Leaving care at 16-17<br>• Leaving care with 1 or more GCSE[6]<br>• Truancy rates<br>• Unfit housing |

**Notes:**
1. Annual rate fluctuates due to small numbers.
2. England and Wales data.
3. Now similar rate to other countries.
4. Better than rate in England.
5. Child poverty rates are worse in Wales before housing costs and before and after housing costs at 60 per cent threshold and before and after housing costs at 70 per cent threshold.
6. Or Standard Grade/Highers in Scotland.

*Source*: Bradshaw and Mayhew (2005)

How the association of poverty with poor child outcomes plays out can perhaps be better understood when comparing the varying range of opportunities available to children from low-income and more affluent households. The latest Households Below Average Income (HBAI) report presents for the first time, information on the material deprivation experienced by children living in low-income households. The findings provide a reminder of the stark reality of poverty from a child's perspective. For example, 5 per cent of children in the top quintile are lacking outdoor space/facilities to play safely, in contrast to a quarter of children in the bottom quintile who lack such an item. Just 3 per cent of children in the top income quintile do not have at least one week's holiday away from home but more than half of children in the bottom quintile do not have such a holiday (DWP, 2007).

*Through the eyes of a child*

The Welsh Assembly Government has adopted the United Nations Convention on the Rights of the Child as underpinning all its policies relating to children (WAG, 2004b). Under the Convention, children have the right to grow up free from poverty and hunger and should not be disadvantaged or prevented from achieving their full potential because of where they live or family circumstances. Article 4 of the Convention obliges governments to fulfill children's rights 'to the maximum extent of their available resources' (United Nations Committee, 2003).

In this context it is especially important to try to understand the effect of poverty on children themselves, not just to focus on income poverty or the impact of childhood poverty on their later life chances as a future adult. To understand the lived experience of child poverty we need to bring a child's perspective to the analysis of child poverty and social exclusion (Ridge, 2002).

In preparing its advice for the Assembly Government, the Child Poverty Task Group commissioned and reviewed a series of consultations with over 300 children and young people aged 6-25 across Wales. The aim was to ensure that the Assembly Government's strategy was informed by children and young people's own understanding of child poverty and what life without money is like for children as well as to feed in children and young people's own ideas and suggestions for how child poverty should be tackled in Wales (WAG, 2004a). The consultations identified a common set of themes and messages about the effects of poverty on the lives and experiences of children and young people. Different emphases are apparent according to age, for example older young people were more likely than younger children to raise concerns about housing or employment and had a greater understanding and experience of the benefit system. Children and young people of all ages raised issues relating to education, health, crime, drugs, participation, leisure, transport, the unique pressures on families living on a low-income and the profound affects of the stigma and shame that poverty brings.

Children and young people talked about going without clothing and heating because of the lack of money in their household. Some participants mentioned only being able to have one pair of shoes a year, or to have a bath once a week and having to keep warm in cold, unheated bedrooms. Other children and young people in one of the consultations (Crowley and Vulliamy, 2002) were concerned to point out that most parents in low-income households often went without themselves so that their children could have what they needed and prevent their children being singled out by their friends as poor:

> 'My mother would give me how much as she could afford.
> She can't give me all her money... she won't be able to pay
> off her gas and electric bills.' (Nia, aged 7)

Older young people particularly identified the importance of creating decent jobs and employment opportunities in Wales as a means of tackling child poverty. Young people who were working in low-paid jobs felt exploited. Young people wanted to see a minimum wage for the under 18s and more training opportunities and good-quality apprenticeships.

A strong cross-cutting theme relates to the exclusion children and young people living in poverty experience. Children and young people living in low-income households repeatedly described how they are made to feel different to other children and young people. The fact that children begin to experience the reality of their 'different-ness' at an early age has been highlighted by other studies (Middleton, 1994; Horgan 2007).

The clothes young people wear, the place in which they live, their mode of transport – all set children and young people without much money apart from their peers. The visibility of children's poverty is heightened by the manner in which free school meals are administered; and by not being able to afford essential learning items or school trips, discos and activities. Children and young people clearly understand the stigma and shame that living in poverty brings and acutely feel the lack of respect their 'different-ness' evokes in some of their peers and some of the adults around them:

> 'Poor children can't buy the proper kit and if they didn't have the proper kit some people in the school were meanies and kept saying they haven't got the proper uniform, and they haven't got enough money to get sandwiches either.' (Sean, aged 7)

> 'People think you're different and treat you different if you're poor.' (Gemma, aged 13)

Some children and young people commented on the unwelcome attention they get from their peers because they are perceived as being 'poor' by dint of where they live. Some are routinely humiliated and bullied because of the clothes that they wear or because of where they live. They may be seen as undesirable or 'lower class'. The impact of this on children and young people's sense of worth and self-esteem cannot be underestimated. Projects providing community-based support for young people were seen by young people as helping to ameliorate these feelings – giving them the opportunity to succeed and 'better themselves'. Relationships with trusted and concerned adults who do not judge them or expect certain things because of where they lived were seen as important but changes in the attitude and behaviour of the wider community (adults and peers) were also required.

The accessibility of leisure and social activities was a major issue for young people. The cost and availability of transport is a key factor in young people's social exclusion and feelings of isolation. Children and young people complained about how crime and drugs affected their use of public space, by, for example, the proliferation of discarded syringes and the vandalism of play facilities for younger children. One young person illustrated how, on his estate, the vandalism of bored younger people who had no money and had nowhere to go had spoilt facilities for younger children:

> *'Up here now, they don't stick together. Some of the 11 and 12 year olds are on drugs and things like that, younger than that as well doing it... it's about two years ago now we done that out lovely for the play scheme didn't we, it had a lovely park in there as well, and they wrecked it already, they've coloured all over the walls, they've ripped the stuff up. There was a little house for the little ones to go in, and they burnt that and they're wrecking it and that's because there's nothing here for the older ones and they've got no money to get a bus or go somewhere else. The older ones are wrecking it because they got nothing.'* (Craig, aged 15)

In all the consultations reviewed by the Assembly Government's Child Poverty Task Group, children and young people identified education as playing a key role in helping children and young people to get out of poverty and to fulfill their hopes and dreams. Education prepares young people for life and can provide the necessary skills and qualifications to get a good job and do well. How well poor children and young people get on in school is affected by many things but young people observed that poor children can experience a lower level of expectation, a lower quality of education and sometimes a lack of understanding or support by teachers and youth workers. This suggests that teachers and youth workers should be better supported to guide and advise young people; to be sensitive to the background and circumstances of children; and above all to show belief in all children.

The key messages from children and young people illustrate how combating child poverty and social exclusion has to be part of mainstream policies and not just the preserve of special initiatives. They also provide a glimpse of the social and human costs of child poverty in the 'here and now' of childhood and in the longer term.

## Progress towards tackling child poverty in Wales – a balanced score card?

The comments of the Children's Commissioner for Wales in 2002 definitely threw an uncomfortable spotlight on the accolade that Wales did not want. Wales was firmly in possession of the award for being the nation of the UK with the worst child poverty record. The UK itself being pretty near the bottom of the European Union's child poverty league meant there was not much further for a relatively wealthy country to fall in terms of the inequality in its midst.

The comments did spark individual politicians and the National Assembly as a whole to sit up and think about what more could be done. However, in many ways things have not moved quickly enough. It was only in November 2006, nearly four years after the Commissioner spoke out about Wales' 'national disgrace' that a Child Poverty Implementation Plan for Wales was adopted by the National Assembly; the first payouts to local authorities to deliver on *Flying Start* went out in the same month and year. However, Wales can now pride itself on its own impressive set of targets and milestones to drive the eradication of child poverty; some formidable political champions for child poverty; and a tumbling child poverty rate, which now places Wales only on the same bad footing as its neighbours.

When the UK government missed its first target to reduce child poverty by a quarter by 2005, there was a flurry of policy-related research to investigate why this had happened and what was needed to get the UK back on track. It transpired that while the government's 'welfare to work' agenda had lifted 600,000 children over the poverty threshold, these were essentially children living just over the wrong side of the threshold – children that could be described as 'the low-hanging fruit'. If government is serious in its intention to eradicate child poverty by 2020 and halve it by 2010, it has some serious thinking and some serious spending to do.

## What is needed?

Since the late 1990s child poverty in Wales (and across the UK) has started to fall, helped by rising parental employment and by large increases in tax credits and benefits paid to low-income families with children. It is, however, widely agreed that the state is currently way off course and will not meet the targets of halving child poverty by 2010 and eradicating it by 2020 with existing policies (Hirsch, 2006). Leading experts convened by the Joseph Rowntree Foundation have estimated that an extra £4 billion a year (0.3 per cent of GDP) is needed for additional benefits and tax cuts. Getting the second half of children out of poverty between 2010 and 2020 will, it is suggested, be far harder.

To make further in-roads into child poverty, the UK will need to extend its policy of increasing redistribution to low-income families combined with other measures to improve parents' incomes, enabling parents to fare better in the workplace with improved pay and conditions. Long-term policies working in this direction (and also within the power of the National Assembly for Wales) include better education and training for disadvantaged groups, improved childcare and the promotion of equal pay for women. The Rowntree report points out that many of the parents of 2020 are still in school today:

> '... and a decisive effort to improve educational outcomes for disadvantaged groups, and renewed efforts to improve low pay and women's access to child care, would help tomorrow's parents to thrive in the labour market.'
> (Hirsch 2006:5)

There are, the report acknowledges, a number of solutions to child poverty that need to be tackled at a devolved, that is, the National Assembly for Wales, level of Government. There are clear links between poverty and low levels of educational attainment. Social mobility has declined, rather than improved in Britain since 1997 (Blanden et al., 2005) and the link between educational attainment and social mobility is central to this. The percentage of children in Wales leaving school without any qualification has fallen but the rate for both boys and girls in Wales is still the highest in the UK (Bradshaw and Mayhew, 2005). A joint Task Group (WAG, 2002) examined the factors that contribute to the gap in performance between schools in prosperous and deprived areas and found that successful outcomes could be achieved even where school circumstances are challenging and demonstrated that deprivation does not necessarily lead to poor performance. The recommendations in this report have yet to be implemented. From 2006-07, the new RAISE programme supports disadvantaged pupils in schools where 20 per cent or more of school-age pupils are eligible for free school meals; and provides learning support for looked-after children. The funding of £16 million runs for two years (WAG, 2007).

The rising costs of school seem to be a significant barrier. It was estimated in 2004 that the costs per year for one child is £563 in primary and £948 in secondary school (DfES, 2004). Disadvantaged children feel stigmatised because they cannot afford to take part in school trips or buy the proper school uniform (Crowley and Vulliamy, 2002). In Wales there are still wide variations in availability and eligibility of local education authority financial help towards the cost of a school uniform. The Assembly Government has issued guidance to school governing bodies recommending that the cost implications be considered before choosing a particular uniform and has also encouraged schools to provide free meals in non-stigmatising ways. In order to ensure that these guidelines have some impact on policy in individual schools however, they need to be widely publicised and monitored. Current guidance is not adequately monitored and individual school policies vary widely (Aktar, 2006).

More needs to be done to tackle severe and persistent child poverty in Wales – not just by additional spending on tax and benefits to redistribute wealth but also by tackling barriers at the Welsh Assembly and local government levels of governance. A project funded by the Welsh Assembly Government and involving Save the Children, the National Policy Institute and the Bevan Foundation is examining the characteristics of children living in households with below 50 per cent median income and going without necessities and has brought together experts to design targeted policy solutions for those groups most at risk. Access to childcare; improved benefit take-up rates; support in education, training and development to 'narrow the gap'; and access to employment and progressing to better paid jobs are all areas where the National Assembly can make a difference. It seems that the second Assembly Government responded to the gauntlet that Peter Clarke, Wales' first Children's Commissioner laid at its feet. It introduced a strategy (with some limited, additional resources), an action plan and targets and milestones for eradicating child poverty.

Implementing the intentions will now depend on the UK government and the third Assembly Government allocating adequate resources; developing a well-trained workforce; and establishing clear accountability for delivering improved services on the ground (Williams, 2003). The third Assembly Government is expected to announce its intention to propose a measure to enable it to legislate to place a duty on local authorities and other public bodies to make and demonstrate their contribution to tackling child poverty. Time and sustained political will are now of the essence. So far in Wales, action has been too slow and piecemeal. The reality, as Hirsch concludes when he sets out to summarise what is needed to eradicate child poverty in the UK by 2020, is that:

> 'The scale of the long term challenge... shows that no single approach will be enough to meet it. Only by 'firing on all cylinders' can this historic mission be achieved.' (Hirsch, 2006:5)

## References

Adelman, L, Middleton, S and Ashworth, K (2003) *Britain's Poorest children: Severe and Persistent Poverty and Social Exclusions* London, Save the Children.

Aktar, L (2006) 'Child poverty' in Croke, R and Crowley, A (eds.) *Righting the Wrongs: The Reality of Children's Rights in Wales* Cardiff, Save the Children.

Blair, A (1999) Beveridge Lecture, Toynbee Hall, 18 March, reproduced in Walker, R (ed.) *Ending Child Poverty* Bristol, The Policy Press.

Blanden, J, Gregg, P, and Machin, S (2005) *Intergenerational Mobility in Europe and North America* London, Sutton Trust, Centre for Economic Performance and London School of Economics and Political Science.

Bradshaw, J and Mayhew, E (2005) *The Well-being of Children in the UK* London, Save the Children Fund.

Children's Commissioner for Wales (2002) *Report and Accounts 2001-2* Swansea, www.childcom.org.uk

Crowley, A and Vulliamy, C (2002) *Listen Up! Children and Young People Talk About: Poverty* Cardiff, Save the Children Fund.

Darton, D, Hirsch, D and Strelitz, J (2003) *Tackling Disadvantage: A 20-year Enterprise* York, Joseph Rowntree Foundation.

DfES (Department for Education and Skills) (2004) *The Cost of Schooling* London, HMSO.

DWP (Department of Work and Pensions) (2006) *Opportunity for All – Eighth Report*, www.dwp.gov.uk/ofa/

DWP (2007) *Households Below Average Income (HBAI), 1994/5 to 2005/6*, www.dwp.gov.uk/asd/hbai/hbai2006/contents.asp

Goodman, A and Webb, S (1994) *For Richer, For Poorer: The Changing Distribution of Income in the United Kingdom, 1961-1991*, Fiscal Studies, 15(4), pp. 26-62.

Hirsch, D (2006) *What Will It Take to End Child Poverty? Firing on all Cylinders (Findings)*, York, Joseph Rowntree Foundation, www jrf.org.uk

Horgan, G (2007) *Impact of Poverty on Young Children's Experience of School* York, Joseph Rowntree Foundation.

Kenway, P, Parsons, N, Carr J and Palmer, G (2005) *Monitoring Poverty and Social Exclusion in Wales 2005*, York, Joseph Rowntree Foundation, www.jrf.org.uk

Kenway, P (2006) 'Cameron's poverty challenge to Labour' *Bevan Foundation Review*, 8, pp. 36-7, www.npi.org.uk/lites/cameron%20article.pdf

Magadi, M and Middleton, S (2005) *Britain's Poorest Children Revisited: Evidence from BPHS 1994-2002*, CRSP Research Report 3, Loughborough, Loughborough University.

Magadi, M and Middleton, S (2007) *Measuring Severe Child Poverty in the UK* London, Save the Children Fund.

Middleton, S (1994) *Family Fortunes* London, CPAG.

Ridge, T (2002) *Childhood Poverty and Social Exclusion* Bristol, The Policy Press.

Save the Children (2006) *Hard Times* London, Save the Children.

Thomas, N and Crowley, A (2007) 'The state of children's welfare and rights in Wales in 2006' *Contemporary Wales: An Annual Review of*

*Economic and Social Research*, 19, pp. 161-79.

Timmins, N, IPPR, Social Market Foundation, Policy Exchange, Scottish Council Foundation and Institute of Welsh Affairs (2004) *Overcoming Disadvantage: An Agenda for the Next 20 Years* York, Joseph Rowntree Foundation.

United Nations Committee on the Rights of the Child (1995) *Concluding Observations of the Committee on the Rights of the Child: United Kingdom of Great Britain and Northern Ireland* Geneva, United Nations.

United Nations Committee on the Rights of the Child, 34th Session (2003) 'General Comment No 5. General Measures of implementation of the Convention on the Rights of the Child' www.crc/gc/2003/5

UNICEF, Innocenti Research Centre (2007) *Report Card 7: An Overview of Child Well-being in Rich Countries* Florence, p. 1, UNICEF, www.unicef.org/irc

WAG (Welsh Assembly Government) (2002) *Narrowing the Gap in the Performance in School* Cardiff, Welsh Assembly Government.

WAG (2004a) *Report of the Child Poverty Task Group Consultation* Cardiff, Welsh Assembly Government.

WAG (2004b) *Children and Young People: Rights to Action* Cardiff, Welsh Assembly Government.

WAG (2005) *A Fair Future for Our Children* Cardiff, Welsh Assembly Government.

WAG (2006a) *Child Poverty Implementation Plan – Phase 1 Proposal* Cardiff, Welsh Assembly Government, http://new.wales.gov.uk/topics/childrenyoungpeople/publications/strategicplans/implementplanphase1?lang=en

WAG (2006b) *Eradicating Child Poverty in Wales – Measuring Success* Cardiff, Welsh Assembly Government, http://new.wales.gov.uk/topics/childrenyoungpeople/publications/strategicplans/measuresuccess?lang=en

WAG (2006c) *Flying Start Guidance 2006-8* Cardiff, Welsh Assembly Government, http://new.wales.gov.uk/topics/educationandskills/policy_strategy_and_planning/early-wales/flying-start/?lang=en

WAG (2006d) *Interim Evaluation of Communities First* Cardiff, Welsh
Assembly Government, http://new.wales.gov.uk/topics/
housingandcommunity/research/c1stinterim?lang=en

WAG (2007) *Rights in Action: Implementing Children and Young
People's Rights in Wales* Cardiff, Welsh Assembly Government.

Williams, C (2003) 'The impact of Labour on policies for children and
young people in Wales', *Children & Society* 17(3), pp. 247-53.

Chapter 6

# Social services in the Welsh countryside

Richard Pugh

## Introduction

There are several ways in which rural areas may be distinguished from urban areas, but the most common approach is to use some measure of population density (ONS, 2004). According to the Office for National Statistics, from 1981 through to 2001 the rural population of Wales increased from 886,200 to 959,700 people (Hartwell *et al.*, 2007). This represents just over a third of the population at 35 per cent (Gartner *et al.*, 2007), and the most sparsely populated local authority areas are Powys, Ceredigion, Gwynedd and Anglesey (White and Tippireddy, 2005). Interestingly, much of this increase was the result of migration into rural Wales from other parts of Wales and from England, without which there would have been an overall decline over the period from 1991 to 2001 (Hartwell *et al.*, 2007). There are a number of reasons for population changes in rural areas. Many young people leave the countryside to seek higher education, work or suitable housing, while other people return to rural areas after working elsewhere (Hartwell *et al.*, 2007). In rural areas adjacent to larger towns and cities, counter-urbanisation is commonplace as many people have chosen to move to the countryside seeking a better quality of life.

The age structure of the population in Wales shows that rural areas have slightly lower proportions in the age bands below 40-44 years, and above this band, the proportions are slightly higher (Gartner *et al.*, 2007). Every rural county in Wales has an minority ethnic presence, and more recently, the growing numbers of migrant workers from the newer member states of the European Community has increased the diversity of some districts (WRO, 2006a; Hold *et al.*, 2007). The Trades Union Congress in a report in 2004 (TUC, 2004) found that the patterns of settlement of migrant workers were changing, with many more being recruited to work in agriculture, food processing and hospitality, all areas where the work tends to be sited in non-urban areas.

There is little evidence that rural areas in Wales have any higher incidence of poverty as most of the indices show higher levels in urban areas, although of course, deprivation does exist. Unlike urban areas, poor people in rural areas may live in the same areas as relatively comfortable households, which may tend to mask their existence in any statistics that have an averaging effect (Gartner *et al.*, 2007). Housing conditions in some rural areas are poorer (NAW, 2005), and there is sound evidence that some people living in rural areas are comparatively disadvantaged in regard to access to welfare services, education, employment, income and life chances generally (Shucksmith, 2003). Nevertheless, trying to understand the countryside and the lives of those who live there is not always best done by pursuing a simple urban/rural dichotomy, as this can lead to an over-simplification of the variability and complexity of different rural contexts. For example, the social and economic circumstances of someone living in a depopulated former mining community may be very different from a person living on a hill farm in a more isolated location, or in a small fishing village on the coast. Variability can also be seen in the level and quality of rural social services as the Joint Review reports in Wales reveal, with some areas facing serious problems in management and service provision (SSIW, 2006a).

This chapter draws on earlier published work, especially Pugh (2006, 2007) and Pugh *et al.*, (2007). It begins by setting out some of the general features of rurality and rural context that often influence perceptions of rural problems and impede the development of effective services. The second section reviews some of the specific issues that affect service users, while the third section looks at some of the key issues for workers and service providers. The chapter concludes with recommendations for service development and further reading.

## Rurality and the rural context

Historically, the provision of social services in rural areas of the UK has been based on policies that have an implicit urban perspective (Lloyd and Lloyd, 1984; Francis and Henderson, 1992; Pugh, 2000; Turbett, 2004). This urbanist presumption ignores the diversity of rural communities and often fails to recognise that personal and social problems may be experienced differently in the countryside and thus may require different approaches and solutions.

Since devolution, political rhetoric has often acknowledged the importance of rural places and people. Lowe and Ward (2002) in a review of the governance of rural affairs noted that although new institutions of administration had been developed since devolution, agriculturally oriented approaches to rural development were still dominant. In contrast, a more recent review of rural policy across the UK by Woods (2006) suggests that rural politics are changing and that a broader, more social vision of rural affairs is becoming established. However, in regard to rural social services in Wales, aside of developments in terms of Welsh language provision, scrutiny of policy documents and service plans reveal few other substantive developments. For example, while *Fulfilled Lives, Supportive Communitie*s (WAG, 2007), the main strategy document for social services in Wales, acknowledges the importance of services being developed according to the characteristics and needs of particular localities, it still makes no direct reference to the particularities of rural communities.

As well as the tendency to urbanist assumptions and the political neglect, there are two other broad reasons why people in rural areas may be poorly served by public services.

*Idealisation and assumptions*

In the UK there is a tendency to idealise the countryside and see it as a place without problems (Cloke and Little, 1997), and in Wales, the common perception of the rural interior as the heartland of Welsh identity and Welsh language may hinder the recognition of social problems and lead to a reluctance to accept that difficulties exist. Thus, issues such as alcohol and drug misuse or domestic violence may be seen as being predominantly 'urban' problems (Collins and Billingham, 2001), and as such, are thought not to require any local response. Similarly, the apparent lack of diversity in rural areas compared to many urban areas can contribute to a lack of awareness of racism and its deleterious consequences for some rural dwellers (Chakraborti and Garland, 2004; Robinson and Gardner, 2004; Williams, 2007). The presumption that there are problems but 'not round here', bedevils many efforts to initiate appropriate developments in service provision, and as a result other groups such as those in poverty, people with mental health problems, and gay men and lesbians, who may be relatively 'invisible' among the more dispersed population of rural areas, may also find that their presence is not recognised either.

The idealisation of the countryside may be evident in simplistic assumptions about the readiness of family and friendship networks to provide informal care and support. The notion that there are invariably strong networks that will support those who need help can undermine the impetus to provide supportive services (Craig and Manthorpe, 2000). Research in older women's experiences and expectations of friendship and family in rural Wales reveals more variable and complex patterns of dependence and inter-dependence (Wenger, 2001). Similarly, the tendency to idealise rural Wales as a 'community of communities' ignores the changes that have taken place (Day, 2006), and in part, is based on some uncritical assumptions about what constitutes a community in the first place (Charles and Davies, 2005).

Many writers have noted that inaccurate and idealised views of the countryside can play an important symbolic and political role in society (Cloke and Little, 1997) and may influence local responses to particular problems. Sibley (1997) notes that 'discrepant minorities' such as, Gypsies, Travellers and people from minority ethnic groups are often seen as transgressors, as people who do not belong, especially when the countryside is seen as a symbolic heartland in terms of identity. For example, an assumed distinction between insiders and outsiders may lead to the supposition that many problems such as homelessness in rural Wales are caused by outsiders (Milbourne *et al.*, 2006). Thus, the local political and cultural context in which decisions about service policies and priorities are made, may be influenced by some much broader ideas of rurality and belonging. Day (2002) has noted that both Welsh language and rurality are linked in some conceptions of national identity in Wales, and the in-migration of non-Welsh speakers into rural areas may well lead to some tensions in the community (Griffiths, 1992;

Cloke *et al.*, 1997; Hartwell *et al.*, 2007). Specifically, Charles (1995) has noted that women's refuges in some rural areas of Wales such as Gwynedd and Powys tend to take a higher proportion of women from outside of the area largely because of the difficulty of ensuring their safe accommodation within their own home area, and that this was perceived by some local authority officers as encouraging an influx of outsiders.

*Inadequate funding and lack of recognition of rural costs*

Typically, it costs more to provide public services in rural areas because of the geography of rural areas and the dispersed populations within them, which leads to longer journeys and more staff time spent travelling (Asthana *et al.*, 2003; Hindle *et al.*, 2004). These costs are further intensified by the lack of suitable facilities in some areas and by poorer public transport networks, which lead to more home visits by workers. For example, a survey of car mileage and time spent travelling in a mental health team on the Scottish Borders found that rural staff spent about 25-33 per cent of their work time travelling compared to 7-10 per cent among their urban staff (Wilson, 2003). Yet funding for rural services in Wales rarely meets the full costs of provision and the result is a trade-off between the extent of provision, service quality and costs (White *et al.*, 2007).

Local government has struggled for years to persuade central government of the need for fairer funding for rural areas (Hayle, 1996). Part of the problem has been that for many years rural politics has been dominated by agricultural issues (Woods, 2006), although the Welsh Assembly has explicitly recognised that service provision in rural areas is more costly and that levels of service are problematic (White *et al.*, 2007). Nevertheless, putting aside the question of what would be appropriate levels of provision in different areas, the ratios of social workers to local authority populations in the most rural parts of Wales are no better than in many of the more urban areas (ADSS, 2005), and the levels of expenditure per head of local population show that some rural councils spend around £100 less than some urban districts (SSIW, 2006b).

There have been many attempts to find a fair solution to this issue, but most of these do not adequately address the funding shortfall, because they use a simple urban/rural distinction that does not adequately reflect the real differences in costs between different areas (Pugh, 2007). For example, costs are likely to be lower in a compact rural area surrounding a town with good transport networks, than in a more remote upland area. A further difficulty is that attempts to base funding on existing service provision are constrained by the fact that they will be based on *what is* provided rather than *what ought* to be, and so, tend to fossilise existing inadequacies in service provision (Cheers, 1998).

## Issues for service users

Many of the problems facing users of rural services are the same as those facing people in urban areas, but the geography of the countryside, the weaker infrastructure of public services, the absence of alternative provision and the social dynamics of small communities results in rural dwellers facing some further difficulties in accessing and using services. For some potential service users, the degree of social visibility within their small communities poses particular difficulties in regard to confidentiality, risk and recognition of their needs.

*Transport and access to services*

Poor public transport networks in rural areas result in higher levels of car ownership. Consequently, poorer households are likely to spend a higher proportion of their income on transport than their urban counterparts, and access to private transport remains a problem for many people. One study in Wales found that 22 per cent of rural households reported an adult who lacked access to transport and relied on lifts from other people (White *et al.*, 2007). Access remains stratified in other ways too, with many women having difficulty because the family's car is being used by a male partner to travel to work, or by age, as the young and the old, as well as the unemployed, are less likely to have access to private transport. White and his colleagues noted that 16 per cent of those over 65 years reported difficulty in accessing their general practitioner (GP) surgery. Unfortunately, surveys into access to public services do not specifically include access to social care services, but research into health services reveals a phenomenon of 'distance decay'. That is, the use of health services diminishes the further away people live from them (Deaville, 2001; Gibbon *et al.*, 2006). It is likely that the same phenomenon might be found in regard to the use of social services.

The *Wales Spatial Plan* has identified the need to improve access to health services and improve community transport provision (WAG, 2004). Public transport may be too infrequent, perhaps requiring users to spend too long at their destination, or may not be available at convenient times. People with disabilities may have difficulty boarding buses, and many people may be reluctant to wait for long in exposed places or may fear being stranded if services are delayed or cancelled (Scharf and Bartlam, 2006). While access to some services in rural areas of Wales, like childcare and community transport schemes, has improved in recent years (White *et al.,* 2007), poor transport still impedes access to a wide range of social services, with long journey times being a common feature. For example, one man attending a treatment programme for sex offenders spent nearly five hours travelling to and from the venue. Thus, offenders in rural areas may be disadvantaged compared to urban offenders in terms of the time taken to comply with court orders. They may also be may be less likely to complete their programmes, and so find their difficulties exacerbated (Pugh, 2007).

Finally, access to services in Welsh (as noted in Chapter 4) remains a problem in many rural areas. Despite the rural upland areas of mid and north Wales being areas with relatively high proportions of Welsh-speaking households, the chances of them receiving linguistically appropriate services remains patchy (Madoc-Jones and Buchanan, 2003; Pugh and Jones, 1999; Pugh and Williams, 2006).

*Confidentiality, risk and stigma*

In urban areas confidentiality is supported by the relative anonymity of individuals within the larger population that surrounds them. Whereas in smaller communities in rural areas, where people are more likely to notice the comings and goings of other people, or to notice a stranger's car, simply to be seen entering a particular building or driving to a house may compromise confidentiality. This can be especially difficult for those whose problems do not elicit a sympathetic response, or who feel ashamed, or are at risk in some way. For example, a woman wishing to escape domestic violence may be deterred from seeking help at a family centre or Women's Aid office if she fears that her visit might come to the attention of her abuser (MacKay, 2000). In more remote areas, violence towards women and children may be less likely to be observed by others or be deterred by their presence, and those who are victims may find it more difficult to escape their situation. Violent men may restrict their capacity to contact others by removing the telephone, or restricting their access to transport, and threats of violence may be lent added credibility by isolation of location, as well as by the higher levels of gun ownership in rural areas (MacKay, 2000).

Stigmatisation and isolation are widely reported in studies of people with mental health problems in rural areas. The lack of anonymity may deter people from seeking help and fears of local reactions may inhibit the use of even the limited services available (Pugh and Richards, 1996; Philo *et al.*, 2003). Some groups may also experience isolation because of negative ideas held about them. This has been particularly true of travelling peoples like Gypsies whose lifestyles may be stigmatised by providers and the local community (Cemlyn, 2000). The Equality of Opportunity Committee of the National Assembly for Wales (NAW, 2003) has reported that the needs of travelling people are being neglected, and both Cemlyn (2000) and Roberts (2005) stress the importance of multi-agency approaches to developing service provision for Travellers. Interestingly, Roberts (2005) noted that the use of a caravan as a mobile advice centre was perceived by traveller communities as 'private space' in which people would talk about sexual health, domestic violence and mental health problems.

Social isolation by virtue of difference is also experienced by other groups and individuals. For example, informal networks for gay men and women may be sparse in some rural areas. This can create difficulties in establishing contact with other gay men and lesbians. There may be few places where it is possible to meet and talk with others, to try out different identities, or experience different degrees of 'coming out', and Australian research has noted that such isolation may have significant implications for HIV prevention strategies in rural areas (Roberts, 2003).

*Neglect of minority ethnic communities*

While it was noted earlier that racism is widely reported in rural areas, the social and political position of minority ethnic communities in rural Wales is complex. For example, in north Wales they are more likely to have better than average employment, housing and income (Williams, 2006). Thus, any simple assumption that they are necessarily a deprived and marginalised group is likely to be mistaken, or at least to be an over-generalisation, as there is some evidence of a more variable experience (Pugh, 2004a; Williams, 2007). It should be noted that for many minority ethnic individuals, the decision to live in a rural area is an intentional choice, made with the knowledge that the perceived advantages in terms of the comparative safety and security for their children and overall quality of life, are offset by some degree of social marginalisation or isolation.

Nevertheless, while the demographic presence of some minority ethnic groups in rural areas is well established, relatively little is known about their experience of social services, but it is clear from reports from other areas and from in Wales that generally, provision for minority ethnic groups is poor and that their expectations are often correspondingly low (CSCI, 2004, 2006; de Lima, 2001; DH, 2001a, 2001b, 2002; NAW, 2003; Pugh, 2004b; Social Services Inspectorate, 1998). Because of the absence of larger minority ethnic communities and the consequent lack of voluntary organisations, minority ethnic individuals and families who need help are unlikely to have anyone else to advocate for their needs and will have few alternative options for service provision. Elsewhere in the UK, research into rural childcare services found that minority ethnic groups were less likely to use them, partly because of the costs, but also because of the perception that these were aimed at a white clientele (ACRE, 2002).

Recently arrived migrant workers tend to be relatively young adults without dependants (Gilpin *et al.*, 2006) who are unlikely to need much help from health or social services, although low wages and precarious housing may make them more vulnerable to homelessness and problems of isolation. Nevertheless, a study of 60 migrant workers in Flintshire found that about a quarter were married or in civil partnerships (Hold *et al.*, 2007), and most of these had children (81 per cent). About two thirds of them also had at least one of their own parents living with them to help with childcare. This study found that while most respondents (57) knew how to get access to healthcare, less than half were registered with a local doctor. Only seven knew about local authority or housing association provision, and only 26 knew how to get access to translation, although most thought that this was the service that would improve their quality of life. Evidence of increasing linguistic variation was also noted as 96 pupils in local schools were speaking one of 23 languages other than English or Welsh. The researchers estimated that in total, there were around 44 different languages being spoken in the district. Another study undertaken by the Wales Rural Observatory found that in Powys, the number of children in local schools who did not have English or Welsh as their first language had risen from 80 to 143 in the previous eighteen months (WRO, 2006b).

Many of those in rural areas who suffer racism, or other forms of oppression and who would benefit from services, may be reluctant to seek help or 'make a fuss' because they fear that in drawing attention to their problems and needs, they may be blamed for their own situation, or even worse, become subject to further discrimination, perhaps even violence. As de Lima (1999:37), writing in a Scottish context observed, 'there is often a reluctance to become involved in any initiative which they feel would focus attention upon them as individuals, and they are often not keen to discuss their experiences of living in communities'. Workers seeking to develop better services need to be sensitive to these concerns and recognise just how inhibiting this reluctance may be.

*User expectations and satisfaction with services*

It is sometimes assumed that rural dwellers are more stoical about their circumstances and, consequently, have lower expectations of public services, although there is little direct evidence of this. However, it is the case that the rural poor do not always recognise themselves as such (Milbourne and Hughes, 2005; Scharf and Bartlam, 2006) and this may well influence their perceptions of their needs and any subsequent responses to them. User surveys in England have generally found relatively high levels of satisfaction with services (DEFRA, 2004), but caution should be noted in the interpretation of such results. For example, some studies ask users what they think about particular aspects of a service, such as its accessibility, while others enquire about overall satisfaction with a service. Bowden and Moseley (2006) have also noted that the averaging of results across rural populations means that the views of the most disadvantaged rural dwellers may be collapsed with the perceptions of those who have higher incomes, better access to personal transport and better information about services. They also noted that in regard to access to services, users were willing to trade-off some factors against others depending on the nature of the problem and the service concerned. For example, they were prepared to travel for 30 minutes for primary healthcare if this meant that they could have a full-time service, rather than accept shorter journey times to a more local part-time service.

## Issues for workers and agencies

The current context of policy, practice and training in social work takes little account of the demands of rural settings. The urbanist assumptions implicit in much policy and guidance often present social workers as individuals who float free of their local social context. Furthermore, little attention is paid to questions about the training, supervision, support and professional development of rural staff, yet these things may have a considerable bearing on who comes to work in rural areas, whether they stay in post, and how they practise.

### Placing and personalisation

The more personalised basis of formal relationships in many rural areas makes it difficult for workers to maintain professional neutrality, and attempts to maintain professional distance may be rejected by local people. Social workers in rural areas often find that clients wish to 'place' them, that is, to establish who they are and where they come from. This may serve several purposes: to establish some 'safe ground' on which to base the working relationship; to allow the service user to show that despite the current difficulties he or she is nonetheless a competent and functioning member of the community; or perhaps to allow the user to redress the power imbalance that inevitably exists between helper and helped. Most significantly, information about the worker can be used to check out what other people think of the worker and to decide to what extent the worker can be trusted. Professional credibility in small communities often rests on a broader appreciation of the behaviour of workers outside of their work. Their behaviour, as well as that of other family members, may play a part in how the wider community and users view the service and the worker (Pugh, 2000).

*Dual relationships*

Rural workers who live in the area in which they work face some interesting challenges in managing personal and professional boundaries in their relationships within the community, as 'out of hours' contacts are often unavoidable (Gripton and Valentich, 2003; Galbreath, 2005; Pugh, 2006). Dual relationships have received very little attention in the UK generally and professional codes of practice provide no guidance other than to prohibit exploitative relationships between workers and clients. However, there are risks to workers too. When they carry out statutory duties in child protection and mental health work, or become involved in domestic violence work, their social visibility can leave them vulnerable to social pressure, isolation, or even threats and violence. One of the most difficult aspects of rural practice is the question of how social workers should engage with the local community and yet still exercise their formal powers. Experience in Scotland has shown that there are considerable difficulties in carrying out child protection tasks with intimidating adults in small communities (Social Work Inspection Agency, 2005).

*Tensions between organisational and local expectations*

Many social workers in rural areas will have developed ways of working that enable them to operate effectively in their communities and which help them maintain the cooperation of service users, but the 'space' for such local adaptations may be becoming squeezed as practice becomes ever more proceduralised. Thus, tensions may emerge between organisational imperatives and local expectations. Turbett (cited in Pugh, 2006) provides an interesting example of how workers in a remote Scottish location used local knowledge to inform community care assessments, which nevertheless seemed problematic to a temporary worker from the mainland.

Rural social workers may face considerable pressures to share information within their community, especially when it concerns issues of safety and risk. Writing in an Australian context, Green (2003) has noted that a worker undertaking work with a released child sex offender, although bound by professional expectations of confidentiality, could be subject to criticism if the person were to reoffend. As local people might well think that the worker was able to provide some protection for their own children while they remained unaware of the potential risk. These sorts of pressures are likely to increase as Multi-Agency Public Protection Arrangements to manage the risks of more dangerous offenders in the community become more widely used.

*Recruitment, support and supervision*

Rural services often experience difficulty in recruiting suitable staff simply because of the smaller local pool of potential employees. While it may seem to be less problematic when seeking professionally qualified staff who might be expected to seek jobs over a much wider geographical area, recruitment remains problematic across a wide range of public services. Many people who move to rural areas do so to improve their quality of life, but higher living costs, shortages of suitable housing and limited career prospects may deter potential employees. It can also be difficult to recruit local ancillary and part-time workers, as people may be reluctant to undertake work that places them in authority over people whom they know, or whose reputation gives them cause for concern.

In rural areas there is often less opportunity for specialism and workers may have to undertake many different roles with the result that they may not develop their expertise to the same degree as those working in larger urban teams. Rural workers may be professionally isolated and not get the informal support and advice of colleagues that are common in larger teams, nor receive the levels of in-service training and supervision available to their urban counterparts. These factors can affect the quality of service and can also make it more difficult for workers to gain promotion, partly because they find it harder to develop the expertise and experience required for advancement, and partly because of fewer opportunities for promotion. These pressures on workers may be exacerbated by a lack of support from other services who are also likely to be operating under the same sorts of constraints. Staff from minority ethnic groups who come to work in rural areas may feel more isolated within the workplace and, lacking local connections, may be excluded from informal networks.

Social workers in rural areas sometimes comment that they are never off-duty, as they report working longer hours and having to field more out-of-hours calls. These demands may arise from the lack of other workers and other services, but also result from local expectations of informality and approachability. Rural services, because of the smaller staff numbers, are particularly vulnerable to staff illness, absence and departure, and rural agencies often face a dilemma in deciding how best to organise their services. If they centralise them to maintain efficiency and preserve service capability, they incur higher travel costs and run the risk of becoming isolated and distant from the communities they serve. On the other hand, if they localise them, they can find it difficult to respond satisfactorily to specialist needs.

*Service development*

Several writers have noted that it can take longer to establish new developments in service in rural areas (Francis and Henderson, 1992; Edwards *et al.*, 1999). There may be difficulty in gaining local support for initiatives, especially when people are unwilling to acknowledge that there is a problem, or when the proposed initiative is aimed at an unpopular group. This has been evident in anti-racism strategies, in many drug initiatives, and in proposed developments for Gypsies and Travellers (Cemlyn, 2000; Chakraborti and Garland, 2004; McKeganey *et al.*, 2004). The scarcity of local groups who can act as advocates for unpopular and minority interests may require that social workers take a more political role in advocating for their needs. New initiatives also remain more vulnerable to failure in the early stages, either because of continuing opposition or simply because of staff change as project workers move on to other jobs.

It is clear that social workers need to use some of the methods adopted by community development workers. They may need to identify significant local people who wield power and influence within the area and seek their views and suggestions. They may need to undertake an educational role in helping people and organisations such as parish councils, farming organisations and Women's Institutes to understand what is needed and what is being proposed, and use these bodies to canvass opinion and to disseminate information. Initiatives that resonate with local sentiments and perceptions or that are promoted by local people are more likely to succeed.

The weaker infrastructure of other public services and the relative paucity of voluntary and independent sector provision in rural areas that was noted earlier, means that there are fewer alternative sources of service and fewer opportunities for collaborative development with other agencies. Nevertheless, given the problems of inadequate resources and the need for community support for new developments, cooperation and joint working between agencies is desirable. In north Wales, an outreach initiative aimed at the health needs of Gypsies/Travellers successfully adopted a multi-agency approach (Roberts, 2005) and evidence from elsewhere in the UK shows that multi-agency approaches to racism or domestic violence can also be effective, although small voluntary organisations can find their scarce resources over-stretched by the demands of co-operation with statutory agencies (Edwards, *et al.*, 1999; Dhalech 2000; Hague, 2000; Blyth, 2005). Williams (2006:200) has noted how the North Wales Race Equality Network experienced 'consultation overload' and how its work became largely 'pitched towards servicing the consultative needs of "white" organisations' (Williams, 2006:196).

## Conclusion

This chapter has focused on some of the key issues in service delivery in rural areas of Wales, but we should recognise that the question of whether rural social work is different, or requires different approaches than social work in urban areas, has not received much consideration in a UK context (Pugh, 2003; Turbett, 2004). Indeed, most British social work literature makes little or no mention of rural settings. While there have been many small-scale studies of some features of rural provision, many aspects of rural practice have not been researched at all and there is a tendency to carry out uninformed or unproductive repetition of existing work (Craig and Manthorpe, 2000). However, there is much to be learned from the experience of other countries like Australia, Canada and the USA, as rural social work raises crucial issues about how we conceptualise the social work role in small communities.

My view is that working in rural areas re-emphasises the importance of local context in practice, something that also tends to be neglected in urban contexts. It is easy to see why the temporary worker in the example of community care practice in rural Scotland might have thought that the use of local knowledge in the assessment process was unprofessional. Yet such local adaptations may be justifiable if we draw on the conceptual frameworks developed by writers overseas. Martinez-Brawley (2000:221) explicitly addressed this sort of issue when she described the role of rural-based workers as 'translating the vertically generated policies and programs into specific action geared to the civic and sociocultural style of the community'.

Rural practice also challenges notions of professional neutrality and detachment as the separation of workers from the communities in which they live and work is often impractical. The assumption that objectivity follows from detachment is also open to challenge; emancipatory perspectives have challenged assumptions of expertise and power, and as Miller (1998) has noted, have undermined the assumption of formal distance between clients and workers and have legitimated self-disclosure and integration into communities.

Finally, while this chapter has focused on many problematic aspects of rural practice, we should not assume that the daily experience of rural practitioners is a negative one. Most writers on rural social work have noted the high levels of satisfaction expressed by rural workers, who seem to relish the variety of the work and the opportunity to play a bigger role in service development. Research from other countries shows that they value the sense of engagement and achievement that is possible in smaller communities (Martinez-Brawley, 2000; Lonne and Cheers, 2004).

## References

ACRE (Action with Communities in Rural England) (2002) *Challenging Inclusion. Childcare: The Way Forward* Ipswich, ACRE.

ADSS (Association of Directors of Social Services) (2005) *Social Work in Wales; A Profession to Value* Cardiff, ADSS (Cymru).

Asthana, S, Gibson, A, Monn, G and Brigham, P (2003) 'Allocating resources for health and social care: the significance of rurality' *Health and Social Care in the Community*, 11(6), pp. 486-93.

Blyth, L (2005) 'Not behind closed doors: working in partnership against domestic violence' in Carnwell, R and Buchanan, J (eds.) *Effective Practice in Health and Social Care: A Partnership Approach* Maidenhead, Open University Press/McGraw-Hill, pp. 112-25.

Bowden, C and Moseley, M (2006) *The Quality and Accessibility of Services in Rural England: A Survey of the Perspectives of Disadvantaged Residents*, www.defra.gov.uk

Cemlyn, S (2000) 'Assimilation, control, mediation or advocacy? Social work dilemmas in providing anti-oppressive services for Traveller children and families' *Child and Family Social Work*, 5(4), pp. 327-41.

Chakraborti, N and Garland, J (2004) *Rural Racism* Cullompton, Willan.

Charles, N (1995) 'Feminist politics, domestic violence and the state' *The Sociological Review*, 43(4), pp. 617-40.

Charles, N and Davies, C A (2005) 'Studying the particular, illuminating the general: community studies and community in Wales' *The Sociological Review*, 53(4), pp. 672-90.

Cheers, B (1998) *Welfare Bushed: Social Care in Rural Australia* Aldershot, Ashgate.

Cloke, P and Little, J (1997) *Contested Countryside Cultures: Otherness, Marginalisation and Rurality* London, Routledge.

Cloke, P, Goodwin, M and Milbourne, P (1997) *Rural Wales: Community and Marginalisation* Cardiff, University of Wales Press.

Collins, S and Billingham, J (2001) 'Alcohol services in Wales' *Journal of Substance Abuse*, 6, pp. 114-22.

Craig, G and Manthorpe, J (2000) *Fresh Fields: Rural Social Care: Research, Policy and Practice Agendas* York, Joseph Rowntree Foundation.

CSCI (Commission for Social Care Inspection) (2004) *Inspection of Social Care Services for Older People: Herefordshire County Council* www.csci.gov.uk

CSCI (2006) *Inspection of Social Care Services for Older People: Cumbria County Council*, www.csci.gov.uk

Day, G (2002) *Making Sense of Wales: Politics and Society in Wales* Cardiff, University of Wales Press.

Day, G (2006) 'A community of communities? Civil society and rural Wales' in Day, G, Dunkerley, D and Thompson, A (eds.) *Civil Society in Wales: Policy, Politics and People* Cardiff, University of Wales Press, pp. 227-48.

Deaville, J (2001) *The Nature of Rural General Practice in the UK: Preliminary Research* Gregynog, British Medical Association/Institute for Rural Health.

de Lima, P (1999) 'Research and action in the Scottish Highlands' in Henderson, P and Kaur, R (eds.) *Rural Racism in the UK* London, The Community Development Foundation, pp. 33-43.

de Lima, P (2001) *Needs Not Numbers: An Exploration of Minority Ethnic Communities in Scotland* London, Commission for Racial Equality and the Community Development Foundation

DEFRA (Department of the Environment, Food and Rural Affairs) (2004) *Survey of Rural Customers' Satisfaction with Services*, www.defra.gov.uk

DH (Department of Health) (2001a) *Responding to Diversity*, www.dh.gov.uk

DH (2001b) *From Lip Service to Real Service*, www.dh.gov.uk

DH (2002) *Developing Services for Minority Ethnic Older People*, www.dh.gov.uk

Dhalech, M (1999) *Challenging Racism in the Rural Idyll* Exeter, The Rural Race Equality Project.

Edwards, B, Goodwin, M, Pemberton, S and Woods, M (1999) *Partnership Working in Rural Regeneration* Joseph Rowntree Foundation Research Findings 039, www.jrf.org.uk

Francis, D and Henderson, P (1992) *Working with Rural Communities* London, Macmillan.

Galbreath, W (2005) 'Dual relationships in rural communities' Lohmann, N and Lohmann, R (eds.) *Rural Social Work Practice* New York, Columbia University Press, pp. 105-23.

Gartner, A, Gibbon, R and Riley, N (2007) *Rural Health: A Profile of Rural Health in Wales* Cardiff, Wales Centre for Health.

Gibbon, R, Riley, N and Meyrick, J (2006) *Pictures of Health in Wales: A Technical Supplement* Cardiff, Wales Centre for Health.

Gilpin, N, Henty, M, Lemos, S, Portes, J and Bullen, C (2006) *The Impact of Free Movement of Workers from Central and Eastern Europe on the UK Labour Market* Department for Work and Pensions Working Paper 26, London, DWP, www.dwp.gov.uk/asd/asd5/wp2006.asp

Green, R. (2003) 'Social work in rural areas: a personal and professional challenge' *Australian Social Work*, 56(3), pp. 209-19.

Griffiths, D (1992) 'The political consequences of migration into Wales' *Contemporary Wales*, 5, pp. 65-80.

Gripton, J and Valentich, M (2003) 'Dealing with non-sexual professional – client dual relationships in rural communities', Paper presented at the International Conference on Human Services in Rural Communities, 29-30 May, Halifax, Canada.

Hague, G (2000) *Reducing Domestic Violence: What Works – Multi-Agency Fora* London, Home Office.

Hartwell, S, Kitchen, L, Milbourne, P and Morgan, S (2007) *Population Change in Rural Wales: Social and Cultural Impacts* Research Report No. 12, Cardiff, Wales Rural Observatory.

Hayle, R (1996) *Fair Shares for Rural Areas? An Assessment of Public Resource Allocation Systems* London, Rural Development Commission.

Hindle, T, Spollen, M and Dixon, P (2004) *Review of the Evidence on Additional Costs of Delivering Services to Rural Communities* London, SECTA, www.defra.gov.uk

Hold, M, Korszon, S, Kotchekova, E and Grzesiak, F (2007) *Migrant Workers in Flintshire* Conwy, North East Wales Race Equality Network.

Lloyd, G and Lloyd, S (1984) 'The changing context of rural social work and service delivery' in *Social Work in Rural and Urban Areas*, Research Highlights No. 9 Aberdeen, University of Aberdeen.

Lonne, B and Cheers, B (2004) 'Practitioners speak – balanced account of rural practice recruitment and retention' *Rural Social Work* 9, pp. 244 -54.

Lowe, P and Ward, N (2002) 'Devolution and the governance of rural affairs in the UK' in Adams, J and Robinson, P (eds.) *Devolution in Practice* London, Institute of Public Policy Research, pp. 117-39.

MacKay, A (2000) *Reaching Out: Women's Aid in a Rural Area* St. Andrews, East Fife Women's Aid.

McKeganey, N, Neale, J, Parkin, S and Mills, C (2004) 'Communities and drugs: Beyond the rhetoric of community action' *Probation Journal* 51(4), pp. 343-61.

Madoc-Jones, I and Buchanan, J (2003) 'Welsh Language, Identity and Probation Practice: The Context for Change' in *Probation Journal*, 50, pp. 225-38.

Martinez-Brawley, E (2000) *Close to Home: Human Services and the Small Community* Washington, DC, NASW Press.

Milbourne, P and Hughes, R (2005) *Poverty and Social Exclusion in Rural Wales* Cardiff, Wales Rural Observatory, www.walesruralobservatory.org.uk

Milbourne, P, Hughes, R and Hartwell, S (2006) *Homelessness in Rural Wales*, Cardiff, Wales Rural Observatory, www.walesruralobservatory.org.uk

Miller, P J (1998) 'Dual relationships in rural practice: a dilemma of ethics and culture' in Ginsberg, L H (ed.) *Social Work in Rural Communities* (3rd edition) Alexandria, VA, CSWE, pp. 55-62.

NAW (National Assembly for Wales) (2003) *Review of Service Provision for Gypsy Travellers* Cardiff, National Assembly for Wales.

NAW (2005) *Welsh Index of Multiple Deprivation* Cardiff, LGDU, National Statistics.

ONS (Office for National Statistics) (2004) *Rural and Urban Area Classification: An Introductory Guide* London, Office for National Statistics, www.statistics.gov

Philo, C, Parr, H and Burns, N (2003) *Social Geographies of Rural Mental Health: Experiencing Inclusion and Exclusion*, http://web.ges.gla.ac.uk/projects/website/main.htm

Pugh, R (2000) *Rural Social Work* Lyme Regis, Russell House.

Pugh, R (2003) 'Considering the countryside: is there a case for rural social work?' *British Journal of Social Work* 33, pp. 67-85.

Pugh, R (2004a) 'Difference and discrimination in rural areas' *Rural Social Work* 9(1), pp. 255-64.

Pugh, R (2004b) 'Responding to racism: delivering local services' in Chackraborti, N and Garland, J (eds.) *Rural Racism* Cullompton, Willan, pp 176-203.

Pugh, R (2006) 'Dual relationships: professional and personal boundaries in rural communities' *British Journal of Social Work* Advance Access, 8 September.

Pugh, R (2007) 'Rurality and the probation service' *Probation Service Journal*, 54(2), pp. 145-59.

Pugh, R and Jones, E (1999) 'Language and social work practice: minority language provision within the Guardian ad Litem service' *British Journal of Social Work,* 29(4), pp. 529-45.

Pugh, R and Richards, M (1996) 'Speaking out: a practical approach to empowerment' in *Practice* 8(2), pp. 35-44.

Pugh, R and Williams, D (2006) 'Language policy and provision in social service organizations' *British Journal of Social Work*, Advance Access 10 March.

Pugh, R, Scharf, T and Williams, C (2007) *Obstacles to Using and Providing Rural Social Care*, Research Briefing for the Social Care Institute of Excellence, www.socialcareonline.org.uk

Roberts, A (2005) 'Working with Gypsy travellers: A partnership approach' in Carnwell, R and Buchanan, J (eds.) *Effective Practice in Health and Social Care: A Partnership Approach* Maidenhead, Open University Press, pp. 97-111.

Roberts, R (2003) *Men who have Sex with Men in the Bush: Impediments to the Formation of Gay Communities in Some Rural Areas*, www.csu.edu/research/crsr/ruralsoc/v2n3p13.htm

Robinson, V and Gardner, H (2004) 'Unravelling a stereotype: the lived experience of black and minority ethnic people in rural Wales' in Chakraborti, N and Garland, J (eds.) *Rural Racism* Cullompton, Willan.

Scharf, T and Bartlam, B (2006) *Rural Disadvantage: Quality of Life and Disadvantage Amongst Older People – A Pilot Study* Cheltenham, Commission for Rural Communities

Shucksmith, M (2003) *Social Exclusion in Rural Areas: A Review of Recent Research* Aberdeen, Arkleton Centre, www.defra.gov.uk

Sibley, D (1997) 'Endangering the sacred: nomads, youth cultures and the Countryside' in Cloke, P and Little, J (eds.) *Contested Countryside Cultures: Otherness, Marginalisation and Rurality* London, Routledge, pp. 218-231.

Social Work Inspection Agency (2005) *An Inspection into the Care and Protection of Children in Eilean Siar* Edinburgh, Scottish Executive.

SSI (Social Services Inspectorate) (1998) *They Look After Their Own, Don't They?* London, Department of Health.

SSIW (Social Services Inspectorate for Wales) (2006a) *Joint Review of Powys County Council Social Services* SSIS, www.joint-reviews.gov.uk

SSIW (2006b) *Social Services in Wales 2004-2005: The Report of the Chief Inspector Wales,* SSIW, http://new.wales.gov.uk/social_services/?lang=en

TUC (Trades Union Congress) (2004) *Propping Up Rural and Small Town Britain: Migrant Workers in Britain* London, TUC.

Turbett, C (2004) 'A decade after Orkney: towards a practice model for social work in the remoter areas of Scotland' *British Journal of Social Work* 34, pp. 981-95.

WAG (Welsh Assembly Government) (2004) *Wales Spatial Plan* Cardiff, Welsh Assembly Government.

WAG (2007) *Fulfilled Lives, Supportive Communities: A Strategy for Social Services Over the Next Decade*, Cardiff, Welsh Assembly Government.

Wenger, C (2001) 'Myths and realities of ageing in rural Britain' *Ageing and Society* 21(1), pp. 117-30.

White, S and Tippireddy, H (2005) *Statistical Report on Rural Wales: Volume 1* Cardiff, Wales Rural Observatory, www.walesruralobservatory.org.uk

White, S, Walkley, C, Radcliffe, J and Edwards, B (2007) *Coping with Access to Services* Cardiff, Wales Rural Observatory, www.walesruralobservatory.org.uk

Williams, C (2006) 'Black and ethnic minority associations in Wales', in Day, G, Dunkerley, M and Thompson A (eds.) *Civil Society in Wales: Policy, Politics and People* Cardiff, University of Wales Press, pp. 183-205.

Williams, C (2007) 'Revisiting the rural/race debates: a view from the Welsh countryside' *Ethnic and Racial Studies*, 30(5), pp. 741-65.

Wilson, F (2003) *Key Issues for Rural Areas in Northumberland* (First Draft) Newcastle, North Tyneside and Northumberland Mental Health Trust.

Woods, M (2006) 'Redefining the "rural question": the new 'politics of rural' and social policy' *Social Policy and Administration* 40(6), pp. 579-95.

WRO (Wales Rural Observatory) (2006a) *Scoping Study on Eastern and Central European Migrant Workers in Rural Wales* Cardiff, Wales Rural Observatory, www.walesruralobservatory.org.uk

WRO (2006b) *A Survey of Rural Services in Wales* Cardiff, Wales Rural Observatory, www.walesruralobservatory.org.uk

# Chapter 7

# Equalities and social justice

Charlotte Williams

## Introduction

This chapter is being written against the backdrop of widespread change in the equalities field. The UK government has introduced a new approach to equalities under the 'single equality framework', a new enforcement body is being set up, the Commission for Equality and Human Rights (CEHR) and a new infrastructure for delivering on equality duties at local level is to be created. These developments are being put in place in Wales alongside the existing architecture for promoting equality established under the Welsh Assembly Government. This chapter will outline the major changes initiated by the UK government on equalities. It will explore the legal framework for advancing equalities within Wales and review aspects of the approach taken by the Assembly to implementing its equality duties. The chapter concludes by discussing these developments within the wider context of the social justice ambitions of the Assembly Government and raising issues for consideration by social welfare and equalities practitioners.

## New Labour and equalities

The framework for advancing equalities is undergoing major change. Since 1997 the Labour government has introduced a significant tranche of reforms in the field of equalities and equality of opportunity has been placed at the heart of the New Labour modernising agenda in public services. It is not too difficult to assert that the climate for taking forward issues of equality of opportunity has never been better. UK equality law now leads the way in Europe as the new framework for the 'single equality approach' is put into place. The single equality framework signals a generic approach to legislation, policy and institutions relating to inequality and discrimination rather than treating each minority status as distinct. Established under the Equality Act 2006 the CEHR which came into being in October 2007 will replace the existing Commission for Racial Equality (CRE), the Equal Opportunities Commission (EOC) and the Disibility Rights Commission (DRC). The CEHR will bring together the expertise and resources to promote equality and tackle discrimination in relation to gender, gender reassignment, disability, sexual orientation, religion or belief, age, race and promote human rights. Alongside this development the Labour government is undertaking a major review of discrimination law with a view to establishing the Single Equality Act and has published a comprehensive report on its independent review into the persistence of discrimination and inequality in British society: *Fairness and Freedom* (Equalities Review, 2007). *Fairness and Freedom* proclaims Britain as having the most advanced and effective equality legislation, now 'unrivalled in Europe' (2007:1)

Under ten years of the Labour government there has been a fundamental shift within discrimination law from 'negative' equality duties to 'positive' equality duties. In its first term of office New Labour took the forthright step of strengthening race relations legislation following the MacPherson Inquiry (1999) in order to require public authorities to *promote* good race relations as well as provide protection against discrimination. These duties have now been extended to disability legislation under the Disability Discrimination Act 2005 and since early 2007 these duties have also applied to gender equality. Now employers have to take anticipatory actions to prevent and pre-empt inequality by taking positive steps to promote equality within the workplace and in service delivery. With regard to race, for example, public authorities are obliged to take steps to promote integration and social cohesion in their communities, to consult with minority ethnic groups and to conduct ethnic monitoring (for a good discussion of negative and positive equality duties, see Mclaughlin, 2007). The establishment of positive duties considerably strengthens the potential for real and effective change as authorities must now not merely react to issues to discrimination, but have a duty to be *proactive* in working towards equality.

To coincide with the establishment of the CEHR, 2007 has been designated 'European Year of Equal Opportunities for All' with the aim of launching a major debate on the benefits of diversity for all European societies. A nationwide dialogue during 2007 is focusing on the matrix of issues at the heart of contemporary equalities: rights, representation, recognition and respect.

There can be little doubting that New Labour's forthright approach to equalities is unprecedented. The explicit acknowledgement of the concept of 'institutional discrimination' following the MacPherson Report and the systematic approach to requiring public bodies to be responsive and to be held to account for their actions means that there can be nowhere in the country where issues of equality are not ringing in the ears of public servants. The approach of New Labour is not, however, without criticism. The New Labour approach to equality is based on the achievement of equality of *opportunity* through the removal of barriers hindering people's potential rather than a more radical ambition of producing equality of *outcomes* through redistributing resources in society. The government's definition of an equal society is set out in *Fairness and Freedom* (Equalities Review, 2007:6) as:

> 'An equal society protects and promotes equal, real freedom and substantive opportunity to live in the ways people value and would choose, so that everyone can flourish. An equal society recognises people's different needs, situations and goals and removes the barriers that limit what people can do and can be.'

This approach embraces the myth of an open and meritocratic society in which removing 'barriers' that limit opportunity allows people to realise their potential. This type of approach denies or at best seeks to shift attention away from systemised structural inequalities in society (Ellison and Ellison, 2006). People's choice and agency are constrained in a constellation of ways that limit their ability to take up opportunities even when they may be offered to them. These are not simply the product of individual propensities or idiosyncrasies, but deeply embedded in societal arrangements. For Labour, equality is portrayed as a matter of individual agency and choice and as a consequence the twin strategies of opening access to the labour market and the appearance of greater participation in policy-making become the formula for redress. Such a strategy itself obscures the fact of limited opportunities in some territorial areas and limited opportunities for some groups of people and proffers a rather simplistic view of the exercise of choice.

The approach flagged in *Fairness and Freedom* (Equalities Review, 2007) also serves to fragment issues of inequality. The analysis it adopts disaggregates the impacts of unequal chances as they affect individual chances into different policy fields such as education, housing or health in order to prioritise for action the most pressing and thus target effort and resources: the so-called '*Equalities Scorecard*'. So, for example, it prioritises early years education, employment, health and crime for targeted action, while housing and income support fall quietly off the equalities agenda. This disaggregation has two effects. First, it blurs the complex inter-relationship between dimensions of inequality in individuals' lives. Second, it shifts attention away from systemised and persistent inequalities as experienced collectively by certain status groups across the spectrum of policy areas. On the broader front of social justice, McClaughlin and Baker (2007:60) argue that New Labour's approach 'has been strong in discourses of well-being and need but weak in terms of discourses of rights and social solidarity'. Their targeted, as opposed to universalistic, approach to policy necessarily hampers their ability to deliver on equality and social justice (Ellison and Ellison, 2006).

Against the backdrop of New Labour policy on equalities, the approach taken by the Welsh Assembly Government (WAG) appears markedly distinctive. The WAG agenda has been driven by an equalities mandate embedded within its constitutional arrangements, one that is unique in the whole of the UK. Now the WAG is poised to mesh the new UK equalities apparatus into the framework that it has established post-devolution. This transitional moment will not be without difficulties – not least because of differences in approach – and it will be interesting to see the ways in which the WAG steers a course through what is a sea change in equalities practice.

## The equalities challenge

The principle of equality is fundamental to the work of the Assembly and has far-reaching implications for those working within or in association with public services in Wales. Prior to devolution, no coherent approach to issues of inequality in Wales existed. Indeed, a widespread lethargy on the part of government bodies prior to the establishment of the Assembly casts a long shadow forward. The vision set out in *Wales: A Better Country* (WAG, 2003) suggests that:

> 'We will promote gender equality, good race relations and race equality and tackle discrimination on grounds of age and disability. We want to see people in public life reflecting the diversity in the population as a whole. We will comply with our Welsh Language Scheme, thus ensuring that Welsh and English are treated on a basis of equality in the conduct of public business.'

Wales is a profoundly unequal society. Overarching economic disparities affect people from a range of status backgrounds producing widespread poverty for older people, disabled people, black and minority ethnic (BME) people and for children, among others. Fundamental inequalities of income and wealth cannot be disassociated from life chances but for some groups of individuals deep and persistent discriminations reduce their freedoms, well-being and ability to participate in society. The systemised patterning of these discriminations becomes evident in even the most superficial look at the statistics.

The pay gap between men and women in Wales is doggedly resistant to change with a differential between women's and men's full-time earnings of 12%, rising to 31% for women working part-time (EOC, 2006). Women are by and large concentrated in low-pay, low-skilled sectors of the economy and a lifetime of disadvantage results in poverty in older age. Women's access to work is hampered by a lack of childcare in Wales. There is only one childcare place to every seven children in Wales and in some areas, such as Blaenau Gwent, there is only one place for every 20 children (EOC, 2006a). Of the 340,000 people providing unpaid care in Wales the majority are women (EOC, 2006a). Lack of support for caring responsibilities seriously disadvantages their prospects. On International Women's Day in 2006 the EOC published its report *Who Runs Wales* (EOC, 2006b), a review of women's representation in key decision-making roles in Wales. Despite strong representation as members of the Assembly (52%) women are largely absent from the committee rooms and council chambers of Wales. One striking example is that only 9% of local authority chief executives are women.

Some of the most profound inequalities in terms of race in Wales relate to employment. Based on 2002/03 figures the CRE notes that employment rates for all ethnic groups were lower in Wales and Scotland than in England, with people of Pakistani and Bangladeshi backgrounds being the least likely to be in employment (CRE, 2007). Employment and unemployment are, however, just one indicator of the ways in which BME groups experience inequalities in Wales. Another is educational opportunity. Black African and Pakistani pupils are less likely than average to reach the expected level across primary and secondary schooling in Wales (Equalities Review, 2007).

In terms of disability the evidence is equally stark. Wales has the highest proportion of disabled people in the whole of Britain, with 23% of the working-age population having a work-limiting disability. The DRC's (2006a) document *Disability in Wales: Impact Report 2005-6* indicates that Wales has a higher proportion of young people not in education, employment or training by the age of 16 and by the age of 19 they are still twice as likely as their peers to be in this predicament. In 2006 the DRC launched its most provocative campaign under the banner *Are we taking the Dis?* which featured the startling facts of the nature of discrimination and disadvantage faced daily by disabled people (DRC, 2006b).

While the pattern and persistence of gender, race and disability disadvantage are amenable to monitoring, new fields of discrimination such as age, sexuality and religion are more difficult to demonstrate in quantitative terms due to lack of available data. This is not to suggest they are any less trenchant in Wales. For example, Stonewall Cymru continues to document its concerns about hate crimes and workplace discriminations against gay, lesbian and bi-sexual people. A 2003 survey undertaken by Stonewall noted that one in three of its respondents had been the victim of physical violence or bullying and 25% of respondents had been dismissed from a job because of their sexuality. It is only since 1999 that the Sex Discrimination (Gender Reassignment) Regulations provided for the recognition of transgender people for the first time in UK legislation but their voiced experiences of discrimination have been known for sometime. The relationship between religion and disadvantage is more difficult to establish. The emergence of British Muslims as a group widely recognised as being systematically disadvantaged can be extrapolated from the high number of Bangladeshis and Pakistanis among this group. Evidence suggests that these are highly represented among people living in the most deprived areas of the UK (Equalities Review, 2007:35).

While the Welsh language has not traditionally been viewed as an equal opportunities issue it is nevertheless clearly associated with discriminations and disadvantage (see Chapter 4) and forms an important – and at times complex – interface with other equalities issues such as disability and age.

The difficulty of demonstrating the interplay between major sources of inequality should be noted when reading these bare facts of inequality. To isolate, for example, education and skills disadvantage of young disabled people in Wales from facts relating to their health chances is to miss the profound impact of inequality across people's life experiences. Or to disassociate workplace discrimination of women from the facts of poverty across the life course is to over-simplify the nature and effects of inequality. It is also very clear that people may be disadvantaged on a number of levels relating to their multiple status and identities. They may not simply be women but older women, BME women and/or disabled women. This multi-dimensional nature of inequality demands approaches that tackle change across a range of social policy spheres in an integrated way and that utilise a range of methods. It is also worth reiterating the much noted point that all kinds of disadvantage are bad for those who experience them but they are also very bad for a society.

## The Assembly's equality duties and powers

The National Assembly for Wales has a panoply of duties and powers at its disposal in pursuing equality objectives. The range of legal, constitutional, governance and structural arrangements unique to Wales indicates that Welsh policy in respect of equalities has a significant degree of divergence from practices elsewhere in Britain. The Assembly has a unique statutory duty (under Sections 120 and 48 of the Government of Wales Act 1998 and Section 77 of the Government of Wales Act 2006) to:

> *'... make appropriate arrangements with a view to securing that its functions are exercised with due regard to the principle that there should be equality of opportunity for all people'.*
> (Section 120)

and to:

> *'... make appropriate arrangements with a view to securing that its business is conducted with due regard to the principle that there should be equality of opportunity for all people.'*
> (Section 48)

The new Government of Wales Act (2006) will place this duty specifically upon the Welsh Assembly Government as opposed to the earlier statute that placed the duty on the National Assembly for Wales as a whole. The new legislation separates the legislative and executive branches of the Assembly and Section 77 of the 2006 Act lays a clear equality duty on the executive to *'make appropriate arrangements'* to exercise its functions *'with due regard to the principle of equality of opportunity for all people'*. This twin arrangement, wherein the government is duty bound to plan and deliver action and report on it on an annual basis to the Assembly and the Assembly's duty to scrutinise the government's actions, provides a powerful platform for driving through equality achievements in Wales.

The nature of this equality duty goes beyond the legal equalities framework applying to the government in Scotland and England (Chaney and Fevre, 2002). Such is the reach of these powers that they apply to all people in Wales, irrespective of status, and to all of the Assembly's functions, including those carried out on behalf of the Assembly. This means that in delivering on its core functions of education, health, local government, social services, economic development, transport, housing and industry, the Assembly must ensure equality of opportunity for all. Clements and Thomas (1999:8) have noted that the Assembly's equality duty means that 'the people of Wales are the first in the UK to be given a series of positive rights to exercise and, if necessary, enforced through the courts in Wales'. They illustrate the ways in which the human rights obligations set out in the Government of Wales Act (2006, s. 79) have distinct implications for Wales. For example, in respect of: the timing of enactments (Section 79, s. 4); in terms of the requirement for UK ministers to consult Welsh Ministers before making an order (Cf, Section 79, s. 5); and in terms of the compliance by Welsh ministers to the human rights obligations. They indicate: 'Welsh Ministers have no power… to make, confirm or approve any subordinate legislation, or … to do any other act … [that] is incompatible with (European) Community law' (Section 80, s.1). This confers considerable protective rights for the individual citizen in Wales.

This in itself is an extensive application of equality law, but in addition, as Chaney (2004:67) has rightly pointed out, the duty implies *distributive* as well as rights-based actions. This foregrounds public service provision as a key instrument in producing fairer outcomes for individual citizens, by redistributing opportunities and resources between those who have and those who have not. McLaughlin (2007:111) has used the concept of 'equality regime' to describe the combination of a country's equality law together with the total redistributive or equalising impact of its social welfare system. She suggests that the equality regimes apparent in the various UK countries differ from each other in significant respects, both in terms of their legislative mandate and in terms of their approach to equality issues. This combination of strong legal duties and the specific remit of the Assembly over core social policy areas is therefore conducive to making significant inroads on issues of inequality.

A number of other aspects of the constitutional settlement favour equalities work. The Assembly is not the only actor in delivering on equalities and work with a range of public and private bodies is important in achieving change. The Government of Wales Acts (1998 and 2006) place unique statutory duties on the Assembly to implement formal partnership schemes with local government and the voluntary sector, and schemes of co-working with police authorities, fire authorities and national parks in Wales, and to carry out consultations and legislative impact assessments relating to future legal enactments with organisations representative of business. These arrangements have no direct constitutional parallel in Scotland or England. Thus the statutory framework itself promotes partnership across sectors that can be used as a powerful lever for change. An example of this in action is the Assembly's efforts to engage private businesses in Wales in its equality ambitions using the mechanism of 'contract compliance'. The Assembly has £3 billion to spend in the procurement of services (National Assembly for Wales, 2004) and requiring those tendering to offer services to comply with equality standards is an important mechanism in effecting change. The Assembly has developed a voluntary code of equality practice encouraging its suppliers to subscribe to these good practice guidelines. It has also used its relationship with local government to drive forward change. The Welsh Local Government Association's (2002) *Equality Standard* sets the benchmark for local authority equality practices.

The powers of the Assembly have also enabled it to have an impact on areas of government policy that are reserved matters, for example in interventions made by the Minister for Social Justice on the issue of detention of asylum seekers in prisons in Wales (see Chapter 8). In addition, as with the case of the Scottish Parliament, existing legislation passed by the Assembly can have a significant impact on the prevailing legal equalities framework, for example The *School Government (Wales) Regulations (2000)* which provide for the instituting of multi-cultural education in the Welsh school curriculum.

In post-devolution Wales there is also a new and extensive state regulatory framework. These unique, statutory Wales-only regulatory bodies are required to include equality assessments in their inspection reports. They include the Wales Audit Office, the Welsh Public Services

Ombudsman, the Care Standards Inspectorate for Wales, the National Assembly for Wales Ombudsman, the Welsh Schools Inspectorate (ESTYN), General Teaching Council Wales, Social Services Inspectorate for Wales and the Health Service Ombudsman for Wales – as well as the offices of the Welsh Commissioners for Children and Older People. These bodies are charged with monitoring and reviewing performance on equality issues.

Finally, the Assembly can use concordats and Memorandum of Understanding (MOU) in its relationships with public bodies, which provide protocols of how they will work together. These concordats establish a framework for working arrangements between central government and the devolved administrations and operate within the overarching MOU, which sets out the common principles and practices that will underlie relations. There are, for example, these arrangements with the existing Equality Commissions who are bound by the concordat between their sponsor UK governmental department and the devolved institutions. These arrangements will most likely underpin the relationship between the Assembly and the new CEHR.

This gamut of powers will be supplemented by the framework being rolled out UK wide under the steer of the new Commission.

## The CEHR in Wales

The new Commission, the CEHR, operates fully in Wales from October 2007. Recognising the unique nature and duties of the devolved governance has been explicit in the development of the new Commission with the intention that Wales will have its own CEHR Committee and its own CEHR Commissioner with the mandate to set priorities for work in the devolved nation. The CEHR Great Britain Board will delegate functions and establish procedural and governance practices applying in Wales that are complementary to the elected body. While the Equality Act (2006) does not give the CEHR enforcement powers to Wales in relation to this statutory duty, the operation and the actions of the CEHR in Wales will take into account the distinct legal context. The intentions have been made explicit but it is yet to be seen how this will work in practice. A Chair of the Commission in Wales has been appointed along with a Wales Board of Commissioners.

A measure of continuity is inevitably assured by the fact that many employees in the new Commission and people appointed to the Board will be drawn from existing equalities practitioners and activists across Wales.

Wales has a strong tradition of collaborative working on equalities issues. As a small nation, equalities practitioners, advice workers and social welfare workers have been able to work to build informal networks and establish close working relationships (Williams, 2004). There is a lot of evidence to suggest that bodies in Wales have been able to work 'cross strand' quite effectively at the same time as strongly retaining the profile of their statutory responsibilities. As Wales gears up to the introduction of the new Commission, new partnerships and coalitions are emerging such as the Equalities Reference Group, a partnership of 20 voluntary organisations, which has been lobbying hard to influence the equalities agenda of Wales. In March 2007 this group launched a groundbreaking and unique Equality Manifesto for Wales (Equalities Reference Group, 2007) in advance of the Assembly elections, to influence policy-makers' agendas on equality. They lobbied for an agenda that will address identified needs such as:

- assisting disabled and older people to live independently if they wish to;
- closing the pay gap between women and men;
- removing all forms of discrimination from the health service;
- extending the availability of Welsh medium education from early years to higher education;
- tackling bullying, including homophobic bullying, in schools and colleges;
- assisting a more diverse range of people to get into positions of power in politics and public life;
- tackling violence in the home and community including domestic violence and hate crime against older and disabled people, minority ethnic communities and religions, lesbians and gay people.

(Equalities Reference Group, 2007)

The generic approach heralded by the CEHR will undoubtedly have an impact on the ways in which the Assembly has approached and funded its equality agenda. The institution of the WAG, like any other public body in Wales, will have to make the shift from a 'strand' approach focusing on issues of race, gender, disability as discrete mandates, to working with equality issues in the round. The statutory context for taking forward equalities issues in Wales is undoubtedly strong and potentially strengthened by the new Equality Act and there is a lot of goodwill at grassroots level. Progress on implementing and delivering on these requirements, however, reveals a more sketchy picture.

## Implementing equality

The Assembly's first term of office flagged issues of social justice and equality as priority themes. Equality of opportunity was established as one of three cross-cutting themes that would shape policy-making, the other two being sustainable development and social inclusion/justice. The evolution of the equality duty and evidence of its implementation have indicated a political culture willing to embrace a much broader concept of equality than the more narrow definition of equality of opportunity used in England. The working definition of equality highlighted by the Assembly in its 2004 review of progress stands in contrast to that adopted by the UK government in the report *Fairness and Freedom* (cited above) with its emphasis on achieve equality of outcome rather that removing barriers:

> *'Equality, in the context of this report, is about treating people equally in status, rights and opportunities through a set of policies and actions, with the aim of securing equality of outcome for all'*
> (WAG, 2004:7)

The First Minister has not shied away from flagging key differences in the approach to equality. In his 2002 *Clear Red Water Speech*, hailing the second term of office of the Assembly as a period of implementation, Rhodri Morgan (2002) stated:

> *'Equality of provision must be underpinned by equality of access, and equality of opportunity. But most importantly of all, we match the emphasis on opportunity with what has been described as the fundamentally socialist aim of equality of outcome'*

This more radical approach to equality is firmly linked to the wider social justice ambitions of the Assembly. To this end the Assembly has adopted a mainstreaming approach to the development of its equalities strategy. The mainstreaming approach, now the dominant methodology in use by governments across Europe, has attracted considerable applications and in its wake, critical debate. It is described as follows:

> *'Mainstreaming equality is about the integration of respect for diversity and equality of opportunity principles, strategies and practices into the everyday work of the Assembly and other public bodies. It means that equality issues should be included from the outset as an integral part of the policy-making and service delivery process and the achievement of equality should inform all aspects of the work of every individual within an organisation. The success of mainstreaming should be measured by evaluating whether inequalities have been reduced.'*
> (WAG, 2004:6)

It represents a shift away from seeing equality of opportunity as a special measure to seeing it as an approach fully integrated into the functioning of all policy areas of an institution. The approach implies a pro-active and comprehensive commitment to equalities, taking the long view as a change strategy rather than quick fix measures. A number of commentators are somewhat critical of this approach, seeing it as locked into the existing capacities and functions of institutions that may not necessarily be equality enhancing (Williams, 2001; Chaney and Rees, 2004). Despite such concerns there is little doubt that the mainstreaming of the statutory equality duty has had a significant and positive impact and resulted in a number of reforms being initiated in most of the policy areas within the remit of the Welsh Assembly.

In his overview of the initial phase of implementation of the equality duty, Chaney (2004) notes a number of developments flagging the Assembly as actively pursuing its intention to '*mainstream*' equality. In the first term of office it took steps to signal itself as a lead organisation by getting its own house in order, establishing its Equality Policy Unit, conducting internal equality audits and carrying out equality awareness training. One of its critical developmental tools has been the cross-party Standing Committee on Equal Opportunities, one of only two standing committees specified in the Government of Wales Act (1998). The purpose of the Equal Opportunities Committee is to monitor and audit the Assembly's compliance with the statutory equality duties set out in the devolution statutes. Under the National Assembly's procedural law a number of equal opportunities organisations including the three Commissions, Stonewall Cymru and the Welsh Language Board have a standing invitation to attend these meetings as advisers. The Committee meets once a month when the Assembly is in session and all of its proceedings are held in public, televised and full transcripts are made available online. The annual reports of this Committee provide a transparent documentation on the Assembly's progress on its ideals and can easily be consulted by stakeholders and the general public.

A number of achievements stem from the Equality of Opportunity Committee's policy development work, in conjunction with the Assembly Government. Examples are the establishment and funding of consultative policy networks to seek the views of different social groups across Wales. These include the All Wales Ethnic Minority Association (AWEMA), the Wales Women's National Coalition, Disability Wales, the Lesbian, Gay and Bisexual (LGB) Forum Cymru and the Interfaith Council. A major study tracking the effectiveness of these engagement and consultation strategies with minority groups in Wales found evidence of a sense of greater access to policy makers and policy-making, if not necessarily a direct influence on policy outcomes (Fevre, *et al.*, 2004). Other examples of the development work of this Committee include a joint campaign on equal pay (EOC, 2005), a review of government policy strategy relating to Gypsies and Travellers in Wales (WAG, 2007) and a strategy for refugees and asylum seekers (WAG, 2004a).

In addition, the Welsh Assembly Government has implemented a number of innovative social policy initiatives that impact on equalities issues. These include the appointment of the UK's first Children's Commissioner, a Strategy for Older People, which has included newly-passed legislation for the appointment of an Older People's Commissioner for Wales, the development of multicultural education and recently *Making the Connections* (WAG, 2004b), which sets out the Welsh Assembly Government's vision of a prosperous, sustainable, bilingual, healthier and better-educated Wales. This package of public sector reform has equality and social justice as one of its four key pillars in the delivery of better public services.

The National Assembly's statutory duty and its actions on equality indicate a clear break from the past. A systematic attempt is being made to tackle inequalities using a broad range of measures (Williams and de Lima, 2006). The political climate is conducive to these developments with strong proclamations in evidence across the political spectrum. Chaney (2004) has given evidence of the willingness of the Assembly to go beyond the Westminster approach towards the development of a distinctly Welsh response and suggests that the Welsh approach may prove instructive to other parts of the UK and beyond.

There are, however, a number of reservations to be noted. The Assembly's own assessment of its progress reveals considerable frustrations. In 2004 its review *Mainstreaming Equality in the work of the National Assembly* (National Assembly for Wales, 2004) found the Assembly lacking in a coherent strategy towards equality with *ad hoc* gains, but with a lack of leadership. It stated:

> *'We are left with a sense that people generally regard equality as important and know that they need to be proactive, but that they are not always sure how to apply mainstreaming principles in their particular policy area'*
> (National Assembly for Wales, 2004:31)

Despite the Assembly's efforts the report found internal co-ordination of equality activities (policy integration) to be weak, its consultation processes to be limited in terms of engaging a wide constituency and diversity of interests and its monitoring of tangible impacts poor.

While a number of tangible achievements can be identified it is clear from more recent deliberations of the Equality of Opportunity Committee that there is still a long way to go and some re-emphasis to be made in the trajectory the Assembly has taken. In January 2006 the Minister Jane Hutt (6th Annual Report on Equality of Opportunity) stressed the need for a more outcome-focused emphasis. It has been suggested that a lot of energy and effort has been expended on 'inputs' in terms of processes such as training, revising procedures and establishing impact assessments, with somewhat less attention given to what the outcomes of these efforts might be in terms of tangible change.

Establishing rights is one thing, exercising and realising them another. Studies undertaken across Wales on rights awareness indicate a largely ill-informed public across a range of rights issues (Williams *et al*., 2003; Williams, 2004; DRC 2006c). The Disability Rights Commission (DRC) document, *Our Rights our Choice* highlights the widespread lack of awareness about black disabled people's rights. In 2002 a collaboration between the DRC, the EOC and the CRE commissioned research on advice and support in cases of workplace discrimination for women, disabled people and black and ethnic minorities. The report *Snakes and Ladders: Advice and Support in Employment Discrimination Cases in Wales* (Williams, *et al.*, 2003) assessed the available evidence on advice provision across the three equality strands and found:

- a lack of accessible information about rights and sources of advice;
- a weak infrastructure for delivering advice, support and representation, revealing significant 'advice deserts' across Wales;
- a lack of training and quality accreditation among major advice providers;
- a poor system of referral and co-ordination between agencies, including a failure to transfer expertise between agencies such that people in need were passed from pillar to post;
- ineffective systems of client support with no formalised protocols on pathways to advice and support;
- a lack of bilingual provision for advice giving;
- a lack of accurate statistical information disaggregated for Wales.

*Snakes and Ladders* provided important baseline information on the nature and extent of the delivery system for rights-based work in Wales. While the report did not cover the new equality strands or human rights provision, nor offer any discussion of non-employment discrimination, it is important in signalling the huge gulf between the establishment of positive rights for all citizens in Wales and their ability to realise them (Williams, 2004).

## Social welfare practitioners and equality issues in Wales

The philosophy and approach of the Welsh Assembly to issues of equality, and the more prominent profile that has been given to these issues over the last eight years, will be instrumental in reshaping the opportunities for anti-discriminatory/anti-oppressive practice by social work and social welfare professionals. This new enabling context for proactive work on equalities is matched at local level. In each local authority in Wales there is a designated individual with responsibility for equality issues and clear standards are available to guide performance on equalities issues. All local authorities are obliged to produce a Race Equality Code of Practice, a Disability Code of Practice and since 2007 a Gender Code of Practice. The broad philosophy of the Assembly that values 'voice' over 'choice' in its approach to the user of services (see Chapter 2) provides a bolster to the push towards greater user participation and user involvement in social work, health and social care. The challenge will be to establish appropriate and effective user engagement that delivers on these intentions. In addition, as the new CEHR infrastructure for delivering on equality at the local level (local equality bodies) emerges, there will be additional resources and support for social welfare workers in signposting users to appropriate help and advice and in offering support to practitioners.

Despite this framework, there are concerns at the local level that local authorities and Local Health Boards are not meeting their statutory duties (see, for example, CRE Annual Report, 2006). Developments are patchy and uneven and there is still a long way to go. There are a number of explanations put forward for the implementation gulf ranging from 'initiative overload' to lack of political will and leadership. It is clear that there are a number of countervailing forces undermining bureaucratic equality strategies that will impinge on the goodwill and efforts of frontline practitioners. The tension between the neo-liberal managerialist aims of New Labour and delivering on equality and fairness for all strikes to the heart of contemporary social welfare practice (Jones, 2001). It is professionals at the interface of service delivery that have to engage with and navigate these tensions to work in the interests of service users. Early social policy academics such as Titmuss (1958) recognised the discretion in the hands of public service professionals that could promote or restrict equality aims. He saw professionals as key arbiters of welfare, determining the pattern, nature and extent of welfare services. The equalities responsibilities have never been greater as social welfare practice manages the tension between the demands of the bureaucracy and the social justice concerns of the professions.

Opportunities for social welfare practitioners in Wales to take a more proactive stance in relation to equalities and social justice issues are being opened up within a wider culture of welfare resistant to the neo-liberal mandate (see Chapter 11). Practitioners will need to move beyond minimalist, bureaucratic requirements in their interventions in order to ensure that equality and social justice principles are realised in practice. In the context of Welsh public service delivery the First Minister Rhodri Morgan's stance is steering a path towards greater recognition of social solidarity and citizenship rights, underpinned by the principle of 'progressive universalism' (see Chapter 2). It is the attempt to provide a coherent framework for tackling equality that is embedded in the wider social justice ambitions that marks the distinctiveness of the Welsh approach.

## References

Chaney, P (2004) 'The post-devolution equality agenda: the case of the Welsh Assembly's statutory duty to promote equality of opportunity' *Policy and Politics* 32(1), pp. 63-77.

Chaney, P and Fevre, R (2002) *An Absolute Duty: The Equality Policies of the Government of the National Assembly for Wales and their implementation: July 1999-2002* Report for the Equal Opportunities Commission, the Disability Rights Commission and the

Commission for Racial Equality, Cardiff, Institute of Welsh Affairs.

Chaney, P and Rees, T (2004) 'The Northern Ireland Section 75 Duty: an international perspective' in McLaughlin, E and Faris, N. (eds) *The Section 75 Equality Duty – An Operational Review* Belfast, Northern Ireland Office, 2, pp. 1-51.

Clements, L and Thomas, P (1999) 'Human rights and the Welsh Assembly' *Planet* 136, pp: 7-11.

CRE (Commission for Racial Equality) (2007) Factfiles, www.cre.gov.uk

CRE 2006 annual report, www.cre.gov.uk

DRC (Disability Rights Commission) (2006a) *Disability in Wales: Impact Report 2005-6*, www.drc.org.uk

DRC (2006b) *Are We Taking The Dis? Campaign*, www.drc.org.uk

DRC (2006c) *Our Rights Our Choice*, www.drc.org.uk

Ellison, N and Ellison, S (2006) 'Creating opportunity for all? New Labour, the new localism and the opportunity society' *Social Policy and Society* 5(3), pp. 337-48.

EOC (Equal Opportunities Commission) (2005) *Close the Pay Gap Campaign*, www.eoc.org.uk

EOC (2006a) *Facts about Women and Men in Wales 2006*, www.eoc.org.uk

EOC (2006b) *Who Runs Wales?*, www.eoc.org.uk/pdf/who%20runs%20wales%202006.pdf

Equalities Reference Group (2007) *Equality Manifesto for Wales*, www.eoc.org.uk/PDF/Equality_Manifesto_for_Wales.pdf

Equalities Review (2007) *Fairness and Freedom: The Final Report of the Equalities Review* London, HMSO.

Fevre, R, Chaney, P, Betts S and Williams C (2004) *Social Capital and the Participation of Marginalised Groups in Government* Swindon, Economic and Social Research Council, ESRC R000239410.

Jones, C (2001) 'Voices from the front line: state social workers and New Labour' *British Journal of Social Work* 31, pp.547-682.

McLaughlin, E (2007) 'From negative to positive equality duties: the development and constitutionalisation of equality provisions in the UK' *Social Policy and Society* 6(1), pp.111-21.

McLaughlin, E and Baker, J (2007) 'Equality, social justice and social welfare: a road map to the new egalitarians' *Social Policy and Society* 6(1) pp. 53-66.

MacPherson, W (1999) *The Stephen Lawrence Inquiry: Report of an Inquiry by Sir William MacPherson of Cluny* London, HMSO.

Morgan, R (2002) Speech to the University of Wales, Swansea, National Centre for Public Policy Third Anniversary Lecture, 11 December.

National Assembly for Wales (2004) *Equality of Opportunity Committee: Report on Mainstreaming Equality in the Work of the National Assembly* Cardiff, Welsh Assembly Government.

Stonewall Cymru (2003) *Counted Out*, www.stonewall.org.uk/cymru

Titmuss, R (1958) *Essays on the Welfare State* 2nd edition (1963), London, Unwin University Books.

WAG (Welsh Assembly Government) (2007) *Review of Service Provision for Gypsy and Travellers Report LD2070* Cardiff, Welsh Assembly Government.

WAG (2004a) *Report of the Equal Opportunities Committee: Asylum Issues* 15 July, EOC(2)06-04 (p. 4).

WAG (2004b) *Making the Connections* Cardiff, Welsh Assembly Government.

WAG (2003) *Wales: A Better Country*, Cardiff, Welsh Assembly Government.

Welsh Local Government Association (2002) *Equality Standard*, www.wlga.gov.uk

Williams, C (2004) 'Access to justice and social inclusion: the policy challenges in Wales' *Journal of Social Welfare and Family Law* 26(1) pp. 53-68.

Williams, C (2001) 'Can mainstreaming deliver? the equal opportunities agenda and the National Assembly for Wales' *Contemporary Wales* 14, pp. 57-79.

Williams, C; Borland J; Griffiths A; Roberts, G; Bradshaw, H and Morris, E (2003) *'Snakes and Ladders' Advice and Support in Employment Discrimination Cases in Wales*, www.eoc.org.uk

Williams, C and de Lima, P (2006) 'Devolution, multicultural citizenship and race equality: from laissez-faire to nationally responsible policies' *Critical Social Policy* 26(3) pp. 498-522.

# SECTION THREE

## Service Delivery Areas

Chapter 8

# Children's policy in Wales

Ian Butler

## Introduction

The Government of Wales Act (GOWA) 1998, perhaps inadvertently, settled on the Welsh Assembly and subsequently the Welsh Assembly Government, legislative authority in relation to almost all of those 'traditional' policy areas that bear directly on children; namely education, social care and health. There are some notable areas where the policy lead remains with the UK government, for example, youth justice and immigration, and some of these are discussed in detail elsewhere in this volume but, to all intents and purposes, almost all public policy explicitly directed towards children and young people in Wales that has emerged since the 1998 Act is 'made in Wales'. This point is just as often missed in Wales as it is elsewhere in the UK.

It is with frustrating regularity that major policy initiatives that have their origin in Westminster or Whitehall but which do not extend to Wales are assumed to apply on both sides of Offa's Dyke. Notable among these is the *Every Child Matters* agenda, a collection of policies and programmes that has developed, largely by the Department for Education and Skills (DfES), after the Laming Inquiry into the Climbié case (Laming, 2003). *Every Child Matters* (DfES, 2003) is England specific, as was its precursor (*Quality Protects*; DH, 1999). Neither have effect in Wales.

Similarly, the Children Act 2004 is carefully divided into those parts that relate to Wales and those that do not. This is not to say that there are not considerable and important similarities with arrangements in England and elsewhere in the UK and, of course, there is a substantial common heritage in terms of service delivery structures and the knowledge base of professional engagement with children and families but it is the differences between children's policies and programmes in Wales and those operating elsewhere in the UK (in England specifically) that this chapter will address.

It remains a moot point as to whether in Wales it is a defensible proposition to talk about 'children's policy'. How far children and young people have come to occupy a distinctive and coherent 'policy space' is an important question and one that this chapter seeks to address. Clearly, lives of children in Wales are as much subject to the renegotiations that have taken place in the politics and structures of welfare over recent years as any other section of the population living anywhere in the UK.

Similarly, childhood in Wales, understood as a social artefact and as a set of lived experiences, can not be isolated from the constructions and experiences of childhood and of children elsewhere in the UK and beyond. (For a detailed account of the 'new sociology of childhood' and an exploration of childhood as a social construction, see Foley *et al.,* 2001; James and James, 2004; Prout, 2004.) The dynamics of social change, especially the changing balance of inter-generational relations and of developing trends in household formation, structure and dissolution have run through Wales as surely as they have run through the rest of the Britain and northern Europe. For example, despite an overall increase in the population of Wales over the period from 1971, in 2005 there were 19 per cent fewer children aged 0-14 in Wales than there had been in 1971 and 1 per cent fewer aged 15-29 (WAG, 2006a, figure 5:6). As a proportion of the population, children (aged 0-15) have fallen from approximately one in four to one in five. In contrast, the proportion of pensioners has increased from approximately 17 per cent of the population to 21 per cent (WAG, 2006a, table 3:8). In terms of household structure and family formation, in 1971, 93 per cent of the 43,000 children born in Wales were born to married parents. In 2005, 52 per cent of the 32,500 children born in Wales were born outside of marriage (WAG, 2006a, figure 2:18). Rates of marriage in Wales have fluctuated but overall have declined sharply from 1971. Divorce rates have, overall, increased markedly over the same period (WAG, 2006a, table 1:32).

Arguably, given their declining literal and demographic visibility and the shift of political 'weight' in favour of the older citizen, children may be thought to have lost the vanguard status that they once possessed in public policy terms. In England in particular, children, other than in relation to economic dependency ratios (or 'education, education, education' in the mantra of New Labour) and their perennial potential to jeopardise the social order (the so-called 'respect agenda' of Westminster), present less of a policy profile than would have been recognised by the architects of the post-war welfare settlement. This encompassed a much more ambitious set of policy objectives to enrich the lives of the nation's children, from free school milk to playing fields.

A long historical perspective is beyond the scope of this chapter however. This chapter will focus on the policy outcomes aimed at children and young people that have been produced in Wales, for Wales, since devolution. In passing, one might note that this process of gradual divergence and nuancing of children's policy is observable across all four of the devolved administrations of the UK. For present purposes, it is the differences that are emerging between England and Wales that will occupy our attention. For, although still in the process of development, these differences are fundamental. They turn on the question of citizenship and the civil status of children but they relate also to the politically dominant conception of what constitutes a 'welfare state' at this and the far end of the M4.

The issue of child poverty is a specific but illustrative instance of the developing character of children's policy in Wales (see also Crowley, Chapter 5 in this volume).

## The politics of child poverty: New Labour and Welsh Labour

In March 1999, at Toynbee Hall, the previous residents of which include Clement Attlee and William Beveridge and which was the birthplace of the Child Poverty Action Group some 30 years previously, Prime Minister Tony Blair committed the New Labour government to an ambitious programme to tackle child poverty. He declared its 'historic aim that ours is the first generation to end child poverty for ever' (Blair, 1999). (Further quotations from the Prime Minister in this section are taken from the same Beveridge Lecture, 18 March 1999.) He cast his vision in terms of his wider ambitions to 'make the welfare state popular again', based on a particular vision of 'social justice', which is 'about ... decency ... merit ... mutual responsibility ... fairness ... values'. The New Labour vision for the welfare state would be quite different from that with which the electorate was in danger of losing faith; one that was associated with 'fraud, abuse, laziness, a dependency culture, social irresponsibility'. By reconnecting 'social justice to economic vision', the New Labour welfare state would tackle the root causes of social exclusion, poverty and community decay and offer a 'hand-up not a hand-out'. This would be achieved through a mixture of targeted and universal services delivered through an expanded range of service providers, including a 'modernised' public sector.

Approvingly quoting his Chancellor's recent Budget speech, the Prime Minister represented the conventional developmentalist view that while children may be 'only 20% of the population ... they are 100 per cent of the future'. He identified key targets including 'lifting 700,000 children out of poverty by the end of the Parliament'. This would help 'sow the seeds of ambition in the young' in the belief that,

> *'... the role of the welfare state is to help people to help themselves, to give people the means to be independent. We are creating an active welfare state focussed on giving people the opportunities they need to support themselves, principally through work.'*

The success or otherwise of this workfare as much as welfare strategy awaits a final judgement and both the nature and the effectiveness of New Labour's underlying commitment to ending child poverty is open to debate. Taken with the increasing authoritarianism, instrumentalism and conditionality that have come to characterise welfare policy towards children and young people in England, starting with Thatcherism in the 1980s and continued under New Labour to the present day (see Butler and Drakeford, 2001), this may be doubted. Of primary interest to us is the difference in both form, style and content with which the anti-poverty agenda for children has been developed in Wales against the blueprint offered by Tony Blair.

In 2003, the Assembly Government commissioned an independently chaired Task Group to map out its contribution to the UK child poverty strategy. The Task Group's Report resulted in the publication in February 2005 of *A Fair Future for Our Children: The Strategy of the Welsh Assembly Government for Tackling Child Poverty* (WAG, 2005). The specifics of *A Fair Future* are considered elsewhere in this volume. What is important for our present purposes is to understand the different rhetorics around poverty employed in England and Wales and how these speak to a distinctive approach to children's policy in Wales.

*A Fair Future* is unambiguously 'built on a set of core values in line with the UN Convention on the Rights of the Child' (WAG, 2005:9). While this reflects the position taken by the Task Group, in introducing the Plenary Debate on *A Fair Future*, the Minister for Children, Jane Hutt (Labour; Vale of Glamorgan) emphasised that as far as the Assembly Government was concerned:

> '*Our duty as a Government is to use our powers to their maximum potential and effect on behalf of those children who face poverty in their daily lives in Wales. It is a matter of both entitlement and social justice. Freedom from poverty is a basic human right.*'
> (The Official Record of the National Assembly for Wales: 9/02/05:34)

In responding on behalf of the Conservative Party, their spokesman expressed himself as 'pleased' at the reference to the United Nations Convention on the Rights of the Child (UNCRC) made in the Strategy (The National Assembly for Wales; The Official Record of the National Assembly for Wales: 9/02/05:48) and tabled an amendment to the substantive motion under debate to 'commend the Welsh Assembly Government on basing its strategy on the core principles of the UNCRC' (The Official Record of the National Assembly for Wales: 9/02/05:42). The amendment was subsequently agreed by every Assembly member present.

He demurs (unsurprisingly!) from endorsing a commitment to redistributive socialism advocated by other speakers in the debate. On the other hand, perhaps more surprisingly to those less familiar with Welsh Labour than New Labour, in winding up for the government, the Minister for Social Justice, Edwina Hart (Labour; Gower) is happy to make clear that she has 'always stood as a socialist and ha[s] always believed in the redistribution of wealth' and that she does 'not care about upsetting the UK Government if there are policy issues in Wales that we want to take forward' (The Official Record of the National Assembly for Wales: 9/02/05:53 ff.). Even from this position, the Minister for Social Justice was quick to point out her willingness to work in partnership with those in Wales who had a genuine interest in the subject:

> '... *we must get the partnerships right. This is about creating a strategy for all, involving everybody and getting everything signposted and integrated.*'
> (The Official Record of the National Assembly for Wales: 9/02/05:52 ff.)

Earlier, the Minister for Children in her opening speech had gone on to 'reaffirm' the Assembly Government's 'commitment to listen and respond to children and young people' (The Official Record of the National Assembly for Wales: 9/02/05:35) and stated that the Government 'will continue our dialogue with children and young people and seek their views on how we deliver this strategy' (The Official Record of the National Assembly for Wales: 9/02/05:36). The Minister for Children had also made reference to the close attention with which the Children's Commissioner for Wales would keep the Assembly Government's progress under review. She emphasised that the Cabinet Sub-Committee on Children and Young People, which she chaired, would focus on delivering the strategy. There is a commitment to tackling poverty through improving universal services but with a greater commitment to 'Assembly programmes to direct additional resources to areas facing multiple deprivation' (The Official Record of the National Assembly for Wales: 9/02/05:34). *A Fair Future* itself emphasises the view of the Assembly Government that, 'Within a framework of universal services the most disadvantaged and vulnerable groups will need positive action to promote equality' (WAG, 2005:11). In the debate, the Minister for Children emphasised that 'The Assembly Government has many powers that can ensure that children and families in poverty get the services they need' (The Official Record of the National Assembly for Wales: 9/02/05:36).

In this one debate on a particular strategy one can see the outlines of what has become distinctive about the first and second National

Assembly/Assembly Government's approach to children and young people's policy: an unambiguous and explicit commitment to a rights-based agenda that crosses conventional party political lines; a determination to provide Wales-relevant solutions to Wales-specific problems even if this required a break with Westminster and Whitehall; a commitment to work in partnership rather than in competition with all of those who have a contribution to make and to actively engage with young people as part of that process; a commitment to transparency and external scrutiny of the Government's record, including by the first children's independent rights institution to be established in the UK (the Children's Commissioner for Wales); a commitment to ensure continuity and coherence in children's policy making through maintaining a high-profile presence in Cabinet discussions and structures; and a continuing confidence in the capacity of the institutions and instruments of government to shape the lives of individuals and communities, including those of children and young people.

Much of this is of a piece with the Assembly Government's ambitions for Wales more generally (see Drakeford, Chapter 2 in this volume). Welsh Labour's commitments to promoting 'openness, partnership and participation' had been set out in *Wales: A Better Country* (WAG, 2003:11), repeating the commitment to:

> *'... work across boundaries, communicate consistently and give responsibility to those who are best placed to take decisions. We will be clear about what we want to achieve and how we will measure success. We will continue to develop a distinctively Welsh approach to improving the delivery of public services.'*
> (WAG, 2003:12)

Interestingly, *Wales: A Better Country* expresses its specific ambitions for children quite differently from the way in which the Prime Minister had done some years earlier. Whereas for Blair, the burden of the future rests on succeeding generations, for Welsh Labour, the future is clearly the responsibility of the current generation. The Assembly Government's vision is to ensure that:

*'... all our children and future generations enjoy better prospects in life, and are not landed with a legacy of problems bequeathed by us.'*
(WAG, 2003:15)

These key themes of more citizen-focused public services that are more responsive to the needs of communities; more focus on equality and social justice; and more efficient and effective were taken up and developed in *Making the Connections: Delivering Better Services for Wales – The Welsh Assembly Government Vision for Public Services*, published in October 2004 (WAG, 2004a) and have been developed subsequently in the review of local service delivery, *Beyond Boundaries: Citizen Centred Local Services for Wales* published in June 2006 (WAG, 2006b, *The Beecham Report*).

While such overarching strategic considerations are beyond the scope of this chapter, it is important to understand that any specific policy initiatives towards children that have been developed during the first two terms of the Assembly Government must be located in this very particular political and policy context; a policy context that is much more Welsh Labour than New Labour. The fundamental distinguishing characteristic of children and young people's policy in Wales since 1999 is its strong foundations in a commitment to children's rights. This in turn is of a piece with Welsh Labour's broader political traditions and understanding of what constitutes a modern welfare state and its proper relationship to its citizens. (For a more detailed account of the conceptual and political origins of children's rights, see Franklin, 2001; Archard, 2004).

## Rights to action

Arguably the first major statement of children's policy made by the Assembly Government was published in November 2000 as *Children and Young People: A Framework for Partnership* (National Assembly for Wales, 2000). Intended primarily to bring coherence and focus to the planning and funding of services for children at local level, the *Framework* established early the Government's commitment to children's rights and, in particular, its endorsement of the UNCRC:

> *'Over the past 10 years [the UNCRC] has helped to establish an internationally accepted framework for the treatment of all children, encouraged a positive and optimistic image of children and young people as active holders of rights and stimulated a greater global commitment to safeguarding those rights. The Assembly believes that the Convention should provide a foundation of principle for dealings with children.'*
> (National Assembly for Wales, 2000:10)

This commitment was given real substance when on the 14th January 2004, the National Assembly, in plenary, formally, and again with no votes cast against the motion:

> *'Reaffirm[ed] the priority which it attaches to safeguarding and promoting the rights and welfare of children and young people in Wales, particularly those who are vulnerable;*
> [*and*]
> *Formally adopt[ed] the United Nations convention on the rights of the child as the basis of policy making in this area*
> ...'
> (The Official Record of the National Assembly for Wales: 14/01/04:44).

The subsequent debate contained some discordant notes, along predictable party lines, on the Government's record in office, especially in relation to its capacity to ensure delivery of its aims and objectives by local authority 'partners'. Arguably, however, this was fuelled by a continuing and sincere commitment, on all sides of the chamber, to improve services for children, particularly vulnerable children. It should be remembered that this debate was taking place in the context of the post-Climbié period of high anxiety that had provided the momentum for the *Every Child Matters* programme in England and the Children Act of 2004. The Minister for Children chose to make reference to the Assembly Government's own 'Safeguarding Vulnerable Children Review' that it had commissioned some weeks earlier, in December 2003. This Review would publish its report, *Keeping us Safe* in June

2006 (WAG, 2006c). In the debate, the situation of looked-after children in particular drew critical attention from Assembly members (AMs), over which another significant inquiry report, that of Sir Ronald Waterhouse (2000), still casts a long shadow.

The cross-party consensus on a rights-based approach might be considered remarkable enough by itself but this Plenary debate was remarkable also for an amendment that was made to the substantive motion. Welsh Liberal Democrat AM Kirsty Williams (Brecon and Radnorshire) proposed that the Assembly:

> *'Regrets that the UK Government continues to retain the defence of reasonable chastisement and has taken no significant action towards prohibiting the physical punishment of children in the family.'*

The Assembly had already established its opposition to corporal punishment during a short debate introduced by a Labour AM, Christine Chapman (Cynon Valley), some two years previously. What is interesting to note is that AMs from Plaid Cymru, the Welsh Liberal Democrats as well as the Labour government located the issue squarely in the context of the protection of vulnerable children, frequently citing the Climbié case. Even Welsh Conservative AMs who voted against the amendment itself, voted for the amended substantive motion. This is indicative once again, not only of the Government's preparedness to put 'clear red water' between itself and Westminster but also of a progressive, largely consensual approach to policy making on behalf of children and young people. At the start of the Assembly's third term, this opposition to corporal punishment of children is, if anything, more strongly felt.

By the time of the debate, progress had been made in giving the UNCRC a distinctively Welsh cast. This found expression in the publication, later in the same year of *Children and Young People: Rights to Action* (WAG, 2004b). Here the Convention was translated into what the Government was to call its Seven Core Aims, which would, in turn, form the basis for all of the Assembly Government's policies and programmes for children and young people throughout its second term. The Seven Core Aims are designed to ensure that all children and young people:

- have a flying start in life;
- have a comprehensive range of education and learning opportunities;
- enjoy the best possible health and are free from abuse, victimisation and exploitation;
- have access to play, leisure, sporting and cultural activities;
- are listened to, treated with respect and have their race and cultural identity recognised;
- have a safe home and a community which supports physical and emotional wellbeing;
- are not disadvantaged by poverty.

*Rights to Action* describes the programmes that have been put in place to deliver under these core aims and looks forward to the Assembly's second term. A more comprehensive and detailed account of the Assembly's achievements in delivering its programme has been set out in *Rights in Action: Implementing Children and Young People's Rights in Wales* (WAG, 2006d). (See also *Righting the Wrongs: The Reality of Children's Rights in Wales*; Croke and Crowley, 2006. This is the [interim] report of the UNCRC Monitoring Group, an alliance of non-governmental agencies, academics and others, founded in 2002, which will also submit a report to the Committee of the UNCRC as part of the periodic reporting process as will the Children's Commissioner for Wales, along with representatives of young people's organisations).

In many ways this is a landmark document in that its publication had to be negotiated by the Assembly Government as its contribution to the periodic reporting required of signatories to the UNCRC. In law, it is the 'state party' that is the signatory to the Convention rather than any constituent countries, dependencies or territories. With Whitehall officials initially reluctant, the UK Children's Minister agreed to a request by the Assembly Government's Minister for Children to publish, in effect, a separate 'country report'. Scotland and Northern Ireland have also subsequently published 'country reports'. These would ultimately be combined into a single 'metropolitan report' to represent the UK's position. What this demonstrates is not only the growing divergence in children's policy between Cardiff and Westminster but also an explicit recognition of the fact of devolution by Whitehall.

As indicated already, this recognition continues to be hard won. However, the GOWA 2006 provides the National Assembly with a range of additional powers including the power to seek to extend its jurisdiction over key areas of public policy. Prior to the election of the Third Assembly (May 2007), the Labour government in Wales was actively considering, as a priority, a number of 'legislative competency orders' directly affecting children and young people, including the possibility of measures to consolidate a wide range of statutes that bear on children into a single body of, effectively, Welsh children and young people's law.

## Representation and participation

Central to any human rights agenda are the issues of representation and participation. In Wales, in relation to children and young people, perhaps the most distinctive contributions to ensuring something more than a rhetorical commitment to children's rights have been the appointment of a Commissioner for Children and the establishment of *Funky Dragon*, the Children and Young People's Assembly for Wales.

Although often traced back to a specific recommendation of the Waterhouse Inquiry into child abuse in North Wales (2000), the idea of a Commissioner for Children had been gathering momentum since the Staffordshire 'pindown inquiry' almost 10 years earlier (Staffordshire County Council, 1991). Rather than provide the *case* for a Commissioner, 'Waterhouse' provided the *opportunity* for the Assembly Government to establish the UK's first independent human rights institution specifically for children. In other words, the choice to make such an appointment had been available to the UK government for some time. This appointment was a conscious act of the National Assembly in Wales that might easily have been deferred, as it was in England, for several more years. The post was established by the Care Standards Act 2000 and extended by the Children's Commissioner for Wales Act 2001.

The Commissioner's primary duties are to safeguard and promote the rights and welfare of children in Wales and, in so doing, to have regard to the UNCRC. His functions include reviewing the effect on children and young people of the activities of the National

Assembly/Assembly Government or for those public bodies for which it has responsibility. The Commissioner also has the power to examine particular cases if this involves an issue that could have a wider application to the lives of children in Wales. He can also make representations to the Assembly Government about any matter affecting the rights and welfare of children in Wales, including in relation to non-devolved matters.

The Commissioner's published reports have dealt with such topics as school toilets (*Lifting the Lid*, 2004a); safe journeys to school (*As Long as I Get There Safe*, 2004b); a review of complaints, advocacy and whistle-blowing procedures in social services departments and local education authorities (*Telling Concerns*, 2003; *Children Don't Complain... Parents Do*, 2005) and *Clwych* (2004c), the report of an inquiry into child sexual abuse in a school setting. The Commissioner has also published a series of Annual Reports in which he has raised such issues as:

- respect for children and young people (2001/02);
- child and adolescent mental health services (2001/02);
- anti-social behaviour (2002/03);
- bullying (2002/03);
- asylum-seeking children (2003/04);
- advocacy services (2004/05);
- school nurses (2004/05);
- the education of looked-after children(2005/06);
- safe use of the internet (2005/06).

These Annual Reports are subject to plenary debates by the National Assembly in addition to the scrutiny provided by an annual special joint session of the Health and Social Care, Social Justice and Education and Lifelong Learning Committees. The Assembly must prepare and publish a *Response to the Children's Commissioner's Annual Report* by the 31st March each year.

At the outset, expectations of the Commissioner both in the National Assembly and more widely among the children's workforce in Wales were high, perhaps unreasonably so, and a longer period may be required to make any judgement of the effectiveness of the term of office of the first Commissioner, Peter Clarke, who died in office in January 2007. What is clear, however, is that his office has received considerable support from government, not least financially; his budget for 2006-07 was established at over £1.6 million. The formal and informal means he has had at his disposal to access government are unsurpassed by those of his fellow commissioners now established in Scotland, Northern Ireland and England. As such, the Assembly Government's commitment to establishing an effective, independent champion of children's rights who is well-resourced to carry out his functions, including holding the government to account, gains some substance.

Representation is an important safeguard for children and young people but central to achieving unconditional status as a rights-holding citizen, especially where suffrage is not a likelihood, is the question of participation. Article 12 of the UNCRC states:

> 'Parties shall assure to the child who is capable of forming his or her own views the right to express those views freely in all matters affecting the child, the views of the child being given due weight in accordance with the age and maturity of the child.'

As already indicated, from the outset, the Assembly Government demonstrated a positive interest in listening to children and to securing their active participation in the process of policy formation.

The 2000 key policy statement *Framework for Partnership* devoted a whole chapter to 'Listening to Children'. It noted the 'strongly held view' (National Welsh Assembly for Wales, 2000:26) across Wales of 'listening more closely to the voices of children and young people' and continued:

> 'The Assembly believes that the framework should ensure that children and young people are listened to and enabled to play an active part in decision making and in determining the services they receive.'

The Government had previously launched an ambitious project, *Llais Ifanc/Young Voice* to find ways of engaging with young people on a sustainable long-term basis and there already existed in Wales a relatively small number of local 'youth forums' as well as a number of *ad hoc* and 'single-issue' groups of young people that were consulted from time to time. Beginning at a conference in July 1999 ('Bite Back'), organised by members of local youth forums, and continued later that year at a residential event, the outlines of a national organisation that could represent the views of young people across Wales began to take shape. In July 2000, following another conference ('Breaking Barriers'), this embryonic organisation joined with *Llais Ifanc/Young Voice* and subsequently, after a process of consultation with children and young people across Wales, The Children and Young People's Assembly For Wales (known as *Funky Dragon*) was established with funding from the Assembly Government.

Both in its origins and in its operation, *Funky Dragon* is a peer-led organisation; of young people and by young people. Its stated aims are:

> '... to give 0-25 year olds the opportunity to get their voices heard on issues that affect them. The opportunity to participate and be listened to is a fundamental right under the United Nations Convention Rights of the Child. Funky Dragon will try to represent as wide a range as possible and work with decision-makers to achieve change. Funky Dragon's main tasks are to make sure that the views of children and young people are heard, particularly by the Welsh Assembly Government, and to support participation in decision-making at national level.' (*Funky Dragon*, 2003)

The Assembly Government has fostered the participation of children and young people in other ways too. Wales is the first country to have introduced a statutory requirement for all primary, secondary and special schools to have a school council. In secondary schools, two students can be nominated to serve as associate governors on the school's governing body; the governing body being required to accept such nominations. Also, in 2002, the Assembly Government commissioned a national voluntary organisation to establish a Children and Young People's Participation Consortium for Wales. The Consortium has subsequently received European Structural Fund support to accelerate its work. As a result of the Consortium's work, in

January 2007, the Government published national standards for involving children and young people in decision making.

## Programmes and delivery

Table 8.1 provides a brief description of some of the specific policies and programmes adopted and implemented by the Assembly Government during its first two terms, very broadly grouped under the Seven Core Aims.

At national level, this considerable range of programmes and initiatives has largely been taken forward by individual, portfolio ministers. However, co-ordination has been achieved by a variety of means including a Standing Children and Young People's Cabinet Sub-Committee. This Cabinet Sub-Committee, chaired by the Minister for Children and attended by the First Minister and relevant portfolio ministers, met monthly while the Assembly was in session during the first two terms of the Assembly. Its terms of reference were:

- to oversee the implementation of the UN Convention on the Rights of the Child in Wales and the Assembly Government's Seven Core Aims for Children and Young People;
- to ensure that the interests of children and young people are given due priority in all Cabinet and Assembly policy-making;
- to promote the health, well-being, educational, social and personal development of all children and young people in Wales;
- to combat social disadvantage arising from poverty, disability or lack of educational opportunity; and
- to help all children and young people in Wales to maximise their potential in adult life.

**Table 8.1: Specific policies and programmes for children's services**

| Core Aim | Policy | Brief Description |
|---|---|---|
| 1 | *Childcare is for Children:* The Childcare Strategy for Wales | Seeks to improve the quantity, quality and capacity of childcare provision. |
| 1 | *Cymorth* (Children and Youth Support Fund) | Funding for projects and programmes that support children, young people and their families, particularly those in disadvantaged areas, with a range of preventative interventions including family support, health promotion, participation, childcare, children's information services, training and mentoring, play. |
| 1 | *Flying Start* | Targeted at 0 to 3-year-olds and their families in the most deprived communities. Interventions include free, good-quality childcare, additional health visiting, and parenting programmes. |
| 1 | Breastfeeding Strategy | Intended to increase initiation and continuation rates of breastfeeding. |
| 1 | *Parenting Action Plan* | Seeks to raise the profile of parenting by setting out key actions to support parents and carers. |
| 2 | 14-19 Learning Pathways | Intended to transform and extend options and opportunities for 14 to 19-year-olds; includes individual learning pathways designed to meet the learners' needs. |
| 2 | Foundation Phase | The Assembly Government is committed to provide all 3 to 7-year-olds with high-quality early years education. |
| 2 | Youth Service Strategy | A vision for youth work in Wales, including an action plan to enable youth work to make an effective contribution to Extending Entitlement. |
| 2 | Safe Route to Schools | An initiative involving 50 projects across Wales promoting opportunities for walking and cycling to school. |

| 3 | *National Service Framework for Children, Young People and Maternity Services* | A 10-year strategy that sets national standards to improve quality and reduce variation in service delivery for children and young people. |
|---|---|---|
| 3 | *Everybody's Business* | A 10-year strategy for improving child and adolescent mental health services (CAMHS) in Wales. |
| 3 | *Food and Fitness: Promoting Healthy Diets and Physical Activity for Children and Young People in Wales* | A 5-year implementation plan for promoting healthier lifestyles. It includes a target that by 2010 all schools in Wales should be involved in the Welsh Network of Healthy Schools Scheme. |
| 3 | *Appetite for Life* | A strategy to improve the quality and nutritional standards of school food. |
| 3 | *Sexual Health Strategy* | Designed to ensure that young people have appropriate sex and relationship education, information, and access to sexual health advice services. |
| 4 | *Play Strategy* | Designed to implement the Assembly Government's Play policy by developing play provision across Wales. |
| 4 | *Climbing Higher: Strategy for Sport and Physical Activity* | A strategy to increase participation in sport and physical activity in Wales; includes free swimming scheme and programme to increase secondary school extra-curriculum participation in sport and physical activity. The PE and School Sport Action Plan aims to raise standards in PE and school sport. |
| 5 | *Advocacy Strategy* | The Assembly Government is committed to the development of a new model of advocacy for children and young people across health, education and social care settings. |

| 5 | *Extending Entitlement* | The overarching policy for young people aged 11-25 based around 10 basic entitlements including the entitlement to exercise one's rights, to be heard, have access to education and employment and to participate and get involved in the local community. |
| 6 | All-Wales Youth Offending Strategy | A national framework for preventing offending and re-offending by children and young people. |
| 6 | All-Wales Refugee Inclusion Strategy | Provides a framework for those working towards refugee inclusion and sets out key actions over the three years from 2007. |
| 6 | Iaith Pawb: A National Action Plan for a Bilingual Wales cultural activities. | Sets targets up to 2011 to bring about increased use and visibility of the Welsh language in all aspects of everyday life, including education, leisure and |
| 7 | *A Fair Future for our Children: Child Poverty Strategy and Implementation Plan* | Sets out measures, targets and milestones to deliver on the Assembly Government's commitment to eradicate child poverty in Wales by 2020. |
| 7 | Communities First | A long-term strategy for improving the living conditions and prospects for people in the most disadvantaged communities in Wales. Aims to involve people of all ages so as to secure sustainability, development of skills, physical and environmental improvements, health and well-being gains and reduction in crime. |

As the National Assembly commences its third term, it is impossible to predict with any great accuracy which of the specific initiatives set out in Table 8.1 will continue and which will come to an end, either before or after their due date; nor to be certain as to what new policies and programmes will emerge. However, the structures established for delivering direct services tend to be more enduring and to define the policy possibilities over a longer period. The second Assembly Government began designing a framework for delivering children's services that also captures the government's specific approach to children's policy as much as any individual initiative or policy outcome, although, as has been previously noted, such arrangements also reflect Welsh Labour's wider policy goal of providing public services with public bodies at the forefront of delivery.

Part 3 of the Children Act 2004 applies exclusively to Wales and establishes a new statutory framework for the delivery of services and for the planning necessary at local level to ensure that those services are appropriate to local need and consistent with national policy objectives. The model is one of local partnerships of statutory and other relevant bodies with the power to pool budgets and other non-financial resources (Children Act, 2004, S. 25). There is no requirement in Wales, as there is in England, for any radical reconfiguration of children's services and no provision for children's trusts.

A single local plan (the Children and Young People's Plan) should guide the delivery of such services (Children Act 2004, S. 26). Section 27 of the Act requires each local authority to appoint (from September 2006) a lead director for children and young people's services. It also requires NHS Trusts and Local Health Boards (note that the structure of health service authorities is not the same as in England) to appoint a lead executive and non-executive directors/member to oversee the arrangements established under Section 25.

Statutory Guidance issued by the Assembly Government in relation both to local co-operation and to the Children and Young People's Plan rests on a set of common principles. These include a formal requirement that 'local authorities and their relevant partners should have regard to [the UNCRC's] principles in providing services' (WAG, 2006e:4). The Guidance also makes clear that:

*'Children and young people must be able to influence the planning and provision of services affecting them. It is vital, both for the quality and safety of services, that individual children and young people are able to express their views and have complaints heard when things go wrong.'*
(WAG, 2006:4)

The content of the Children and Young People's Plan is organised under the Seven Core Aims and cross-referenced to the UNCRC in order to demonstrate how local services will help to meet national objectives. The Plan is intended to reflect a detailed local analysis of need and existing provision and to:

- provide strategic vision and state the agreed priorities that will direct the work of all partners;
- describe how requirements of national and local strategies, policies and priorities will be tackled locally;
- set out agreed joint objectives for services that can act as milestones to enable progress in improving outcomes to be measured over the planning timescale;
- identify the contribution made by individual partners towards meeting joint objectives, ensuring that they are consistent and mutually supportive;
- provide a basis for the joint commissioning of services and sharing of all available funding, including core budgets of statutory partners and resource or financial contributions from the voluntary sector.

The plans will require the involvement of children and young people and will become critical documents in holding to account those responsible for delivering children's services.

## Conclusion

The question was raised at the beginning of this chapter as to how far the Welsh Assembly Government could claim to have established a distinctive and coherent 'policy space' for children and young people.

While accepting that this can not fully be considered without reference to a more extensive analysis of the broader political objectives of the Welsh Labour Party, the party that has dominated the first two Assemblies, it is the argument of this chapter that such a space has indeed been constructed.

Children and young people's policy in Wales has been founded on the assumption that children are rights holders with an entitlement to participate in decisions on matters that affect them. Such an assumption is deeply rooted in Welsh radicalism and in the progressive ideals and democratic socialism of the Welsh Labour Party as well as in the emancipatory rhetoric of the specific children's rights 'movement'.

The Assembly Government has used its powers to the full, including showing a willingness to take a different political as well as policy direction to the UK government, to give substance to such an approach. Sharp divisions between Cardiff and Whitehall have arisen, often in private, over the approach taken on particular issues (such as corporal punishment) or in relation to particular groups of children; for example in relation to the status of asylum-seeking and refugee children. The position of the Assembly Government has been clearly articulated in its consultation on an *All-Wales Refugee Inclusion Policy* (WAG, 2006f:44):

> '*The Welsh Assembly Government recognises that asylum seeker and refugee children are children first and foremost and, due to their circumstances, are among the most vulnerable children in Wales. The Welsh Assembly Government is committed to the principles of the United Nations Convention on the Rights of the Child (UNCRC), which inform all of its work in respect of children. This includes an aspirational commitment to Article 22, which requires that such children receive appropriate protection and humanitarian assistance in the exercise of their rights under the convention.*'

It is hard to imagine such a statement finding approving echo anywhere in the Home Office.

This has been much more than a rhetorical commitment to children's policies and programmes. An analysis of spending on children by the

Assembly Government (WAG, 2007) has indicated that approximately 30 per cent  of Assembly Government and local authority budgets are used for the benefit of children (aged 0-17) – representing some £4.4 billion annually. This reflects the leadership that has been given on children's issues at the highest levels of government and indeed across the whole of the National Assembly.

That political leadership has enabled the Assembly Government to innovate and to pioneer. It was the first in the UK to decide to appoint a Children's Commissioner; it was one of the first in the world to publish an integrated policy for play. It has also persevered with policies and programmes of known effectiveness and value but which have fallen out of favour elsewhere; notable among these is the commitment to retain a statutory youth service.

This distinctive approach has been recognised beyond the shores of the UK. In the 2002 'Concluding Observations' made by the Committee on the UNCRC as part of the last round of periodic reporting under the Convention, particular attention was paid to certain developments in Wales. As well as noting approvingly the National Assembly's position in relation to corporal punishment (UNCRC, 2002:§8 and §35) and the appointment of a Children's Commissioner (UNCRC, 2002:§16):

> 'The Committee welcomes that the Convention has been used as a framework in the Strategy for Children and Young People developed by the National Assembly of Wales but it remains concerned that this has not been the case throughout the State party.'

In approving of the position in Wales, the Committee went on to mark the difference between this position and that of the UK government:

> '... the Committee remains concerned at the lack of a rights-based approach to policy development and that the Convention has not been recognised as the appropriate framework for the development of strategies at all levels of the government throughout the State party. The Committee is also concerned at the absence of a global vision of children's rights and its translation onto national plan of action.' (UNCRC, 2002:§14)

The same was not and could not be said of Wales.

The work is far from over, however. A future policy agenda will need to address the considerable number of challenges facing children and young people in Wales. These include:

- The growing numbers of looked-after children and their life chances.
- Services for children with disabilities are in need of urgent review.
- Teenage pregnancy rates in Wales, although falling, are the highest in Western Europe.
- Little impact on the numbers of children held on child protection registers has been made in recent years and the Assembly is committed to delivering on the recommendations of its own review of children's safeguards.
- There is an urgent need to develop an appropriately qualified workforce to deliver on existing policy commitments.
- Services for children and adolescents with mental health problems need to be enhanced.

One must not assume the continuing hegemony of the Welsh Labour Party in relation to the National Assembly for Wales nor of the Assembly Government. At some point, the effects of an electoral system based on proportional representation will no doubt make themselves felt. However, recognition that 'the inherent dignity and ... the equal and inalienable rights of all members of the human family is the foundation of freedom, justice and peace in the world' (preamble to the UNCRC) has been the principle guiding all of the major parties thus far and would seem a reasonable ground for continuing optimism.

## References:

Archard, D (2004) *Children Rights & Childhood* (2nd Edition) London, Routledge.

Blair, A (1999) Beveridge Lecture, 18 March.

Butler, I and Drakeford, M (2001) 'Which Blair project? Communitarianism, social authoritarianism and social work' *Journal of Social Work* 1(1), pp. 7- 20.

Children's Commissioner for Wales (2003) *Telling Concerns* Swansea, Children's Commissioner for Wales.

Children's Commissioner for Wales (2004a) *Lifting the Lid* Swansea, Children's Commissioner for Wales.

Children's Commissioner for Wales (2004b) *As Long as I Get There Safe* Swansea, Children's Commissioner for Wales.

Children's Commissioner for Wales (2004c) *Clwych* Swansea, Children's Commissioner for Wales.

Children's Commissioner for Wales (2005) *Children Don't Complain... Parents Do* Swansea, Children's Commissioner for Wales.

Croke, R and Crowley, A (2006) (eds.) *Righting the Wrongs: The Reality of Children's Rights in Wales* UNCRC Monitoring Group, Cardiff, Save the Children.

DfES (Department for Education and Skills) (2003) *Every Child Matters* Cm 5860, London, HMSO.

DH (Department of Health) (1999) *Quality Protects* London, DH.

Foley, P, Roche, J and Tucker, S (2001) (eds.) *Children in Society: Contemporary Theory, Policy and Practice* Basingstoke, Palgrave/Open University.

Franklin, B (2001) (ed.) *The New Handbook of Children's Rights: Comparative Policy and Practice* (2nd Edition) London, Routledge.

Funky Dragon (2003) *Inventing the Wheel: Annual Report and Accounts 2002-03* p. 4, Cardiff, Funky Dragon.

James, A and James, A L (2004) *Constructing Childhood: Theory, Policy and Social Practice* Basingstoke, Palgrave Macmillan.

Laming Report (2003) *The Victoria Climbié Inquiry: Report of an Inquiry by Lord Laming* Cm 5730, London, HMSO.

National Assembly for Wales (2000) *Children and Young People: A Framework for Partnership* Cardiff, NAW.

Prout, A (ed.) (2004) *The Future of Childhood* London, Routledge Falmer.

Staffordshire County Council (1991) *The Pindown Experience and the Protection of Children* (Allan Levy and Barbara Kahan) Stafford, Staffordshire County Council

UNCRC (United Nations Committee on the Rights of the Child) (2002) *Concluding Observations of the Committee on the Rights of the Child: United Kingdom of Great Britain & Northern Ireland* CRC/C/15/Add.188, Geneva, UNCRC.

WAG (Welsh Assembly Government) (2003) *Wales: A Better Country* Cardiff, Welsh Assembly Government.

WAG (2004a) *Making the Connections: Delivering Better Services for Wales, The Welsh Assembly Government Vision for Public Services* Cardiff, Welsh Assembly Government.

WAG (2004b) *Children and Young People: Rights to Action* Cardiff, Welsh Assembly Government.

WAG (2005) *A Fair Future for Our Children: The Strategy of the Welsh Assembly Government for Tackling Child Poverty* Cardiff, Welsh Assembly Government.

WAG (2006a) *Wales's Population: A Demographic Overview* Cardiff, Welsh Assembly Government.

WAG (2006b) *Beyond Boundaries: Citizen Centred Local Services for Wales* ('The Beecham Report') Cardiff, Welsh Assembly Government.

WAG (2006c) *Keeping us Safe* Cardiff, Welsh Assembly Government.

WAG (2006d) *Rights in Action: Implementing Children and Young People's Rights in Wales* Cardiff, Welsh Assembly Government

WAG (2006e) *Stronger Partnerships for Better Outcomes: Guidance on Local Co-operation Under the Children Act 2004* Cardiff, Welsh Assembly Government.

WAG (2006f) *Refugee Inclusion Strategy: Consultation Document* Cardiff, Welsh Assembly Government.

WAG (2007) *Financial Provision for Children within the Assembly Government Budget: A Technical Note* Cardiff, WAG.

Waterhouse, R (2000) *Lost in Care: report of the Tribunal of Inquiry into the Abuse of Children in Care in the Former County Council Areas of Gwynedd and Clwyd Since 1974* London, The Stationery Office.

Chapter 9

# Youth policy and youth justice

Jayne Neal

## Introduction

This chapter will consider the way that Welsh Assembly policy has influenced services for young people in Wales. It will look at the underpinning ethos displayed in key documents such as *Extending Entitlement* (National Assembly for Wales, 2000a) and compare it against Westminster government policies for young people detailed previously in the *Connexions* strategy (DfEE, 1999) and more recently in the Green Paper *Youth Matters* (HM Government, 2005). It will then go onto examine a practice example – the youth justice system in Wales.

Due to the piecemeal nature of the devolution settlement for Wales, Westminster legislation continues to have an impact on social policy in Wales. For the Welsh youth justice system, this is explicitly felt as responsibility for criminal justice remains at the Home Office in London. There is a long-held argument over how young people at risk of offending should be treated and this manifests in the 'welfare versus justice' debate. How do youth justice workers in Wales ensure that all young people in their care receive their full welfare entitlement as required by the Welsh Assembly and, at the same time, meet the criminal justice concerns of the Home Office?

This chapter will explore policy developments in post-devolution Wales and contrast them with New Labour youth policy in England. It will consider the context of service delivery in Wales and the implications for service users and professionals working in the youth justice system in Wales.

## Policy developments

*Post-devolution developments in Welsh youth policy*

The Welsh Assembly Government signalled its recognition of the needs of young people in Wales early in its development. Only a year after the transfer of powers, the Policy Unit commissioned the report *Extending Entitlement: Supporting Young People in Wales* (National Assembly for Wales, 2000a). The Welsh Assembly has sought to underpin its strategies for children and young people with the United Nations Convention on the Rights of the Child and the report showed a clear emphasis on user consultation; young people's voices were evident throughout the document alongside those of professionals working in youth services in Wales. Williams (2003:250) sees this as a 'striking development' and something enshrined by Article 12 of the Children Act 2004 whereby: 'Children have the right to say what they think should happen, when adults are making decisions that affect them, and to have their opinions taken into account'.

The process had invited over 400 organisations to comment and there was wide publicity through website, youth service and voluntary service publications. The resulting focus groups told a story with a 'powerful theme of disenfranchisement' where young people spoke of 'the lack of respect given by adults, the suspicion they were dealt with in many social settings and the general feeling of not belonging' (Annex 3:4).

In its response, the report recommended an 'entitlement model' to create an environment where all young people could be valued and encouraged to achieve their potential (see figure 9.1). As such, services would be available to everyone and, in an attempt to limit stigmatisation or exclusion, those requiring extra help would receive it from an inclusive, rather than targeted service.

> **Figure 9.1: Extending entitlement key principles**
>
> - to support and encourage all young people to develop as individuals and to enthuse them with the value of learning;
> - to develop a proportionate response to those in need of extra support;
> - to focus on what young people can contribute and give them opportunities to influence services that affect them;
> - to raise the quality and extend the diversity of what is offered to young people so that they are motivated to participate in learning and as citizens;
> - to recognise the diverse nature of Wales' communities in order to produce better outcomes for all our young people.
>
> *Source*: National Assembly for Wales Youth Policy Unit (2000)

*Extending Entitlement* justifies this universal approach by noting:

> *'Support for young people is likely to be most effective where it is part of a broad network, open to all young people, with opportunities to respond to problems as early as possible and tackle them intelligently and flexibly in the context of the individual's wider needs and those of the group and the community.'* (1.8:6)

However, an initial government intention is a long way from the implementation of policy into practice. In their evaluation report, Haines *et al.* (2004a:5) see *Extending Entitlement* as 'a comprehensive long-term strategic policy'. They argue (2004a:6) the value of the strategy 'cannot be underestimated' and that it has 'the capacity to not only impact on the lives of individual young people but also on the future economic and social state of Wales as a whole.'

To guide *Extending Entitlement* into practice, the Welsh Assembly Government laid out recommendations in the 2000 document *Children and Young People: A Framework for Partnership* (WAG, 2000b). Subsequently, all local authorities in Wales employed a Young People's Partnership (YPP) co-ordinator in order to set up a YPP committee for their local area. By 2003, the system was in position throughout Wales and the first strategy meetings were taking place. The role of the YPP is to provide and manage a local strategy and evaluation process that brings existing providers together to work towards the same goals (see Figure 9.2).

---

**Figure 9.2 Young Person Partnership tasks**

- Establish a partnership.
- Agree the broad aims of the partnership and begin to identify key objectives.
- Undertake an audit of need, provision and resources.
- Consult with young people.
- Develop a draft five-year strategy.
- Identify a small number of local priorities.
- Produce an annual delivery plan.
- Finalise and publish the strategy.

*Source:* Haines *et al.* (2005:5)

---

Clearly, however, this is only a first step as the committees need to prove they can be effective in achieving their aims. The YPPs rely on working co-operation between services and require representatives from all welfare agencies and organisations to make up its membership (see figure 9.3). Often those involved come from very different specialisms, with their own particular training and professional ethos. Maintaining the balance of a partnership is particularly difficult where organisations (for example the charitable sector) are funded or managed differently.

---

**Figure 9.3: Membership of Young People's Partnerships**

*'Coherent local frameworks will depend on strong local partnerships which include representatives of all the relevant groups, including local authorities, the NHS, schools, voluntary organisations and children and young people themselves.'*
(NAW, 2000b, 5:11)

---

---

**Example:**

***Membership of Conwy County's Young People's Partnership***

- Education
- NW Police
- Voluntary organisations
- Nacro

- Tourism and leisure
- Health
- ELWa
- SureStart

- Social Services
- Youth Offending Team
- Careers Wales
- Communities First

*Source*: Conwy Council Website

---

In theory, voluntary and community agencies have as much right to contribute to local strategies as anyone else. However, when they are put alongside public sector departments such as social services, an imbalance of power can often be identified with the statutory agency in danger of leading the decisions. The need for co-ordinated working practices is widely recognised and supported by research (see Sloper, 2004:572) and power imbalance is just one factor that prevents it from being a universal panacea for welfare provision. Sloper (2004:572) also recognises that partnership working requires change at all levels and this 'challenges professional cultures'. He notes the resistance to change and defensiveness that may develop. Fortunately, Haines *et. al* (2004b:67) do identify projects in Wales that have been successful in their aims for a 'cultural shift amongst all service providers'.

The fact that youth policy in Wales aspires to pull together existing providers rather than re-invent the wheel by putting a new agency into service is a key indicator of potential divergence in policy between Cardiff and Westminster. It has been said that the *Extending Entitlement* report was more concerned with the flaws to be found in the working practices of the agencies involved with young people than the much-hyped flaws of young people themselves (Holmes, 2001). This chapter will now go on to investigate the idea that, in contrast, policy in England appears to place more focus on the perceived failures of young people than measures to ensure full entitlement and equality of service.

*New Labour developments in youth policy in England*

When Tony Blair's New Labour government came into power in 1997, it was with great expectations of renewal and regeneration, in particular for the youth of the country. Prominence was given to the relatively young age of the Prime Minister and an air of excitement was encouraged by the 'Cool Britannia' tag and media coverage of pop stars visiting 10 Downing Street for tea and biscuits. Quite early on, this promise turned into something of an embarrassment; the Labour peer, Chris Smith (2003:6) assessed that it 'was never more than a rather crude attempt to convey a sense of cultural innovation and because it laid itself open so readily to parody, it failed'. Young people tend to be notoriously good at 'keeping it real' and so positive notions about the relationship between youth and government are soon discarded if actions do not support the rhetorical words. Youth policy and practice has to take full account of this, so when the *Connexions* youth strategy was launched in 1999, it was of great interest to everyone in the field of youth provision.

In the first place, it is significant that a strategy for a new service was published before an overarching youth policy document and as such criticism can be made about a lack of underlying theory or philosophy. Second, its positioning within government was an indicator of where the emphasis would lie. The strategy, although said to be cross-departmental in spirit, came out of the Department for Education and Employment and education, training and employment issues were repeatedly underlined. While a cursory look at the title of the document *Connexions – The Best Start in Life for Every Young Person* (DfEE, 1999) would seem to suggest a universal policy, subtle differences can be identified even before the end of chapter one. The concept of 'entitlement' is replaced by a fixation on participation and educational success:

> *'The key aim of the Service will be to enable all young people to participate effectively in appropriate learning – whether in school, FE college, training provider or other community setting – by raising their aspirations so that they reach their full potential.'* (DfEE, 1999:31.6.2)

Overall, the strategy implies a service that will support young people, not because they have a right to services but because they must not be allowed to fail. Williamson (2006:4) writes of the change in young people's transitions from narrow and prescribed routes prior to the 1970s to a complex array of opportunity and options in the late 20th century. As youth transitions have become more complicated, the emphasis on troubled youth and risk of failure has burgeoned. There is a sense that successful transitions now occur against a background of potential troubles and risks. Without a clear statement on entitlement, *Connexions* inevitably falls into a risk reduction youth policy. Although primarily an education welfare document, the strategy's heritage lies in the early Social Exclusion Unit reports (*Bridging the Gap*, 1999; *Rough Sleeping*, 1998; *Teenage Pregnancy*, 1999 and so on). When the Social Exclusion Unit was set up soon after the elections in 1997, the Blair government's growing pre-occupation with risk groups was already evident. There has been widespread criticism of this and Kemshall points to flaws in the ideology of risk reduction:

> 'Within this approach the primary function of the welfare state is not the alleviation of poverty or the reduction of social exclusion, but the identification, classification and regulation of deviant individuals and groups.'
> (Kemshall 2003:120)

*Bridging the Gap* (SEU, 1999) itself is guilty of making false assertions about social exclusion. Colley and Hodkinson (2001:342) write about an underlying emphasis on deficits and 'aggregates those individuals as generalized, and pathologised, social groupings'. As they point out this is somewhat similar to theories of an underclass that were popular in the 1980s when the previous Conservative government was in power. This categorisation of young people at risk of social exclusion provided a marker for the future development of Connexions and this is illustrated by the categorisations used for operational purposes in the 'Connexions triangle' (Figure 9.4).

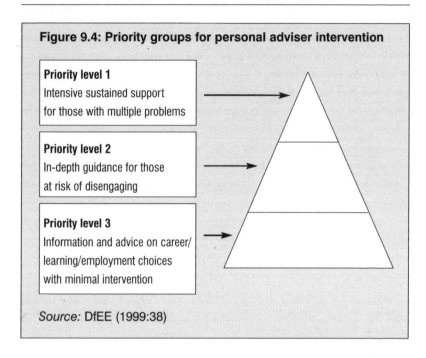

**Figure 9.4: Priority groups for personal adviser intervention**

**Priority level 1**
Intensive sustained support
for those with multiple problems

**Priority level 2**
In-depth guidance for those
at risk of disengaging

**Priority level 3**
Information and advice on career/
learning/employment choices
with minimal intervention

*Source:* DfEE (1999:38)

Using Kemshall's analysis of social policy in a risk society, the higher up the triangle the more 'deviant' you become in the eyes of the government policy. The more 'deviant' you become the more money government is willing to spend to ensure you do not turn out to be a risk to society. Thus, although it is the smallest percentage group, the largest proportion of funding goes to the top triangle for intensive interventions. Jeffs and Smith (2001: internet page) recognise that 'This means that resources are being taken away from the vast bulk of young people who do not pose a threat to order and to economic development'. Although there was a considerable amount of money available to *Connexions Partnerships*, it is clear that those in less risk would be in danger of being left out completely when funding became tight.

Operationally, *Connexions* was to replace the Careers Service in England with a new personal advisory system that would at the low end of need offer basic careers advice and at the high end, present a collection of services offering anything from drug advice and teenage pregnancy support to information on local amenities. Local areas would form *Connexions Partnerships* with a similar membership to the Young People's Partnerships in Wales. However, in England, the partnerships were to be steered and part financed by the new cuckoo in the nest of welfare support services. With an influx of funding to the *Connexions Partnerships* it was inevitable that existing agencies such as the Youth Service would feel somewhat under pressure. The government again expected partnership working to overcome any problems and issued guidance: *Working Together: Connexions and the Statutory Youth Services*:

> 'We would expect to see ALL 13-19 youth work and resources planned, managed and delivered as part of a joint working agreement between the Youth Service and the Connexions Partnership.' (DfES, 2002:13)

This sounds like a rather forced and unequal partnership and it is this type of language that led Davies (1999), in his book on the history of the service in England, to suggest that *Connexions* could have signalled the end of the universal youth service. As it happens, with the passage of time came the growing awareness that *Connexions Partnerships* would not be in a position to solve all the problems and would be unable to fully meet their universal requirement.  The 2004 *Connexions* evaluation report by Joyce and White supported the view that the service:

> 'Despite being introduced as a universal and holistic service for all young people aged 13-19, it is designed to provide more intensive help and support to those young people with multiple barriers to learning and those who are at risk of dropping-out of education.'
> (Joyce and White, 2004:93:6.1)

Joyce and White (2004:100:6.2.9) note that their data suggest that 'the service is better equipped to meet the needs of young people with more intensive support needs rather than those following other more straightforward routes', and they discuss how this could lead to problems. Those assessed as priority three today, if lacking in basic careers advice on jobs and courses, could become a priority one or two level case tomorrow. Other operational difficulties were also identified: some partnerships had failed to work effectively with other organisations, which created worrying gaps of service; continuity could be a problem if young people had to see a number of different advisers and re-tell their story each time; access in the first place was not always easy and there was an identified need for more detailed information and advice within a wider range of opportunities. Despite these misgivings, *Connexions* was found to offer the opportunity for young people to talk openly in a confidential environment and personal advisers, while often judged on their personality and character, were generally thought to be a welcome source of support: 'simply having someone to talk to was valued for being 'comforting', 'supportive' and reassuring' (Joyce and White, 2004:102:6.2.11). The main problem with *Connexions* appears to be its inconsistency – some areas had good services for young people and others were not so good. Wylie (2005:64) writes that, 'despite individual examples of good practice, *Connexions* became an "artificial sovereignty": like the old Austro-Hungarian or ottoman empires, no-one quite knew what it stood for'.

It may be argued that a strongly philosophical document such as *Extending Entitlement* could have helped to steer it more effectively but it was not until 2005 that the Westminster government finally produced anything like a comparable document. The *Youth Matters* Green Paper (HM Government, 2005) was therefore belatedly launched to a somewhat muted response from academics and youth work professionals. Wylie (2005:64) notes that it is 'hard to avoid scepticism regarding another government initiative about young people'. However, there is no doubt that *Youth Matters* does have a different and more inclusive tone to it, even if its ideas are somewhat lacking in innovation. Importantly, it sets out a legal duty for all services to work towards five outcomes that had been suggested in consultation with children and young people (see Figure 9.5). These had already been seen in the strategy document for children, *Every Child Matters* (DfES, 2003) that had been produced in 2003. Wylie (2005:64) notes that 'Youth Matters is intended to nest work with young people inside the range of actions which sprang from Every Child Matters'.

**Figure 9.5:** *Every Child Matters/Youth Matters* **Five Outcomes**

1. Be healthy.
2. Stay safe.
3. Enjoy and achieve.
4. Make a positive contribution.
5. Achieve economic well-being.

*Sources:* DfES (2003); HM Government (2005)

This sharing of intended outcomes seems to mirror the approach taken earlier by the Welsh Assembly Government with the *Extending Entitlement* (National Assembly for Wales, 2000a) and the *Early Entitlement* (WAG, 2002) documents for children. It is early days for *Youth Matters*; how far it will redress the balance between traditional youth service provision and *Connexions* remains to be seen and whether it will make a significant impact on youth provision is still to be tested.

A comparison between youth policy in England and Wales shows some divergence in spirit. Although recent developments do suggest a slight repositioning towards an entitlement model, English policy has spent some considerable time pre-occupied with the re-engagement of disaffected youth. It has relied on the introduction of a new agency to lead an integrated service, thus inviting negativity from existing services and difficulties in partnership working. The Welsh Assembly Government declared its full intentions from the beginning and justified its position by referring to existing human rights legislation, while utilising traditional services to implement its policy. As Williams (2003:252) remarks:

> 'For Wales the key challenge is to meet the gap between the admirable principles and aspirations of the Welsh Assembly Government and the reality for children and young people at local level'.

Would universal services be well equipped (and well funded) enough to protect the entitlement of all young people, including those who had disengaged themselves from society and its rules and regulations? Inevitably, these are the young people who often have a multiplicity of problems and can find themselves involved with the youth justice system. It is for this reason that a review of youth justice practice has been chosen to test the efficacy of the intentions of *Extending Entitlement*.

## Service delivery in Wales

*Wales in context*

A review on the implementation process of *Extending Entitlement* within the youth justice system must take into account the fact that there is a considerable lack of appropriate data on both the current and past experience of youth provision in Wales. Haines *et al.* (2004b:66) noted that evaluation is hampered by the 'patchy and in some cases non existent' availability of data. There is statistical evidence on demographics and this does help to provide a basic picture of young people in Wales. In the recent Census for England and Wales (ONS, 2001), the number of young people in Wales (551,000) against the whole population (2,903,085) was around one in five, similar to ratios in England and Scotland. The gender of the youth population was evenly split: 51 per cent were boys and 49 per cent were girls. There was some variation in where young people lived with 13 per cent living in Cardiff alone (70,737). These figures had not changed much in the ten years following the last Census and so projections can be assessed to be fairly stable in numbers. In other words, policy-makers in Wales are not expecting any major changes. Therefore, rather than any demographic surprise, it is the geographical spread of the general population in Wales throughout its most rural areas that presents a greater challenge for services dealing with young people (or any welfare service user group for that matter). In addition to this, a large part of Wales has been designated by the European Union (EU) as in need of Objective One funding – the highest priority for investment to reduce the differential in social and economic conditions within the EU. While this translates into the availability of extra funding for services related to welfare, it also signals problems with low income, high levels of economic inactivity and child poverty. Taken alongside the disenfranchisement of young people already identified earlier, the Young People Partnerships (YPPs), therefore, face considerable challenges in their quest to ensure full entitlement. For professionals working in the youth justice system in Wales, there are further complications

*Implications for service users and professionals in the youth justice system*

For social policy in Wales, devolution and the powers held by the Welsh Assembly Government in Cardiff have offered an opportunity to develop innovative projects aimed to meet the needs of Welsh communities. However, responsibility for youth justice remains in Westminster with the Home Office and Youth Justice Board (YJB) and this has created tensions in working practice. The Home Office drafts legislation to underpin the youth justice system in England and Wales and the YJB oversees working practice. Using performance management measures, it monitors and gives guidance on effective practice, distributes funding for projects designed to reduce offending behaviour and conducts research into best practice from a 'what works' agenda. Therefore, youth justice practice in Wales is accountable to a number of different documents all with their own key aim and objectives (see figure 9.6).

There are nineteen Youth Offending Teams (YOTs) in Wales dealing with, in 2005, around 6 per cent (11,977) of total national court disposals for young people (212,242) [It is important to note that this figure does not correspond with the number of young people who offended in Wales in 2005 as individuals might commit more than one crime and be subject to more than one court disposal]. Comparing this with the London area, which has over 30 teams working with around 10 per cent of national court disposals (21,157), it is possible to place Wales' youth justice system in some sort of context. Geography has already been mentioned as a factor in the provision of services and this can be further illustrated by considering the differences in size between London (1,579 km$^2$/609 sq mile) and Wales (20,779 km$^2$/8,022 square mile). With a population of well over seven million, London holds much more than double the number of people within an area that is only around eight per cent of the size of Wales. The figures display the disparity between the circumstances in rural Wales and the urban capital. In its research on rural youth crime, the Howard League for Prison Reform (2005:9) points out that the 'vast majority of work on crime, exclusion, probation and resettlement fails to incorporate a rural element'. However, in the everyday working practices of youth justice professionals this difference can be all too evident.

---

**Figure 9.6: Legislative and policy documents relevant to youth justice in Wales**

**Key Welsh Assembly Government documents**

- *Extending Entitlement* (National Assembly for Wales, 2000)
- *The Learning Country* (WAG, 2001) + associated education documents
- *Well-being in Wales* (WAG, 2002b) + associated health documents
- *A Winning Wales* (WAG, 2002c) + associated enterprise documents
- *All-Wales Youth Offending Strategy* (WAG, 2004)

**Key Westminster government documents**

- Crime and Disorder Act (1998)
- Youth Justice and Criminal Evidence Act (1999)
- Criminal Justice Act (2003)
- Anti-social Behaviour Act (2003)
- *Every Child Matters* (DfES) and *Youth Justice – The Next Steps* (2003)
- *Youth Offending: the Delivery of Community and Custodial Sentences* (2004)

---

Youth Offending Teams are responsible for supervising all convicted cases involving ten to seventeen-year-olds referred by the courts and are also increasingly tasked with preventing young people 'at risk of offending' from following a pathway into crime. The prevention remit can include children as young as eight-years-old, providing they meet the required criteria. Another area of responsibility is young people who are under an Anti-Social Behaviour Order or ASBO. Importantly, these orders come in from the civil court and, therefore, blur the line been criminal and civil justice. Thus YOTs do not only work with children and young people who have committed a crime but also those who are considered to be a nuisance to society and those who *may* commit a crime in the future. To place these children in a 'risk of offending' framework is particularly problematical for a rural area such as Wales. The Howard League for Penal Reform (2005:31) notes 'visibility' as an issue for rural youth. In a community where everyone knows each other, those who are attending a YOT may be stigmatised as troublesome, when previously they may have been dealt with by educational or social services. The All-Wales Youth Offending Strategy (WAG, 2004:3) 'supports the view that there is no contradiction between protecting the welfare of young people in trouble and the prevention of offending and re-offending'. Indeed, Welsh YOTs are supported to some degree by the strong assertion that 'young people should be treated as children first and offenders second' (WAG, 2004:3), something that is not so explicitly stated in anything produced by the Westminster government.

The robust use of performance management by the Youth Justice Board is one way that the welfare focus from the Welsh Assembly Government can be undermined. The first step in any YOT intervention, whether in Wales or England, is the completion of the standard YOT assessment tool – ASSET (see Youth Justice Board website for an example: www.yjb.gov.uk). This must be completed at the beginning and end of an intervention (also in the middle if it is a custodial sentence). The 2004 National Audit Commission review recognised ASSET as a 'major step forward in providing a comprehensive risk and needs assessment'. However, although the document does identify areas and intensity of welfare need, the focus is on how this affects behaviour and an eventual risk of offending score is used. In the Annual Youth Justice Statistics 2005 (YJB, 2005) the YJB note that 'a large proportion of cases show "no change" in scores between the beginning and end of an order' and it says it would perhaps 'expect more change in the longer, more intensive community or custodial options'. This could be rather challenging for a practitioner as there is often a correlation between high welfare need and more serious offending and intensive court orders (NACRO, 2003). In fact, the chaotic nature of many of these young people would suggest that ASSET scores taken over the period of an order are likely to be just as unpredictable. It is therefore not surprising that while most YOT managers have been positive about using ASSET, practitioners have been more cautious. Using a scoring system might suggest that simple solutions are possible; for example, a young person identified in ASSET as having a mental health problem, would be referred to Child and Adolescent Mental Health Services and 'cured' and the risk of offending score would be reduced. Unfortunately, this is not so easy in the real world; for a young person to effect change with a mental health issue, a long road lays ahead, full of ups and downs, and there are no guarantees that when the final ASSET is completed, the news will be positive.

A second way in which a welfare approach can be weakened is the access – or lack of it – to other services. ASSET may have identified a mental health issue, but what can the YOT worker actually do to encourage change? Generally, a YOT cannot buy in services by exchange of money but has to rely on quality standards and policy statements to ensure that its young people gain services. Unfortunately, in a climate of financial constraint and increasing demand, services must have priority groups and criteria to assess who should receive a service. For example, a young person who has a mental health issue and has just been discharged from prison is clearly within a priority group with regard to gaining emergency housing according to local authority guidelines. However, they may not be able to access housing because of challenging behaviour in a previous emergency placement. Thus they might be deemed intentionally homeless and it would be left to the young person and their worker to prove that their behaviour may not have been intentional and was due to their health condition. That is not to say that these decisions are wholly bureaucratic; the housing worker may very well be prepared to try and place the young person but the landlords of the emergency accommodation may be unwilling to take a chance on a difficult young person. Ultimately, whoever owns the housing has the final say and no government pronouncement on who should benefit from the service will make any difference. It is for this reason that the mixed economy of welfare is sometimes unresponsive to extreme social need. The move away from public sector provision towards a mix of providers has diluted the power of policy statements. Unlike the public sector, private or voluntary sector providers have their own agendas and constitutions and, most importantly, the right of refusal. Therefore gaining access to services is all about negotiation and this of course returns to the question of partnership working.

Haines *et al.* (2004a:23/24) found that their respondents were cautiously optimistic about the future of welfare provision for young people in Wales. They identify a 'common multi-agency commitment through the YPPs to achieve Extending Entitlement outcomes'. Respondents talked of 'having a common aim', no longer 'working in isolation' and 'it has brought our attention to those groups we were not accessing' (Haines *et al.*, 2004a:19). Importantly, 21 per cent of the respondents felt that 'Extending Entitlement made a positive difference to youth offending'. Concerns were voiced over resource issues and they stated this may be an inhibitor to effective implementation of the process. Respondents were clear that universality should not be compromised by the development of targeted interventions and did have some concerns that sacrifices might be made. Haines *et al.* (2004a:24) suggested that there 'may be a need for reassurances'. In the end, when assessing the effectiveness of partnership working under *Extending Entitlement* it is important to accept that YPPs are a new phenomenon that will take time to make a difference. In addition to this, the YOT structure itself is only six-years-old and so it will be some time before effectiveness can be ascertained. Despite this it is vitally important that practice in Wales starts to be properly evaluated so that baseline data can be created. The 2005 Estyn Inspectorate for Education and Training in Wales report looked at the quality of education and training for Welsh young people in the youth justice system. While it must be read in the context of comments made above, it provides valuable information on how educational policy has started to be translated into practice in Wales. The main findings from the Estyn report on provisions for young people being supervised in the community are summarised in Figure 9.7.

**Figure 9.7: 2005 Estyn Report main findings
(supervision in the community only)**

✔ There are good examples of informal learning opportunities where young people are supervised by YOTs and remain or return to the community.

✔ Where teaching is good, teachers make use of assessment to plan lessons well and match work to abilities, needs and interests.

✔ Young people receive regular and helpful guidance and support from careers advisers.

✘ YOT education workers do not always have enough influence over schools and local education authorities in order to secure full-time educational placements.

✘ Communication between YOTs, educational settings and the secure estate* is not good enough. This poor liaison leads to a lack of continuity and difficulties with planning effectively for young people.

✘ Standards of achievement are not evaluated or recorded as Youth Justice Board criteria looks at only levels of participation. Therefore, it is not possible to give information on the educational attainments of young people.

✘ Although YOTs show an awareness of YPPs and attend partnership meetings, as yet YPPs have made little contribution to the provision for educational targets.

✘ YOT Annual Youth Justice Plans do not have enough detail and specific targets to improve education and training for young people.

\* secure estate = youth justice custodial establishments

*Source:* Estyn (2005:4-6)

It can be seen that practice at that time was far from consistent and did not extend 'an entitlement for all young people in Wales to education training and work experience – tailored to their needs' (National Assembly for Wales, 2000a:6). Considering the assertion in the *All-Wales Youth Offending Strategy* that it 'supports the principle of the universal entitlement for all children and young people including those children and young people at risk of offending and those who do offend' (WAG, 2004:3), it can be said that *Extending Entitlement* policy and YPPs have a long way to go.

What *Extending Entitlement* and the welfare ethos of the Welsh Assembly Government do achieve is to give some hope that universal services focused on social need, rather than targeted services aimed at reducing social risk, can be realised. However, the partial settlement of devolution ensures that this doctrine is restricted by the risk agenda that is being more seriously pursued on a GB level.

Add this to the accepted challenges of partnership working and financial constraints and *Extending Entitlement* could be in danger of being a worthy example of modern day rhetoric.

## References

Colley, H and Hodgkinson, P (2001), 'Problems with "bridging the gap": the reversal of structure and agency in addressing social exclusion' *Critical Social Policy*, 21(3), pp. 335-59.

Davies, B (1999) *History of the Youth Service in England Vol. 2*, Leicester: Youth Work Press.

DfEE (Department for Education and Employment) (1999) *Connexions: The Best Start in Life for Every Young Person* Nottingham, DfEE Publications.

DfES (Department for Education and Skills) (2002) *Working Together* London: DfES.

DfES (2003) *Every Child Matters* London, DfES.

Estyn (2005) *The Quality of the Education and Training Provided for Welsh Young People in the Youth Justice System* Cardiff, Her Majesty's Inspectorate for Education and Training in Wales.

Haines, K, Case, S, Isle, E, Rees, I and Hancock, A (2004a) *Extending Entitlement: Making it Real* Cardiff, Welsh Assembly Government.

Haines, K, Case, S and Portwood, J (2004b) Extending *Entitlement: Creating Visions of Effective Practice for Young People in Wales* Cardiff, Welsh Assembly Government.

Holmes, J (2001) 'The Youth Service alternative to Connexions' *The Encyclopaedia of Informal Education*, www.infed.org/youthwork/extending_entitlement.htm (accessed: 24.01.07).

HM Government (2005) *Youth Matters* London, The Stationery Office.

Howard League for Penal Reform (2005) *Once Upon a Time in the West: Social Deprivation and Rural Youth Crime* London, Howard League.

Jeffs, T and Smith, M (2001) 'Social exclusion, joined-up thinking and individualization: New Labour's Connexions strategy' *The Encyclopedia of Informal Education*, www.infed.org/personaladvisers/connexions_strategy.htm (accessed: 24.01.07).

Joyce, L and White, C (2004) *Assessing Connexions: Qualitative Research with Young People* BMRB Research Report 577, London, BMRB.

Kemshall, H (2002) *Risk, Social Policy and Welfare* Buckingham, Open University Press.

NACRO (2003) *Some Facts about Young People who Offend – 2001* Youth Crime Briefing, London, NACRO.

National Assembly for Wales (2000a) *Extending Entitlement: Supporting Young People in Wales: A Report by the Policy Unit* Cardiff, National Assembly for Wales.

National Assembly for Wales (2000b) *Children and Young People: A Framework for Partnership*, http://new.wales.gov.uk/docrepos/40382/40382313/childrenyoungpeople/403821/623995/q262a360_english1.pdf?lang=en. (accessed: 22/01/2007).

National Audit Commission (2004) Youth *Justice 2004: A Review of the New Youth Justice System* London, NAO, www.audit-commission.gov.uk/reports/NATIONAL-REPORT.asp?CategoryID=&ProdID=7C75C6C3-DFAE-472d-A820-262DD49580BF (accessed: 18.2.07).

ONS (Office of National Statistics) (2001) Census – *Wales – Population Figures*, www.statistics.gov.uk/census2001/pyramids/pages/w.asp. (accessed: 19/01/2007).

Sloper, P (2004) 'Facilitators and barriers for co-ordinated multi-agency services' *Child: Care, Health and Development* 30(6), pp. 571-80.

Smith, C, Lord (2003) 'Beyond Cool Britannia' *Destination Review 12* London, Locum Publishing, www.locum-destination.com/ pdf/LDR12BeyondCoolBrit.pdf. (accessed: 24.01.07)

Social Exclusion Unit (1998) *Rough Sleeping* London: The Stationery Office.

Social Exclusion Unit (1999) *Bridging the Gap: New Opportunities for 16-18 year-olds Not in Education, Employment or Training* London: The Stationery Office.

Social Exclusion Unit (1999) *Teenage Pregnancy* London: The Stationery Office.

WAG (Welsh Assembly Government) (2001) *Learning Country: A Paving Document. A Comprehensive Education and Lifelong Learning Programme to 2010 in Wales* Cardiff, Welsh Assembly Government.

WAG (2002a) *Early Entitlement: Supporting Children and Families in Wales* Cardiff, Welsh Assembly Government.

WAG (2002b) *Well being in Wales* consultation document, Cardiff, Welsh Assembly Government.

WAG (2002c) *A Winning Wales Strategy* Cardiff, Welsh Assembly Government.

WAG (2004) *All-Wales Youth Offending Strategy* Cardiff, Welsh Assembly Government/Youth Justice Board.

Williams, C (2003) 'The impact of Labour on policies for children and young people in Wales' *Children and Society* 17, pp. 247-53 London, Wiley.

Williamson, H (2006) *Spending Wisely. Youth Work and the Changing Policy Environment for Young People* Leicester, National Youth Agency.

Wylie, T (2005) 'Testing a Green Paper' *Youth and Policy 89*, pp. 64-9 Leicester, National Youth Agency.

YJB (Youth Justice Board) (2005) *Youth Justice Annual Statistics 2005/6* (B316) London, Youth Justice Board.

Chapter 10

# Social services for adults

Hefin Gwilym

## Introduction

The establishment of the Welsh Assembly in 1999 created new opportunities for policy makers, academics and practitioners in the field of social care in Wales. The devolution of social care was not new, this had happened previously during the years following the establishment of the Welsh Office in 1963. What was new was the opportunity to expand the Welsh dimension in research, analysis and policy development in the care field. The seeds for some of the most significant developments had been planted during the 1980s. The development of the All-Wales Strategy for Mental Handicap in 1983 (Welsh Office, 1983), subsequently revised in 1993, and still in force today, was a pioneering development of international importance. This strategy showed that an all-Wales approach to policy and service development in other important areas of social care was possible and it set the scene for a clearer vision of how the Welsh Assembly Government would approach the challenges that undeniably existed to raise the standards in other service areas, most notably services for people with mental health problems and services for older people in Wales. This chapter will take a considered view of these important developments in the provision of social services in Wales with particular focus on developments since the establishment of the Welsh Assembly. It will seek to clarify the intention of politicians and policy makers in social care policy. But it will also take a realistic and evaluative look at the successes and the elusive nature of the challenges that face those who grapple with these issues in Wales.

The first essential task is to set the scene in Wales by looking briefly at the social make-up of the nation of Wales. It is in the light of these realities that politicians, policy-makers and practitioners have to respond. Services for adults in Wales should correspond to the needs of the people of Wales, and should be tailored to match the specific needs of localities and communities. There is no one size to fit all, indeed there are particular needs in particular areas of Wales. Wales has a population of 2.9m million. Nearly one in four (23 per cent) of Wales' population of 2.9 million, has a limiting long-term illness. This is slightly lower at one in five (18.4 per cent) among people of working age. Compared to England the figures in Wales are about 5 per cent higher, and 3 per cent higher than Scotland and Northern Ireland. It has been estimated that 9 per cent of the adult population are being treated for mental illness (WAG, 2006a). Wales has a higher concentration of older people compared to the rest of the UK, with 20 per cent of the population aged over 60 (WAG, 2006b – OPLTC4). These statistics on their own would be a far too simplistic way of looking at the social needs of Welsh society. Although social services organise their services according to groups, the reality is that there is a web of complex and intricate links between groups and social problems. The issues of mental health cannot be viewed separately from the issues of stigma and discrimination; the issues of learning disabilities cannot be viewed separately from social exclusion and employment; and the issues of older people cannot be viewed separately from the need for social housing and from age discrimination. Each group encompasses much diversity in terms of gender, ethnicity, language, income and orientation.

## Learning disabilities

The first pioneering attempt at creating a response to some of these needs at a local level started with the All-Wales Strategy for Mental Handicap in 1983 (Welsh Office, 1983). This was most certainly a radical document that was published by the Welsh Office under the leadership of the Secretary of State for Wales, Nicholas Edwards, during the era of a Conservative government led by Margaret Thatcher. There was increasing awareness at this time that keeping the old institutions going was financially unviable in the long run. The focus of care for people with learning disabilities had been in large hospitals, and most of the resources went to these places, despite the fact that the need was in the community where four-fifths of people with learning disabilities lived with their families, with virtually no support (Felce *et al.*, 1998). Many of these people depended entirely on the support of their families, mostly elderly parents, until they were in their 40s and the parents had themselves become too frail to look after them.

But there was also an awareness change taking place at this time. Contrary to common assumptions about people with learning disabilities being incapable of developmental change, there was increasing evidence from research showing that people with learning disabilities were capable of living valued lives and even of holding down a job. New ways of thinking were emerging from people like Wulf Wolfensberger at Saracuse University in the USA. These ideas were collectively known as the normalisation principle, Social Role Valorisation, developed by Wolfensberger (1992), being only a part of this shift towards raising expectations about what people with learning disabilities were capable of achieving with their lives. These ideas eventually influenced service providers with the publication of John O'Brien's Service Accomplishments in 1981. Another major philosophical change at this time that had a bearing on future services for people with learning disabilities was the emergence and growth of the equal opportunities movement and social justice generally. By this time institutional care in large hospitals with all the negative connotations of uniformity of routines and restrictions of choice, was becoming less acceptable. In countries such as Denmark, care had shifted much further into the community with services being as close to normal patterns of living as possible (Felce *et al.*, 1998). In Wales, the old ways persisted but the costs of keeping the old hospital buildings open was an increasing problem. The will to do so was further eroded with reports of poor conditions and even abuse in some of the institutions, such as the famous mistreatment of people with learning disabilities in Ely Hospital Cardiff during the late 1960s (Butler and Drakeford, 2005).

The All-Wales Strategy for Mental Handicap was a rather slim strategy document, compared to the strategies published later on by the Welsh Assembly Government. The strategy's philosophy of normal patterns of life within the community and the right of people with learning disabilities to be treated as individuals heralded a big change of approach at the national level (Drakeford and Williams, 2002). Some of these ideas had already been put into limited effect earlier with the NIMROD project in Cardiff between 1981 and 1986 (Felce *et al.*, 1998).

The project gave people the opportunity to live in ordinary housing with individual and family support services. The concept of individual programme planning was included in the strategy and was a significant departure from institutional care at the time, which gave scant attention to individual care plans. Individual care planning became seen as an important part of any care provision for people with learning disabilities and it remained a cornerstone of care planning in this field.

The Strategy began to address what was seen as the real needs of people with learning disabilities and their families. The hospitals and asylums of the past had segregated people from the community and had offered a service of one size fits all. However, the Strategy sounded ambitious and even idealistic as it set out to change things for the better. The Strategy had a rich assortment of new ideas and within it one can see the genesis of ideas that were to come into their own later on in the evolution of services for people with learning disabilities, including care management, which was incorporated into legislation in the National Health Service and Community Care Act 1990. The new approach would include respite care for the first time for families who had struggled for years without any support at all. Advocacy schemes would be established throughout Wales to represent the interests of the service users themselves; the concept of the Community Mental Handicap Team (CMHT) was mooted where there would be an identified named worker to coordinate the care provided; the CMHTs would be multi-disciplinary for the first time, with social workers, psychologists, family aides, nurses and health visitors working together.

The ideals of the Strategy were far from fully met during the early years. It would be easy to underestimate how difficult a task it was to implement any strategy that needed effective collaboration between various institutions and the continued support of service users and their families. The Strategy had to be implemented on the local level by the social services departments within the 22 Welsh unitary authorities. Each authority had its own service history regarding the type of service it provided for people with learning disabilities, thus across Wales it was hard to develop services in an equitable manner to the same degree of provision because services had never developed in this way. Despite the fact that £10 million had been ring fenced for the Strategy's first few years, each local authority would have to create project plans and bid for funds for their implementation (Felce *et al.,* 1998). This was a rather slow process and some authorities were better off the mark than others. There were other problems in joint-working between health and social services; jealousies had been created when social services became the lead authority when previously the health service had been dominant in the provision of care through the large hospitals. There was no blueprint for services for the whole of Wales, since services were to be locally determined according to need; this placed a great deal of responsibility for development on the local areas. This helps to explain why some of the ring-fenced money was not fully utilised.

The All-Wales Strategy for Mental Handicap was reviewed in 1993 resulting in reduced expenditure and the end of ring-fenced funding. The priorities also changed with a far greater emphasis now being placed on the closure of the old hospitals. The closure of the old hospitals and the resettlement of people into communities had been a consequence of the All-Wales Strategy rather than its stated aim, but this process did not really begin until the late 1980s (Felce *et al.*, 1998). But it was this process that would be seen as the most important area for future development and investment. Less emphasis was now given to the other things in the Strategy as core services were identified as being required in all the Welsh counties, these included respite care, accommodation in ordinary housing and innovative day-care opportunities such as enrolment in further educational colleges. The next decade was characterised by hospital closures and resettlement into the community. This stage saw the emergence of new voluntary organisations who became providers of support services for people with learning disabilities living in ordinary community housing. Many but not all of these people were resettled from the old hospitals, they were given tenancy agreements and were supported by the new organisations that tended to focus on particular localities in Wales, such as Cartrefi Cymru and Mencap. However, independent living did not necessarily lead to new friendships and staff sometimes filled this vacuum by becoming substitutes for the real thing (Ramcharan *et al.*,1997).

The Welsh Assembly Government when it was established in 1999 was faced with a sense of disappointment in Wales with regards to the high ideals and expectations of the All-Wales Strategy for Mental Handicap. The whole area was revisited when the Welsh Assembly

Government produced a framework document whose title reflected some of the disappointment in Wales. The framework document *Fulfilling the Promises* (NAW, 2001a) was warmly welcomed by practitioners in the field as a necessary review and a new impetus to service development. The framework was produced by the Learning Disabilities Advisory Group, which had been set up to advise the Assembly on the implementation of the All-Wales Strategy. The group recognised the shortcomings of the Strategy that despite its valiant aims of full life opportunities, positive identities and roles, choice and independence, and normal patterns of life within communities, many aspirations and expectations remained to be fulfilled. Other groups such as the Joseph Rowntree Foundation (2002), in its response to the framework, identified that the nature of Welsh society had changed and that policy needed to catch up by dealing with the complexities of multiple discrimination in an ethically diverse society and working in a genuine partnership with people with learning disabilities rather than mere consultation. The framework set out the goals of achieving full citizenship and the right to expect a high quality of life. It also set an aim of resettling everyone into the community by 2010. Moreover it recommitted itself to the cornerstone of the All-Wales Strategy, the fundamental importance of individual planning in addressing the needs and aspirations of people with learning disabilities. This latter point had only been achieved in patches throughout Wales, a major problem when it is considered that new services were expected to arise out of the individual care planning process.

The recommendations made by the Learning Disability Implementation Advisory Group (2006) to the Welsh Assembly Government, carried the weight of the All-Wales People First group, which was made up of people with learning disabilities. They emphasised again the vital importance of an advocacy service in Wales to represent the interests of people with learning disabilities; the crucial role of individual planning, particularly at times of transitions such as the stage between school and adulthood when many people slip through the net; continued development of day opportunities, particularly in education; the strong desire for real wages for real jobs; and a range of good housing and locations. A consensus started to form between the organisations representing people with learning disabilities and the

Welsh Assembly Government that disability is not just about personal impairment but is also about the way society organises itself. People with learning disabilities will continue to strive for an inclusive society with quality of life for all, but as we have seen, the road from the All-Wales Strategy in 1984 to the present has not been an easy one and more obstacles lie ahead before we are nearer to achieving the ideals.

## Physical and sensory disabilities

The adoption of the social model of disability by the Welsh Assembly Government in 2002 was a watershed moment for disabled people in Wales. The social disability model firmly shifts the focus away from the assumption that disability is a personal tragedy, to the requirement that society has to change to allow disabled people to participate fully as equal citizens (Oliver and Sapey, 1999). Equal citizenship was denied by society's discriminatory attitudes and the physical barriers that blocked the access of disabled people to transport services and other public areas. The opportunity to participate fully in an inclusive society was seen as a right. There was statutory support for this in the form of the Disability Discrimination Acts (DDA) of 1995 and 2005. The DDA 2005 requires public bodies including the Welsh Assembly and local authorities to promote disability equality through Disability Equality Schemes. The Welsh Assembly Government's Disability Equality Scheme (WAG, 2006a), requires all government departments to produce an equality plan. At this stage, it is too early to judge what real impact this corporate endeavour to mainstream disability equality into the everyday work of the Assembly will have on reducing inequalities. However, the Assembly's aim of providing services for people with physical and sensory disabilities that are flexible and seamless is not without its problems. An area of particular need is the provision of social services for young disabled people in Wales, especially in the area of independent living (WAG Equal Opportunities Committee, 2007).

## Mental health

The establishment of the Welsh Assembly Government in 1999 saw a new impetus in the development of services for adults with mental health problems. There was an increasing realisation that mental illness was a hidden epidemic in Wales as elsewhere in the UK. The rising suicide rates among young men throughout Wales and farmers in the rural areas was causing serious concern. It was calculated that one-in-four would experience a mental health problem at one time in their lives and 25 per cent of all GP consultations had a mental health component. Yet the reality about mental health services in Wales was that they had developed with substantial local variations in the type and quality of the services provided. Psychological treatments in many parts of Wales were poorly developed and there were significant variations in staffing levels and skill mix. One of the aims of any strategy was to set a minimum standard of service that was acceptable throughout Wales. The first attempt had been made in 1989 under the old Welsh Office. This initial strategy had recognised the importance of establishing multi-disciplinary teams in all areas of Wales. It also set the agenda for the closure of the old asylums of which Wales had its fair share, including Sully Hospital in the Vale of Glamorgan, St David's in Carmarthen and the North Wales Hospital in Denbigh (Michael, 2003).

A far more ambitious strategy was issued in 2001 and entitled *Equity, Empowerment, Effectiveness, Efficiency* (NAW, 2001b), which was a ten-year plan to improve mental health services in Wales. Mental good health was no longer seen as dependent on services alone, but the link was firmly made with the social and economic determinants of poor health. The Strategy identified social exclusion as a major problem, especially the effects of stigmatisation of people with mental health problems. Wales had lacked an overarching approach to tackling stigma and building social inclusion, which was essential if prejudices were to be overcome and progress made in the areas of employment, education, housing, access and mobility. Support from services in the areas of housing and employment were seen as particularly important steps for social inclusion. The strong association between home-lessness and mental illness was accepted. The title of the strategy tried to convey its major thrust, equity meant that there should be no postcode lottery or discrimination in service provision; empowerment meant that service users were to be involved in the planning and evaluation of local services; effectiveness meant that symptoms would improve by following the principles of clinical governance and evidence-based practice; and efficiency meant that organisations would need to work together and be accountable for the use of public money.

According to the Strategy, mental health services in Wales for the following ten years would be characterised by high quality and services responsive to the community. There would need to be a sustained public education programme to reduce stigma by showing the public that mental health problems were treatable and that most people recovered from their difficulties; more advocacy services; extended hours and outreach services within Community Mental Health Teams and access to services during weekends and public holidays; a range of employment and occupational opportunities should be provided by linking in to the New Deal for Disabled People in job centres; and a comprehensive range of residential accommodation with varying degrees of support. New services would be developed in partnership between agencies, including health, local authorities, housing associations and the voluntary sector. The Care Programme Approach would be adopted to raise standards nationally in response to a patchy situation. Implementing the Strategy would require more funds to sustain an increased workforce and finance the process of hospital closures. A total of £11 million was allocated for the closure of Sully and St David's Hospitals; a further £4 million was set aside for projects that would take forward the aims of the Strategy and to fund voluntary organisations. This was a relatively small amount of money when compared to the total spending of £220 million on mental health services in Wales in 2000. The aims of the Strategy were reinforced by the National Service Framework for Mental Health. Both documents recognised many of the real needs of service users and their families, including the need to work and live ordinary patterns of life without discrimination.

The desire of service users and their families was for a friendly service that was responsive to their needs and accessible outside the normal working hours of nine-to-five, Mondays to Fridays, and staffed by highly-skilled workers. In this respect, there have been some important local developments, such as the 24-hour Community Treatment Service in north west Wales. This was a multi-disciplinary team that had some notable successes in preventing admissions into an acute psychiatric unit (Saycell et al., 2004). However, by 2005 the national picture on the achievements of the Strategy and Framework documents was far more disappointing. In fact, outreach services to keep contact with those with complex needs had been established in only six out of the 22 Local Health Board (LBH)/Local Authority (LA) areas in Wales. According to the Wales Audit Office (2005), and mental health promotion, a key aim in tackling stigma, had been poorly developed since 2001. Only six LHB/LA areas had developed a mental health promotion strategy, mental health promotion and reducing stigma had been compromised by a lack of capacity and resources. There existed significant variations across Wales in the range and extent of services, for example while some areas had a home treatment service, many other areas had not. Service users and their carers continued to say that support from statutory agencies was only available when a person was in crisis and opportunities for early intervention were missed. As few as three LHB/LA areas claimed to have an adequate range of housing options with appropriate support. Hardly any authority had undertaken a detailed needs assessment to determine the actual level of need for accommodation. The aim of setting up a whole system approach to service development had only been achieved in very few areas. The Wales Audit Office Report (2005) was a baseline on the progress of the All-Wales Strategy and National Service Framework. It clearly identified significant gaps in services and it would not be an exaggeration to say that there have been major shortfalls in its implementation and that there are major challenges for the future if the aims of the Strategy are to be achieved.

Part of the problem with the implementation of the All-Wales Strategy for Mental Health has been the fact that mental health is often the first service area to be squeezed-out when there are conflicting demands for scarce resources. Many of these conflicts exist within the NHS where mental health is sometimes seen less favourably than other areas of medicine for much needed resources. Even within mental health services there are tensions between the needs of the acute psychiatric units and the allocation of services into developing new community services. The hospital-based services are often viewed as bottomless financial pits by people who work within mental health services. But there are other organisational problems when it comes to strategy implementation. Featuring large among these are whether the creators of the strategy at the Welsh Assembly Government level share the same priorities as those managers and practitioners working at the local level. This gap raises issues about the scale and level of partnership between the two levels and whether there had been enough participation and ownership of the strategy by all concerned from the beginning. The other important issue was whether sufficient resources were invested in the Strategy and whether these needed to have been more effectively ring-fenced for the tasks intended. Certainly one of the lessons from the All-Wales Mental Handicap Strategy was that a ring-fenced budget was one of its strengths.

## Older people

The newest of all the strategies is the All-Wales Strategy for Older People (WAG, 2003a), followed by the National Service Framework in 2006 (WAG, 2006c). Arguably, developing a strategy for older people was the most challenging of all service areas because of the huge demographic changes that Welsh society faces in the future. During the past 30 years the number of people aged over 65 in Wales has trebled. This is obviously something to be celebrated since people are living older and healthier lives. But by 2023 the population of Wales is estimated to rise by only 3 per cent, which is less than 100,000 people. However, the number of men aged 65 and over and the number of women aged 60 and over will rise by 11 per cent to 650,000 by 2023, about a quarter of the Welsh population. During the same period the number of people aged 85 and over is expected to rise by over a third to 82,000. As a result, the level of care workers needs to increase by 2-3 per cent annually to meet the needs of an ageing population. New social workers and other care staff need to be attracted into this field as more vacancies inevitably arise in older people's teams throughout Wales.

The Strategy sets out a service response to the challenges of an ageing society. The Strategy identified five areas that adversely affect the lives of older people, namely isolation, poverty, exclusion, discrimination and stereotyping. There was a strong emphasis on a whole systems approach in the Strategy as it reaches out widely to address a range of social problems as well as specific issues such as hospital care and fall prevention. The need for increased social housing and development of community services, such as nursing had already been identified (Wenger *et al.*, 1999). At the centre of the Strategy was the requirement to tackle age discrimination, particularly in the area of employment. Continued employment well into old age was viewed as the surest way of tackling both poverty and isolation. The advantages of continuing to work beyond the age of 65 include making and maintaining friends, more social involvement and community activities, an active lifestyle, very significant economic benefits and consequently less dependency on others and services. The aims of continued employment have, of course, been helped by the Age Discrimination Act 2006 which outlaws discrimination on the basis of age, including in the employment sphere. The Strategy also called for research and a debate about the critically important area of independence and the most appropriate forms of accommodation to meet the age-related needs of older people in Wales. The response to the challenge for good-quality health and social care research in Wales has come with the creation of Clinical Research Collaboration Cymru (CRC Cymru), drawing together centres of research, such as the Older People and Ageing Research and Development Network (OPAN).

To meet the social and health challenges of an ageing population the Strategy document sets a comprehensive agenda for change. Among the community services to be developed from the Strategy were early intervention services to help people live independently for as long as possible; rapid assessment and responses and prompt access to emergency services when required; home adaptations; support for carers; support with activities of daily living; sheltered housing; and integrated transport for older people. Indeed one of the early successes of the Strategy was the provision of free bus travel for all people aged over 60 throughout the whole of Wales. The Free Bus Travel Scheme has helped tackle social exclusion with a 60 per cent increase in the number of trips undertaken by bus. However, a Manifesto commitment to provide free home care for disabled people was abandoned to the dismay of groups representing older disabled people. The Strategy would be implemented in three stages over a ten-year period, with £10 million given for the first three years. Significantly, a Cabinet sub-committee was set up within the Welsh Assembly to oversee progress and sustain political momentum. All Cabinet members were members of the sub-committee except for the First Minister and the Business Minister. A National Partnership Forum was established in 2004 to drive the Strategy forward and to advise the Welsh Assembly Government about issues relating to older people. The Forum was made up of 20 members, 50 per cent of whom were older people and the others were interested parties including gerontologists.

The All-Wales Strategy for Older People was the first of its kind for older people in the UK and has attracted interest worldwide. One of its most interesting innovations was the creation of the office of Commissioner for Older People. The Commissioner for Older People (Wales) Act became law in 2006, and it was expected that the first Commissioner would be appointed during 2007. The Commissioner has the power to consider and make representations to the Assembly about any matter relating to the interests of older people in Wales. The scope of the Commissioner's role is wider-ranging, with responsibilities for promoting opportunities for older people and the elimination of discrimination against older people. This was clearly an important innovation that gave considerable clout to the organisational structure of the Strategy. It enhanced the already existing structure of the National Partnership Forum, Cabinet sub-committee and Older People's Champions in all the local authority areas in Wales, to ensure that older people are represented in local decisions. It is far too early to judge the success or otherwise of the All-Wales Strategy for Older People. However, there are some encouraging signs that the Strategy has had a good start and may be faring better than its predecessors in learning disabilities and mental health (Phillips and Burholt, 2006). While an in-depth baseline evaluation is in progress, initial soundings suggest that there is considerable enthusiasm among those involved in the Strategy and high expectations for the future (Walters, 2005).

## Service users

The service user involvement movement has increased in influence since the 1980s. All the strategies had good intentions about involving service users and their carers. The strategy for learning disabilities stated that service users and their families must play a full part in decisions taken about them. The mental health strategy saw the views of service users and their carers as a fundamental principle of the strategy. The strategy for older people stated the case most powerfully of all when it called for older people to be able to participate fully as citizens in all aspects of society. However, all the strategies have had difficulties in achieving their ideals in this area. The overall picture has varied across Wales with patchy development of advocacy services and systems for the involvement of service users and their families and carers. The Wales Audit Office (2005) had major concerns that only a few areas in Wales had developed protocols for service user and carer participation in mental health services, and that some areas had not gathered the views of service users and carers about their satisfaction with present services and ideas for new ones. In the early days of the learning disabilities strategy it was felt that carers represented their own interests rather than those of people with learning disabilities (Felce *et al.*, 1998). There was a tendency for carers to pressurise for more of the same type of services rather than encourage the development of new ones, to alleviate some of the pressure on themselves. The most promising area for user involvement has been in the field of services for older people with the creation of the National Partnership Forum to provide advice to the Welsh Assembly and statutory bodies in Wales. However, it has been difficult for older people to be heard directly by the Assembly without having to pass through several organisational layers where representation may consist of people who have made a career of the user involvement role (Walters, 2005).

## Carers

An essential element of the care provision for adults is provided by the vast army of carers. According to a 1999 publication, as many as 16 per cent of the Welsh population were carers, this was the second highest figure for the UK. Only the North West of England was higher with 17 per cent of the people in the region being carers (DH, 1999). According to Carers Wales (2006), over 350,000 people experience ill-health, poverty and work-based discrimination as a direct result of being a carer. Mental health problems and physical ill-health as a direct result of the stress involved in caring are experienced by 60,000 people. A startling one in three of those providing continuous care live in poverty and struggle to pay food and other bills. One-fifth of all carers have had to give up their work to care, significantly compounding their financial problems and increasing their isolation. As many as 50 per cent of carers spend five hours or more on informal care, with 20 per cent spending more than 20 hours. The problems faced by black and minority ethnic carers are compounded by societal assumptions about their needs and coping abilities (WAG, 2003b). The *Caring About Carers* strategy document (DH, 1999) and the subsequent *Carers Strategy in Wales: Implementation Plan* (WAG, 2000) recognised the financial costs on and the social exclusion of carers. Maintaining carers' employment was seen as the most effective way of tackling social exclusion and poverty. To this end, employers would need to be more flexible by allowing flexible working, working from home, career breaks and special leave.

## Providers

The delivery and organisation of social services in Wales since 1998 has not differed substantially from England, and any differences have been in the timescale for the implementation of new initiatives. The area of greatest change in policy has been in driving forward joint-working, especially between health and social services. Terms such as partnership and collaborative working were used interchangeably to refer to the process of blurring the boundaries between health and social provision. The Care Programme Approach (CPA) was introduced in the early 1990s following the high-profile death of a social worker by her client in a London hospital. (The Campbell Inquiry - see Sharkey, 2007). The CPA was intended to improve inter-professional communication and collaboration, both of which had been lacking, and would remove the need for separate assessments by health and social services. The CPA became the cornerstone of service delivery for people with serious mental illness who had often slipped through the net (DH, 1996). Its main features were an assessment before people with serious mental illnesses were discharged from hospital; a care plan; a key-worker to coordinate care; and regular reviews of cases. In this respect the CPA was similar to Care Management, and both existed side-by-side, with the CPA being a more specialist approach for people with serious mental illness. Chief among the problems with the CPA in

England were that key components of the CPA were not being fully implemented with wide variations between agencies (Simpson *et al.,* 2003). In Wales, the Wales Audit Office (2005) baseline review of mental health services identified only ten LHBs/LA areas that had introduced the CPA, with three of these being on a pilot basis.

The CPA was generally seen as a specialist assessment within the Unified Assessment Process (UAP) for people with serious mental health problems. The UAP was implemented in Wales between April 2005 for older people and April 2006 for the other adult groups. The UAP was an attempt to standardise eligibility criteria for social care services throughout Wales and to end the duplication in the assessment process between health and social care agencies. Many service users were being asked the same assessment questions more than once by different agencies and this became known as the problem of serial assessments. The UAP would consist of one assessment document for each service user and the information gathered would be shared with all agencies concerned. It is too soon to judge the efficacy of the UAP throughout Wales, but initial indicators suggest that while there have been some improvements in services, there have also been increases in workloads and waiting lists for an assessment. Another major issue has been the development of a joint information technology system between health and social services. The exchange of information through paper documents was viewed as no longer sustainable. A new initiative for social service staff to use the NHS Wales electronic network was introduced.

The Welsh Assembly Government readily admits that social services in Wales are not of a high enough standard, with too many variations across services (WAG, 2006d). While the number of people receiving services grew by 50 per cent between 2001 and 2005, the growth in the workforce has not kept pace with demand. In 2005 nearly 15 per cent of social work posts were unfilled, with an average turnover of 15 per cent. The recruitment crisis in social work is further illustrated when it is considered that the growth in demand for social workers is set at around 12 per cent between 2006 and 2009. In August 2006 the Welsh Assembly Government published a ten-year plan, entitled *Fulfilled Lives, Supporting Communities: A Strategy for Social Services in Wales over the Next Decade – Draft Consultation*, to engage the people of Wales in a discussion about the challenges faced by social services. The strategy's vision of strong social services, at the centre rather than at the margins of local government, working in partnership with other agencies to bring about continuous year-by-year improvements, with service users in the driving seat with services shaped around them, will take an enormous amount of effort and resources to be accomplished by 2016. The driving forces for raising standards throughout Wales will be the Care Council for Wales and the Care Standards Inspectorate for Wales along with national minimum standards and the full implementation of the new three-year degree and new arrangements for post-qualifying education.

## Conclusion

The establishment of the Welsh Assembly in 1999 has been both an evolutionary event and a great impetus in the development of social services in Wales. The roots of service developments in recent times can be traced back to the All-Wales Strategy for Mental Handicap in 1983 (Welsh Office, 1983). The subsequent strategies in the areas of mental health (WAG, 2005), older people, as well as the strategy for carers, have built and learnt from the early experiences. Indeed the most promising of all the strategies, the Strategy for Older People (WAG, 2003a), has evolved far stronger structures for implementation than the earlier strategies. The challenges for social services in Wales during the next ten years remain as great as ever. The lessons from the past have been that plans are very difficult to implement successfully on an all-Wales basis. However, the strategic vision for the future will be less elusive if all organisations remain committed to working together and if adequate resources are made available to implement the plans.

### References

Butler, I and Drakeford, M (2005) *Scandal, Social Policy and Social Welfare* Bristol, BASW/The Policy Press.

Carers Wales (2006) *Looking After Someone: A Guide to Carers' Rights and Benefits*, Cardiff, Carers Wales.

DH (Department of Health) (1995) *Building Bridges*, London, HMSO.

DH (1999) *Caring About Carers: A National Strategy for Carers*, London, HMSO.

Drakeford, M and Williams, C (2002) 'Social work in Wales' in Payne, M, Shardlow, S M (eds.) *Social Work in the British Isles* London, Jessica Kingsley, pp. 156-85.

Joseph Rowntree Foundation (2002) *Fulfilling the Promises: A Response from the Joseph Rowntree Foundation to the Proposed Framework for Services for People with Learning Disabilities in Wales* York, Joseph Rowntree Foundation.

Learning Disability Implementation Advisory Group (2006) *Proposed Statement on Policy and Practice for Adults with a Learning Disability*, Cardiff, Welsh Assembly Government.

Michael, P (2003) *Care and Treatment of the Mentally Ill in North Wales 1800-2000* Cardiff, University of Wales Press.

NAW (National Assembly for Wales) Learning Disabilities Group (2001a) *Fulfilling the Promises: Report to the National Assembly for Wales* Cardiff, National Assembly for Wales.

NAW (2001b) *Equity, Empowerment, Effectiveness, Efficiency Strategy Document* Cardiff: National Assembly for Wales.

O'Brien, J (1981) *The Principle of Normalisation: A Foundation for Effective Services/Written by John O'Brien; Adapted for CMH by Alan Tyne* London, CMH; CMHERA.

Oliver, M and Sapey, B (1999) *Social Work With Disabled People* Basingstoke: BASW/Palgrave MacMillan.

Phillips, J and Burholt, V (2006) 'Ageing in Wales; policy responses to an ageing population' *Contemporary Wales* 19, pp. 180-97.

Ramcharan, P, McGrath, M and Grant G (1997) 'Voices and choices: mapping entitlements to friendships and community contacts' in Ramcharan, P, Roberts, G; Grant, G and Borland, J (eds.) *Empowerment in Everyday Life* London, Jessica Kingsley, pp. 48-70.

Saycell, K, Sims, J, Hugheston-Roberts, J, Hazeldine, K, Lancelot, A, Underwood, P and Williams, H (2004) 'A community treatment paradigm for serious and enduring mental illness in north west Wales' *Mental Health Practice* 8(1), pp. 18-22.

Sharkey, P (2007) *The Essentials of Community Care* London, Palgrave.

Simpson, A, Miller, C and Bowers, L (2003) 'The history of the care programme approach in England: where did it go wrong?' *Journal of Mental Health* 12(5), pp. 489-504.

WAG (Welsh Assembly Government) HSC-OPLTCP (2000) *The Carers Strategy in Wales: Implementation Plan*, Cardiff, Welsh Assembly Government.

WAG (2003a) *The Strategy for Older People in Wales* Cardiff, Welsh Assembly Government.

WAG (2003b) *Challenging the Myth, They Look After Their Own, Black and Minority Ethnic (BME) Carers*, Cardiff, Welsh Assembly Government.

WAG (2005) *Raising the Standards, The Revised Adult Mental Health National Service Framework and Action Plan for Wales*, Cardiff, Welsh Assembly Government.

WAG (2006a) *Disability Equality Scheme*, Cardiff, Welsh Assembly Government.

WAG OPLTC4 (2006b) *Strategy for Older People in Wales: Background and Context*, Cardiff, Welsh Assembly Government.

WAG (2006c) *National Service Framework for Older People in Wales*, Cardiff, Welsh Assembly Government.

WAG (2006d) *Fulfilled Lives, Supportive Communities: A Strategy for Social Services in Wales over the Next Decade* – Draft Consultation, Cardiff, Welsh Assembly Government.

WAG Equal Opportunities Committee (2007) *Why Is It That Disabled Young People are Always Left Until Last?*, Cardiff, Welsh Assembly Government.

Wales Audit Office (2005) *Adult Mental Health Services in Wales: A Baseline Review of Service Provision*, Cardiff, Wales Audit Office.

Walters, V (2005) *The Strategy for Older People in Wales: A Framework for Evaluation* Swansea, University of Wales.

Welsh Office (1983) *All-Wales Strategy for Development of Services for Mentally Handicapped People*, Cardiff, HMSO.

Wenger, G C, Barholt, V and Scott, A (1999) *Bangor Longitudinal Study of Ageing* Bangor, Centre for Social Policy Research and Development, University of Wales.

Wolfensberger, W (1992) *A Brief Introduction to Social Role Valorization as a High-Order Concept for Structuring Human Services* California, Syracuse University.

## Chapter 11

# Social work in a devolved Wales

Charlotte Williams

## Introduction

*'We must create a culture whereby there is a feeling that staff are working for Wales Social Services, which reinforces the principle of social care being one sector with one workforce.'* (Garthwaite Report, 2005:16)

I was trained as a social worker in Wales in the early 1980s in a period of great uncertainty and change. The Barclay Report (Barclay, 1982) on the roles and tasks of social workers pointed to a radical reshuffle of local authority social services departments and their relationship to the communities they served, a model which although rejected may have been eminently suited to the realities of rural social work that we were experiencing in practice. The Thatcher administration had begun what we later came to understand as a radical restructure of the whole context of welfare delivery, opening with a period of retraction of services and financial stringency. Academic forecasters quickly focused on the 'crisis in welfare' (Munday, 1989). If the enemy was not yet named we were led to expect the concomitant 'crisis in social work' (Munday, 1989:34). Brewer and Lait (1980) had presented a trenchant critique of the utility of social work, pointing to the lack of empirical rigour guiding interventions and it had long been clear to us that what we had to offer was not what service users wanted (Mayer and Timms, 1973). In the face of this onslaught we were weak, adrift in a sea change – rudderless and anchorless, graduating into a profession that had clearly lost its way. Things happened to social work and they happened to us in Wales by dint of distant forces. We were relatively powerless to affect our fate or to shape anything that might approximate a 'social work in Wales'. Meanwhile, the experimental initiative of the All-Wales Strategy for Mentally Handicapped People (Welsh Office, 1983) rolled out novel multidisciplinary teams and new ways of working with users and carers. As students we were becoming increasingly politicised as the strategies of the largely English-driven anti-racist agenda fuelled an emerging Welsh language agenda in social work and social care. Despite the potential of these latter initiatives we held little sense of ourselves as a Welsh social work service whatever that might have meant and little confidence to articulate our specific concerns.

In post-devolution Wales the 'crisis of social work' sentiment is still with us, refracting against a backdrop of far-reaching changes that impinge on the nature and functioning of the social work role. Fears expressed about the imposition of the new managerialism and the inability of social work to assert itself against the forces of market-driven practice lie at the heart of the crisis. However, as will be argued in this chapter, negotiating this 'crisis' has never been more in our hands and there is now, more than ever before, an opportunity for social work to be 'a confident participant' rather than 'an apologetic spectator to the social programme of the next century', to borrow Butler and Drakeford's phrase (2000:1). In this chapter I will explore the nature of the changing context for practice under devolution and consider the notion of 'crisis' as it besets contemporary social work in Wales. I will then draw out some of the implications of constitutional change for the development of a 'Wales social services' and the idea of a 'social work in Wales' (Garthwaite, 2005).

## Continuity and change: social work in Wales

There is little doubting that we are in a time of considerable flux and change in social work and social services. Social care services in Wales are a huge enterprise, currently accounting for £1.1 billion in public spending, employing more than 80,000 people and supporting over 150,000 people (WAG, 2007a). Devolution has seen the introduction of wide-ranging policy changes that have resulted not only in new legislative mandates but have led to changes in organisational arrangements and to changes in philosophy, approaches and ways of working. Few areas of social work practice remain untouched by strategies emanating from the Welsh Assembly in relation to specific groups such as *A Strategy for Older People in Wales* (WAG, 2003), *A Fair*

*Future for our Children* (WAG, 2005), *The Review of Service Provision for Gypsies and Travellers* (WAG, 2007*)* and in relation to key areas of need such as homelessness and drugs. New approaches to working have been flagged by policy documents such as the Wanless Report (2002), *Making the Connections* (WAG, 2004) and *Fullfilled Lives, Supportive Communities* (WAG, 2007a). New regulatory bodies have been established, in particular the Care Council for Wales (CCW), the Social Services Inspectorate for Wales (SSIW) and the Care Standards Inspectorate for Wales (CSIW). Statutory registration of social workers and student social workers has been embedded following the Care Standards Act 2000 based on a robust Code of Practice. Efforts are being made to co-ordinate research activity across health and social care in Wales with the establishment of the Clinical Research Collaboration Cymru, which is developing a coherent approach to research and development across the nation. In social work education, the transition has been made from the Diploma in Social Work to the new three-year degree programme with eight programmes in Wales up and running at both undergraduate and postgraduate level. Comprehensive reviews of workforce need have been undertaken that seek to tie training more securely to employer requirements in Wales (see, for example, CCW, 2007) and major inspection reviews of the delivery of services have provided key messages about the state of play (SSIW, 2005). Not all of these activities emanate from Welsh governance. Changes to social work education and the regulation of the profession are standard across the UK and the re-engineering and gearing up of social work to be responsive to national context is happening elsewhere (see Ferguson, 2005; Asquith, *et al.*, 2005, on Scotland for example). A major review of the roles and tasks of social work is being undertaken in England (DH, 2006). What is interesting to explore, however, is the emergence of the idea of a 'social work in Wales' as a coherent entity and to consider how this is being constructed, what the nature of the distinctiveness is and what this might mean for a wider conceptualisation of the profession.

While it is difficult to delineate social work in Wales historically in the way for example it is possible to do in the Scottish context, there are nevertheless ways of viewing the 'old' and the 'new'. The story of social work in Wales emerges from a number of sources. There are the insights of the welfare historians, who have for example illustrated aspects of the treatment of the people with mental health problems in Wales (Michael, 2003) or provided early glimpses of social welfare delivery in rural communities (Grant, 1978). Fascinating, if under-explored, archives exist from the last century of the experiences of people in Butetown, Cardiff, which although controversial, provide the earliest account of the nature of social work with minorities in Wales (Sherwood, 1991). The legacy of scandals in the Welsh context and concomitant reports such as the Howe Report (1969) into the conditions and treatment of patients in Ely hospital in the 1960s, the Waterhouse Inquiry (2001) into the abuse of children in north Wales in the 1990s and the inquiry into the case of Andrew Cole who following discharge from a mid-Wales Hospital in 1996 murdered William Crompton and Fiona Ovis (http://news. bbc.co.uk/2/hi/uk_news/wales/mid_/6193573.stm), illustrate aspects of the highly contentious nature of the terrain and some of the more fundamental failings of social work practice (Butler and Drakeford, 2003). The history of local government reorganisation serves to indicate something about the legacy of fragmentation and problems of co-ordination that beset service delivery in particular in relation to children's services (Drakeford, *et al.*, 1998). An important history exists on the endeavours to establish the principles of Welsh language equality in service delivery, in practice and in terms of the representation of Welsh speakers in the social work workforce (Huws-Williams *et al.*, 1994). The Wales office of the Central Council for Education and Training in Social Work (CCETSW) under the direction of Rhian Huws-Williams from the early 1990s onwards developed a forthright programme on the Welsh language, which included a range of publications and training materials and the facilitation of networks of Welsh-speaking social workers across Wales.

Despite these factors the organisation of social work in Wales largely followed Seebohm lines as in England. The coming of the *All-Wales Strategy for the Development of Services for Mentally Handicapped People* (Welsh Office, 1983) (see Chapter 9) and *The Strategy on Mental Illness* (Welsh Office, 1989) represented a major departure in service delivery and one that was well researched and provided groundbreaking lessons on multidisciplinary working, user involvement and mobilising local resources (Ramchuran, *et al.*, 1997). While many policy strategies subsequently emanated from the Welsh Office pre-devolution, it would be difficult, however, to sustain the argument that they represented any consistent departure from the approach taken in England. In fact, all the evidence suggests that social work in Wales was as subject to the vicissitudes of the Thatcher era as much as anywhere else in the UK, as the series of studies conducted by a team of researchers in the Centre for Social Policy Research and Development (CSPRD) of the University of Wales Bangor in the mid-1990s revealed (McGrath *et. al.*, 1996a, 1996b; Parry-Jones *et. al.*, 1996). These CSPRD studies are significant in that, although they focused on a survey of workers in adult services and an analysis of their roles and tasks, they highlighted the nature of increasing demands on staff under the new care management arrangements and the tensions between their perception of their traditional social work roles and the imposition of market principles on frontline work with users. The studies gave voice to the fears of social workers that they were being deskilled, that they were becoming distanced from service users given the emphasis on 'paperwork', of them experiencing high levels of stress due to lack of support, and a training regime that ill-equipped them for the new roles. A study conducted in 2001 by Parry-Jones and Soulsby in Powys, reiterates the discrepancy between the aim to provide a needs-led service and the realities on the front line, confirming the ongoing tensions in practice.

The findings apparent in the CSPRD studies resonate ten years later with the predicament of workers and their concerns expressed in the recent Garthwaite Report (2005):

> *'Increased scrutiny, joint reviews, inspections and publicly available annual performance evaluations are moving local authorities towards increased target setting often based on process indicators. This is contributing to a shift in the emphasis of the social work role from direct work with clients. Social workers and their managers are expressing concern about increased levels of bureaucracy in their roles which do not necessarily translate into improved outcomes for service users and carers.'*
> (Garthwaite Report, 2005:13)

> 'We heard much disquiet during our research that social
> workers were not ready to practise immediately following
> qualification. Other factors such as inappropriate
> workloads and insufficient levels of support have an impact
> on this.'

(Garthwaite Report, 2005:48)

What might be deduced from the parallels between the accounts in the CSPRD studies and those documented in the Garthwaite review is that the neo-liberal agenda of managerialist and market-driven approaches to social work that have prevailed for over a decade have led to a demoralised workforce and one in which there is serious attrition. While the crisis is formulated as one of recruitment and retention related to pay and conditions, there can be no running away from the fundamental expression of discontent at the mismatch between the motivations for becoming a social worker as a wish to work directly with people and enhance their well-being, the skills and values underpinning their training as social work professionals, and the realities of the changed nature of the job itself.

In this respect, social workers in Wales are saying nothing different from their colleagues elsewhere in the UK. In Scotland, Wilson *et al.*, (2003) noted the predominance of the managerialist over the professional ethos as a source of frustration to workers. Chris Jones' (2001) study 'Voices from the Front Line' exploring state social work in England provided a powerful insight into the nature of these transformations to the social work role under neo-liberal policies. Jones suggests that:

> '... the victims of neo-liberalism seem to be everywhere in
> social work. The clients suffer not only through a reduction
> in welfare but also in the style of welfare... The impacts
> on the state social workers who find themselves
> operationalising what are clearly rationing processes with
> clients whose plight and condition is in many instances
> more dire than before.' (Jones, 2001:358)

He concludes that the 'fragility of state social work' has meant that social service managers have been 'particularly compliant in accommodating the neo-liberal agenda' (Jones, 2001:359).

The Garthwaite Report, *Social Work in Wales: A Profession to Value*, arose from concerns raised by a task and finish group of the Assembly, which reported in 2001. The task and finish group on social care workforce issues identified inadequate pay levels as contributing to social workers leaving the sector. As a result of this, they suggested that a fragmented sector had emerged with individual local authorities responding to staff shortages with initiatives such as 'golden hello' packages to staff to join or stay with them. A system of competition prevailed, which it was felt was detrimental to the principle of what the task and finish group termed 'one sector, one workforce'. Data on the social care workforce of Wales had traditionally been sparse and inconsistent. In 2003 the Skills Foresight Plan described for the first time the social care sector workforce of Wales. The size of the whole workforce including childcare learning and development is currently estimated to be 88,773 which is almost 7 per cent of the entire workforce of Wales (CCW, 2007). This figure does not include foster carers, adult placement carers or volunteers, or those friends and neighbours who provide vital care services. The 2001 Census puts the number of those providing caring services for another person for over 20 hours per week at 132,218 (Labour Force Survey, 2005). Of the total number of social care workers it is estimated that there are 6,136 social workers in Wales working in social care and justice roles. The Care Council's Register for social care workers puts the total of registered social workers at 4,672, which excludes the registered social work students. The Garthwaite Report noted that other than teachers, social workers are the largest single group of qualified workers employed by local authorities and that the demand for social workers was in excess of supply and likely to remain so for some years to come. The vacancy rate of almost 15 per cent, coupled with an equivalent turnover rate as social workers moved through a revolving door between authorities, was regarded as having a damaging effect on the capacity of local authorities to deliver services to those in need. High turnover rates and sickness levels were particular acute in children's services, where the vacancy rate runs at 18.8 per cent (CCW, 2007). Indeed, the recruitment and retention of social workers presents the greatest difficulties for local authorities of any of its occupational groups. Factors affecting the retention of staff are discussed in the Garthwaite Report and among the reasons given for leaving the job are heavy workload, the stressful nature of the job, low pay, lack of appreciation and being taken for granted. The quality and nature of leadership, supervision and support was also cited by many as a reason for leaving.

A number of particular themes and trends emerge from data on the registered social work workforce. Most social workers in Wales are state social workers (62 per cent). The analysis by the Care Council of those on their register reveals perhaps unsurprisingly a broadly white, female, middle-aged and monolingual profile. A large proportion of social workers are approaching retirement age, with 40 per cent of them being over the age of 50 (CCW, 2007) and there is clearly substantial under-representation of disabled people (2.2 per cent), minority ethnic groups (3 per cent), men (23 per cent) and Welsh speakers (17 per cent for the sector as a whole). This under-representation is a feature of both the workforce and the student trainee population. The Care Council is to develop a national action plan to respond to some of these workforce challenges including 'strengthening ways of making social care an attractive and positive proposition for young people setting out on their career' (CCW, 2007:46). The CCW report on the social care workforce refers to these workers as a 'national asset' (CCW, 2007:47) and the Garthwaite Report (2005) calls for a 'relaunch' of the profession in Wales. Tackling the fragmented response to these issues by local authorities is seen as a priority with the push towards a co-ordinated and collaborative approach at an all-Wales level placed within the context of the National Assembly's philosophy of collaboration set out in *Making the Connections* (WAG, 2004). The Garthwaite Report (2005:16) calls for 'a universally applicable set of definitions of roles and responsibilities for social workers' and speaks of developing minimum standards on working conditions and a common approach to workload management:

> *'If vulnerable people in Welsh society are to receive the service they deserve from social services authorities through the contribution of social workers, the social work profession must be re-launched on a new platform of*

*common roles and responsibilities and consistently high standards of working conditions, pay, benefits and career opportunities.'* (Garthwaite Report, 2005:22)

The WAG report *Fullfilled Lives, Supporting Communities* (WAG, 2007) takes forward the agenda for change with targets set for a modernised social services in Wales by the year 2018. The 'single workforce' ideas are reinforced and the idea that 'the social services workforce needs to be involved in the local authority's decision making' is established as a principle (WAG, 2007:9). The WAG philosophy of greater collaboration, partnership and the primacy of 'voice over choice' lies at the heart of the approach set out in this document and opens up considerable opportunities for the profession to be proactive in shaping change.

The notion of 'crisis' is, of course, highly contestable. Inevitably it begs questions about how the nature of the crisis is defined and who is defining it. That change for the profession in Wales is under way is undisputed. What is more disputable are the drivers of that change and the nature of the change. The prevailing discourse on the 'crisis' in contemporary social work is recruitment and retention issues. The workforce agenda argument that we need to attract and retain more social workers in order to respond to growing need, may be, however, to focus on the malaise rather than the symptoms. The voice of the workforce may be telling a different story. Professional formulations of the agenda coined nebulously as 'increasing bureaucracy' as the Garthwaite Report (2005:86) indicates, or feelings of being devalued may reflect the clear unease in practice with being key participants in a neo-liberal welfare framework that is, in Chris Jones (2001) words 'degrading and damaging' to social work practitioners and those whom they seek to serve. The report flags the International Association of Schools of Social Work (IASSW) and the International Federation of Social Workers (IFSW) agreed international definition of social work as part of the bedrock values and principles of social work:

*'The social work profession promotes social change, problem solving in human relationships and the empowerment and liberation of people to enhance well-being. Utilising theories of human behaviour and social*

*systems, social work intervenes at the points where people interact with their environments. Principles of human rights and social justice are fundamental to social work.'*
(Garthwaite Report, 2005:53)

While these social justice ambitions, 'fundamental to social work', are left suspended in the report, there is evidently much in the commitments laid out in *Fulfilling Lives, Supporting Communities* (WAG, 2007) that resonate with these ideals. It has been argued (see Chapters 1 and 2 of this volume) that devolution heralds a welfare regime significantly different in many respects to that of England, with an emphasis on the redistributive and integrative potential of welfare policies. Further, it is advanced that this diversity goes beyond policy differences between nations to incorporate the idea of differences in philosophy (values), style and relationships. Welfare measures in these contexts have become a major instrument in reaching citizens and in defining the contours of national difference. Juliet Cheetham (2001) writing about the Scottish context, has suggested that:

*'What does make a difference – in these still heady days of devolution – is the power to do things which significantly affect individual welfare and which are based on egalitarian principles not always explicitly espoused by New Labour.'*
(Cheetham, 2001:626)

Scotland has badged itself in this way – opting for universalist provision like free University tuition for Scottish students, free nursing care and, indeed, paying school teachers more than their English counterparts.

As their legislative powers increase, the Welsh Assembly is also indicating its willingness to move towards greater universalism. This rhetoric of resistance to market-driven principles in welfare is writ large across a range of government reports aimed at developing the modernised social services post devolution. The philosophy of partnership, collaboration, and high user and citizen involvement characterises political speak. In such a context it is now possible to consider the possibilities and potential for social work to demonstrate 'acts of resistance' and to develop creative practices that translate this distinctiveness into real effects, to develop a welfare *style* that will benefit users and move the profession beyond the perennial sense of 'crisis'.

## Practising nation: tensions and possibilities for social work in a devolved Wales

The way in which social work has evolved in the UK reflects both in its positioning and its role. The central state – the welfare state – defined social work, both given social work's central location within state institutions and the way in which relationships between state services and the independent sector have developed within the mixed economy of welfare. Since the imposition of neo-liberal principles from the early 1980s, the welfare state has increasingly been subject to transformations and limitations and within it, social work has been reshaped and subject to the constraints as a state-led institution. It is frequently argued that social work has been a passive participant in these transformations, unable to muster a level of autonomy necessary to effect critical re-interpretations of government dictat. Writers such as Lorenz (2001) have urged the profession to realise its autonomy by defining its role more clearly and thus being less subject to the contingent and shifting nature of political decisions. Lorenz draws attention to the interplay of welfare regimes with social work methodologies. He argues that welfare regimes reflect the histories and traditions of particular countries and suggests that social work methodologies form a nexus with these regimes, contributing to the development of particular 'welfare cultures' (Lorenz, 2001:606). The notion of welfare culture or what have been called 'ways of life' within a nation (Mooney and Williams, 2006) is key to an understanding of how social work can engage with the reengineering of the welfare state that is under way. In her discussion of social work in a devolved Scotland, Cheetham (2001:628) tentatively suggests: 'I believe there could be a fruitful relationship between politics and social work'. This is no less the case in Wales.

Devolution has brought considerable potential for a repositioning of social work. Opportunities for direct involvement in the political process have been opened up in a number of ways. In a small country, direct access to politicians and civil servants is assured not only at constituency level but the Assembly has sought out ways to make its deliberations more open, transparent and subject to a range of influences, such as, through regional committees, through the establishment of a plethora of consultation fora and through the widespread use of stakeholder representatives in task and finish groups. The Child Poverty Task Group mentioned in Chapter 4 is but one example, drawing its membership largely from practising social workers involved in an existing collaboration between voluntary agencies across Wales (the End Child Poverty Network). Much of this networking and partnership working is not new and comes from a long tradition of close working relationships across agencies, albeit *ad hoc*, and based on voluntarism rather than strategic thinking. Being in a small country, professional groups have built up a certain familiarity with each other alongside informal processes of working across agencies. Some of these existing ways of working are now being mobilised to greater effect and given a strategic push. Consultation on *The Strategy for Older People* (WAG, 2003) is another example of social workers' involvement in shaping policy, and there are examples of practitioners mobilising for acts of resistance over the treatment of children of asylum seekers and refugees. Social workers can be effectively engaged in lobbying as key stakeholders in the activities of a range of decision-making institutions at local, regional and national level. The emphasis on localism in the new public policy model underscores the importance of interventions at this level. In the emergent welfare framework the state is no longer the principal agent of social policy delivery, as its functions are complemented, augmented or replaced by other key stakeholders. The opportunities presented by the shift towards governance (see Chapter 2) and away from government can be illustrated diagrammatically as shown in Figure 11.1.

### Figure 11.1 Policy development pre- and post-devolution

|  | Pre-devolution | Post-devolution |
|---|---|---|
| *Relationship to the centre* | Strong, top-down | Two-way between multiple centres (transnational) |
| *Institutional context* | England (centre) | Realignment/ networks focus |
| *User involvement* | Low | High |
| *Innovations* | Emanate from the central state | From multiple actors in the field |
| *Outcomes* | Rational planning | Experiential and emergent (based on evidence from the field) |
| *Goals* | Standardisation | Particularist |

Within this new framework social work is reconfigured and located within new policy networks that are highly differentiated and in which there are multiple actors. Policies are much more the subject of negotiation and emerge from experiences and evidence on the ground. The search is for responsive and particularist solutions rather than standardisation based on rational planning from the centre. The possibilities for greater user engagement and for developing new partners and allies are greatly increased. This shift away from government to governance (see Chapter 2) brings with it its own challenges and concerns. In such a pluralist framework inevitably some voices will be heard and others muffled and the appearance of involvement and engagement may be more apparent than real.

Undoubtedly, however, more open government has provided a plethora of opportunities for social welfare professionals. There are also increased possibilities for research alliances to be developed with academic institutions and research institutes. Think tanks such as the Institute of Welsh Affairs and the Bevan Foundation welcome contributions, commentary and involvement from those at the front line of public service delivery. As research practices themselves become more inclusive, academics seek partners among practitioners and user groups in determining research agendas, undertaking research and disseminating findings. Voluntary agencies often find themselves at the forefront in identifying research needs, undertaking small-scale studies or acting as partners in academic research. In this way social workers and other welfare professionals can be actively involved in the production of knowledge and influencing policy.

Above all, however, social welfare practitioners are the key implementers of the new public provision model. In Chapter 6 I indicated their critical role in translating equality principles into practices that matter to users and their carers. The underpinning principles of the new approach to public services in Wales (see Chapter 2) have a strong resonance with the fundamental values of social work and with the aspirations of the profession towards social justice ideals. If this is to move beyond political rhetoric it will largely be down to the everyday actions of social welfare practitioners at the front line of services. The leverage this broad approach provides for well-judged 'acts of resistance' to the dictates of neo-liberal managerialism is being tested, as for example in youth justice.

In many respects social work in Wales is well poised for a refreshed role. A renewed politicisation builds on a history of collective action in social welfare, for example, in relation to Welsh language policies and international activism, and builds on a history of innovations in practice, such as the All-Wales Strategy. The fact that many social workers have been trained in Wales and worked within Welsh institutions for many years and that most are state social workers affords them not only familiarity with key decision-making processes but the potential to build a strong collective identity for the profession. The 'One Sector' approach can only enhance this by rejecting individualism and competition in favour of collaborative practices and a sense of common purpose. In addition, registration, which is argued by some to be a double-edged sword, nevertheless provides for a corporate identity at national and trans-national level. Much will depend on how the Care Council for Wales negotiates its twin role of regulation alongside its co-ordinating, support and development roles. Against this must be placed the paucity of a national forum for the consolidation of a sense of a Welsh-*style* social work or even a sense of a social work in Wales. Traditionally, *All-Wales* co-ordination and co-operation has foundered on both sides of the Brecon Beacons as efforts to endure the discomforts of north/south transport links ultimately deter even the most enthusiastic. Membership of the British Association of Social Workers (BASW) in Wales, as elsewhere, has not been strong. Links between academics in higher education institutions, between Welsh-speaking social workers and the co-ordination of practice assessors across Wales and co-ordination for the delivery of post-qualifying programmes are existing avenues varying in strength and capacity that could be mobilised to good effect.

Social work education and training will need to keep apace of these new style requirements. Welsh social policy and attention to aspects of Welsh social life, language and culture have been afforded a profiled place in the social work education curriculum in Wales. Recruitment of students who are Welsh speakers is being carefully monitored by the Care Council for Wales, as is representation from other minority groups. Social work education programmes will also have to work to reflect the public service ethos of social policy in Wales, to underscore its social justice concerns and to develop students' skills in working strategically in the new governance framework.

While opportunities proliferate under devolution, there are also a number of issues that must remain of concern to welfare practice. Large policy swathes that fundamentally affect the well-being of citizens in Wales lie outside the remit of the Welsh Assembly Government. Issues of criminal justice, immigration, income support and thus income poverty, are some key examples. It would be easy to overstate the power of the Welsh Assembly Government in this respect. Neither, as I have argued elsewhere, is the Welsh Assembly Government immune to the flow and influence of overarching neo-liberal ideas, nor as yet shown itself to be in direct conflict with them (Mooney and Williams, 2006). The principle of welfare to work, of social inclusion as labour market inclusion, ideas about entrepreneurship and the balance of the mixed economy of welfare are all powerful neo-liberal mandates that permeate practice in Wales. In some areas of social work practice, for example youth justice (see Chapter 8) and with some areas of children's work (see Chapter 7), social workers will be obliged to struggle with 'serving two masters'.

Devolution also brings to the fore a number of social justice issues as indicated in Chapter 1. Territorial inequalities will inevitably become more acute as factors of place and access to welfare goodies (or not) are now flagged more significantly. Some have argued that superficial 'boutique policies' might generate migrations towards hotspots as people move in search of the good life. Issues of access to key welfare resources such as jobs and housing may become increasingly tied to pre-determined 'national' credentials in ways that may exclude as well as include. For these reasons social welfare professions should develop a critical questioning of national narratives and sufficient confidence and autonomy to critically inspect notions of Welsh citizenship as they develop inclusionary and exclusionary dimensions. In the endeavour to participate in the nation-building project there will always be a danger of losing sight of the ways in which social issues transcend national boundary, for example, issues such as asylum, racism and other discriminations, child poverty, human trafficking and contemporary slavery. In a globalising world, fundamental inequalities between nations can also be ignored in clinging to the certainties of the parochial, to the cosy securities of nation. 'Grasping at nationalistic verities' (McDonald, 2002:508) may mean we lose sight of those who are on the real fringes of societies; those communities subject to persistent and unremitting poverty, excluded from citizenship rights and exploited for the benefit of wealthy nations (Midgely, 2000).

Arguably, a more confident social work in Wales will be in a better position to engage with these concerns, looking outward as well as inward.

## Conclusions: 'the social work project'

The social work project under devolution is intricate and complex. It will require a careful balancing act on the part of the profession. I have suggested that the so-called 'crisis of social work' manifests itself epoch after epoch, foregrounding often differing discourses to explain the over-riding tale of a profession that drifts helplessly in the ebb and flow of political tides. In the early 1980s as I undertook my training the search was on for a better ship in which to sail – the reorganisation of social services. In the late 1980s under Thatcher came the crisis of role as social work functions were up for grabs by a range of associated professionals and in the late 1990s the modernisation mantra emerged, which compromised the fundamental values on which the profession was built under the 'Blair project' (see Butler and Drakeford, 2001). To find ourselves in the 2000s under devolution in a political climate conducive to the aims, values and purposes of social work is one thing. But it may prove to be equally transient if social work in Wales is unable or unwilling to seize the opportunities to gain a more enduring collective sense of role and purpose. At the same time there are tensions to negotiate. Does the development of a Welsh-style social work represent a fundamental fragmentation of professional identity and the political power beyond national boundaries? Will devolution prove to be an even more effective method of technocratic control of the profession? Will it represent a fragmentation of political issues that require UK or international responses? Will constitutional change serve to pave the way for a break-up of the ideology of the welfare state, in particular its integrative potential to build social solidarities?

Earlier in this chapter I made a reference to Butler and Drakeford's (2000) discussion of the social work role in the next century where they explore ideas about the role and purposes of social work. A strong body of work admonishes social work for acquiescence and collusion in the new managerialism of the neo-liberal agenda (Jones, 2001; Ferguson et al., 2005) and for the failure to engage with social justice concerns. The social justice manifesto for a new engaged practice developed by Chris Jones and others (Jones et al., 2006:1) argues that social work in Britain has lost its way and suggests that 'we need to find more effective ways of resisting the dominant trends within social work and map ways forward for a new engaged practice'. They speak of 'new resources of hope that have emerged in recent years' (Jones et al., 2006:2). These resources, it suggests, lie in new engagements with user group movements, with a culture of protest and new-style alliances with service users. A later article by Butler and Drakeford (2005), which reviews the direction of contemporary social work, offers up a plea for the profession to be a confident participant in what they refer to as 'the social work project' for the 21st century, one which, they suggest, will rely heavily on the development of trust:

> *'the most urgent need is to rehabilitate the concept of trust as a social good and as an integral part of a progressive, co-operative practice.'*
> (Butler and Drakeford, 2005:649)

Their argument relies on renewed and productive alliances between practitioners and service users:

> *'The way to ensure we have a form of social work that combines sensitivity to individual needs and circumstances with the confident and articulate pursuit of equality is to understand the contribution both users and workers make to social work encounters.'*
> (Butler and Drakeford, 2005:650)

Opportunities have been opened up within the welfare context and within a new and strengthened recognition of social work in Wales in which social work will have to play a part in asserting itself with a renewed confidence. Devolution represents, in the words of one commentator, the opportunities for experimentation in 'new policy laboratories' (Jeffrey, 2005:5). As key implementers of the new public provision model there is a responsibility to develop new practices and new cultures based on productive alliances with a range of stakeholder groups including service users and their carers, other professional groups, social work students, the army of workers that make up the social care sector, academics as well as politicians and civil servants. In developing a distinctive 'welfare culture' and style, the notion of a Welsh social work can emerge.

## References

Asquith, S, Clark, C and Waterhouse, L (2005) *The Role of the Social Worker in the 21st Century: A Literature Review* Edinburgh, Scottish Executive www.21csocialwork.org.uk

Barclay, P (1982) The Barclay Report *Social Workers: Their Role and Tasks*, London, Bedford Square Press.

Brewer, C and Lait, J (1980) *Can Social Work Survive?* London, Maurice Temple Smith.

Butler, I and Drakeford, M (2000) 'Editorial' *British Journal of Social Work* 30, pp. 1-2.

Butler, I and Drakeford, M (2001) 'Which Blair project: communitarianism, social authoritarianism and social work' *Journal of Social Work*, 1(1), pp. 7-20.

Butler, I and Drakeford, M (2003) *Scandal, Social Policy and Social Welfare* Bristol, BASW/The Policy Press.

Butler, I and Drakeford, M. (2005) 'Trusting in social work' *British Journal of Social Work* 35, pp. 639-53.

CCW (Care Council for Wales) (2007) Annual Report, Cardiff, CCW.

Cheetham, J (2001) 'New Labour, welfare and social work and devolution: a view from Scotland' *British Journal of Social Work* 31, pp. 625-28.

DH (Department of Health) (2006) *Options for Excellence* London, DH www.dh.gov.uk/en/Policyandguidance/Healthandsocialcaretopics/ Socialcare/Socialcareworkforce/DH_4131862

Drakeford, M, Butler I and Pithouse, A (1998) 'Social services' in Osmond, J (ed.) *The National Assembly Agenda: A Handbook for the First Four Years* Cardiff, Institute of Welsh Affairs, pp. 266-80.

Garthwaite Report (2005) *Social Work in Wales: A Profession to Value* ADSS (Association of Directors of Social Services) All-Wales Support Unit, www.allwalesunit.gov.uk/garthwaitereport

Grant, G (1978) 'The provision of social services in rural areas' in Williams, G (ed.) *Social and Cultural Change in Contemporary Wales* London, Routledge and Kegan Paul, pp. 61-75.

Ferguson, I (2005) 'Social work and social care in the "new Scotland"' in Mooney, G and Scott, G (eds.) *Exploring Social Policy in the 'New' Scotland* Bristol, The Policy Press.

Ferguson, I, Lavelette, M and Whitmore, E (eds.) (2005) *Globalisation, Global Justice and Social Work* London, Routledge.

Howe Report (1969) *Report of the committee of inquiry into allegations of ill-treatment of patients and other irregularities at the Ely Hospital, Cardiff* CM3975, London, HMSO.

Huws-Williams, R, Davies, E and Williams, H (1994) *Social Work and the Welsh Language* Cardiff, University of Wales Press.

Jeffrey, C (2005) *Devolution: What Difference Has it Made?* Swindon, ESRC. Research Programme on Constitutional Change, www.dev.ac.uk

Jones, C (2001) 'Voices from the front line: state social workers and New Labour' *British Journal of Social Work* 31, pp. 341-82.

Jones, C, Ferguson, I, Lavalette, M and Penketh, L (2006) *Social Work and Social Justice: A Manifesto for a New Engaged Practice* www.liv.ac.uk/sspsw/Social_Work_Manifesto.html

Labour Force Survey (2005) London, HMSO.

Lorenz, W (2001) 'Social work responses to 'New Labour' in Continental European countries' *British Journal of Social Work* 31, pp. 595-609.

McDonald, D (2002) 'Life on the fringe: nationalism and social work' *British Journal of Social Work* 32, pp. 503-08.

McGrath, M, Grant, G, Ramcharan, P, Caldock, K, Parry-Jones, B and Robinson, C (1996a) *Care Management in Wales: Perceptions of Front Line Workers* CSPRD Report, Bangor, University of Wales Bangor.

McGrath, M, Grant, G, Ramcharan, P, Caldock, K, Parry-Jones, B and Robinson, C (1996b) 'The Roles and Tasks of Care Managers in Wales' *Community Care Management and Practice* 4(6), pp. 185-94.

Mayer, E and Timms, N (1973) *Client Speaks: Working Class Impressions of Casework* London, Routledge.

Michael, P (2003) *Care and Treatment of the Mentally Ill in North Wales 1800-2000* Cardiff, University of Wales Press.

Midgely, J (2000) 'Globalisation, postmodernity and international social work' in Tan, N and Envall, E (eds.) *Social Work around the World* Geneva, International Federation of Social Workers.

Mooney, G and Williams, C (2006) 'Forging new "ways of life"? Social policy and nation building in devolved Scotland and Wales' *Critical Social Policy* 26(3), pp. 608-29.

Munday, B (ed.) (1989) *The Crisis in Welfare* Hertfordshire, Harvester Wheatsheaf.

Parry-Jones, B, Grant, G, McGrath, M, Caldock, K, Ramchuran, P and Robinson, C A (1996) *Stress and Job Satisfaction among Social Workers, Nurses, Community Psychiatric Nurses: Implications for the Care Management Model* CSPRD Report, University of Wales, Bangor.

Parry-Jones, B and Soulsby, J (2001) 'Need-led assessment: the challenges and the reality' *Health and Social Care in the Community*, 9(6), pp.414-28.

Ramcharan, P, McGrath, M and Grant, G (1997) 'Voices and choices: mapping entitlements to friendships and community contacts' in Ramcharan, P, Roberts, G, Grant, G and Borland, J (eds.) *Empowerment in Everyday Life* London, Jessica Kingsley, pp. 48-70.

Sherwood, M (1991) 'Racism and resistance: Cardiff in the 1930s and 1940s' *Welsh History Review* 15(3), pp. 51-70.

SSIW (Social Services Inspectorate for Wales) (2005) *The Report of the Chief Inspector: Social Services in Wales 2004-2005* Cardiff, Social Services Inspectorate for Wales, ssiw@wales.gsi.gov.uk

Waterhouse Report (2000*) Lost in Care: report of the tribunal of inquiry into the abuse of children in care in the former county council areas of Gwynedd and Clwyd since 1974* London: The Stationery Office.

Welsh Office (1983) *All-Wales Strategy for the Development of Services for Mentally Handicapped People* Cardiff, Welsh Office.

Welsh Office (1989) *Mental Illness Services: A Strategy for Wales* Cardiff, Welsh Office.

Wanless Report (2002) *Securing our Future Health, Taking a Long Term View* London, HM Treasury.

WAG (Welsh Assembly Government) (2003) *A Strategy for Older People in Wales,* Cardiff, Welsh Assembly Government.

WAG (2005) *A Fair Future For Our Children* Cardiff, Welsh Assembly Government.

WAG (2004) *Making the Connections* Cardiff, Welsh Assembly Government.

WAG (2007a) *Fullfilled Lives, Supportive Communities* Cardiff, Welsh Assembly Government.

WAG (2007b) *Review of Service Provision for Gypsies and Travellers, Report LD2070* Cardiff, Welsh Assembly Government.

Wilson, M, Walker, M and Stalker, K (2003) *Career Pathways in Scottish Social Services* Stirling, University of Stirling, Social Work Research Centre.